Theistic Psychology - Expanding The Narrative Series
Correspondences, Synchronicity, And Self-Witnessing

Theistic Psychology - Expanding The Narrative Series
A Modern Synthesis Of The Ideas of Jung And Swedenborg

Volume 4
Correspondences, Synchronicity, And Self-Witnessing

Dr. Leon James
Professor of Psychology at the University of Hawaii

Theistic Psychology Series

© 2018 Leon James and Diane Nahl

Theistic Psychology - Expanding The Narrative Series—Volume 4
Correspondences, Synchronicity, And Self-Witnessing

Theistic Psychology - Expanding The Narrative Series
A Modern Synthesis Of The Ideas of Jung And Swedenborg
Dr. Leon James
2018

Volume 1: Individuation And Collective Consciousness: Discovering Our Immortal Self In A Telepathic Universe

Volume 2: Personality And Afterlife Lifestyles: Getting Ready For Eternity

Volume 3: Sacred Scripture, Dreams, And Archetypes: The Secret Connection

Volume 4: Correspondences, Synchronicity, And The Spiritual Discipline Of Self-Witnessing

Volume 5: Regeneration And The Vertical Community: How God Manages Our Psychological States

Volume 6: Natural and Spiritual Marriage: Moving Into Eternity Together

Volume 7: Sayings And Aphorisms In Theistic Psychology
Emanuel Swedenborg, Carl Jung, And Leon James

Volume 8: Topics And References in Theistic Psychology

Volume 9: Schematic Diagrams And Charts In Theistic Psychology

Volume 10: Articles In Theistic Psychology: Part 1 of 3

Volume 11: Articles In Theistic Psychology: Part 2 of 3

Volume 12: Articles In Theistic Psychology: Part 3 of 3

Theistic Psychology - Expanding The Narrative Series—Volume 4
Correspondences, Synchronicity, And Self-Witnessing

Ceiling fresco by Daniel Gran The Miracle of Pentecost

Dedication

The Theistic Psychology Book Series is lovingly dedicated to

Diane M. Nahl

Professor Emerita of Library and Information Science
University of Hawaii

*My angel wife whom God sent into my life
that I too might strive to become an angel by loving her*

"Only what is real matters." ~*Diane Nahl, 2017*

*Conjugial love is the mental state of being oneminded in thought
and conjoined in will.* ~*Leon James, 2017*

Theistic Psychology - Expanding The Narrative Series—Volume 4
Correspondences, Synchronicity, And Self-Witnessing

This publication is in copyright. Subject to statuary exception, no reproduction of any part may take place without the written permission of
Regeneration Media, Kailua
licujames@gmail.com

This is the First Combined Series Kindle Edition of all 12 Volumes
Published in 2018

Theistic Psychology - Expanding The Narrative Series—Volume 4
Correspondences, Synchronicity, And Self-Witnessing

****

Volume 4

Correspondences, Synchronicity, And
The Spiritual Discipline Of Self-Witnessing
****

Content Of Sections

Volume 4 5
Correspondences, Synchronicity, And The Spiritual Discipline Of Self-Witnessing 5
   Preface To The Series 8
   1. Selecting Our Afterlife Society 14
   2. Lifestyles In The Afterlife of Mental Eternity 15
      [There Are Three Heavens] 25
      [Collective Societies] 25
      [There Are Three Heavens] 27
      [Clothes in Heaven] 28
      [What Personality We Need For Heaven] 29
      [Palaces, Streets, And Government In Heaven] 31
      [Children In the Afterlife] 34
      [Marriage In the Afterlife] 34
      [Selfish Traits And Infernal Fire] 35
      [Afterlife Hell Societies] 38
   3. Free Full Text Access To Swedenborg's Writings 39
   4. Jung's Psychology Of The Collective Unconscious 42
   5. The Collective Unconscious 49
   6. Jung On The Thoughts In Our Mind 57
   7. The Archetypes of Afterlife Societies 68
   8. Dual Consciousness And The Unity Of Opposites 71
   9. Explanation Of Key Concepts Used In Theistic Psychology 77
      AFTERLIFE, DYING, DEATH 78
      ARCHEYTPES AND THE SOUL 79
      BORN INTO MENTAL ETERNITY: SPIRITUAL BODY, PHYSICAL BODY 80

5

COLLECTIVE CONSCIOUS AND THE COLLECTIVE UNCONSCIOUS 82
CONSCIOUSNESS 82
FAMILY SPIRITS 83
HEAVEN AND HELL 84
INDIVIDUATION 84
INFINITY, GOD 85
MENTAL SUBSTANCE: LOVE AND TRUTH 87
MENTAL ANATOMY 88
PERSONALITY, SYMBOLISM, AND TALKING WITH GOD 91
PSYCHOLOGY 96
REGENERATION OF PERSONALITY 96
THEISTIC ANIMISM 101
THEISTIC PSYCHOLOGY 101
USES: SELFISH AND ALTRUISTIC 101

10. Conclusions From What Precedes 108
11. Synchronicity And Correspondences 111
12. Archetypes In Sacred Scripture 119
13. Durkheim's Description of Collective Consciousness 127
14. Natural Psychology And Theistic Psychology 133
   Anatomical Chart 1 The Mental World of Eternity Viewed in Successive Order of Discrete Degrees 144
   Anatomical Chart 2 The Mental World of Eternity Viewed in Simultaneous Order of Discrete Degrees 147
   Anatomical Chart 3 Body-Mind Correspondences For Anatomical Layers 4 to 9 148
   Illustration And Application To The Growth Of The Mind 151
15. Post-Materialist Science And Theistic Psychology 157
16. Premises And Methodology In Psychology Science 163
17. Methodology In Theistic Psychology 165
   (1) The Method Of Paraphrastic Transformations 165
   (2) The Method Of Correspondences 167
   (3) The Method Of Substitution 168
   (4) The Method Of Discourse Thinking 173
   (5) The Method Of Self-Witnessing 173
   (6) The Technique Of Graphic Methodology 173
18. Swedenborg And Jung: Foundation Stones For Theistic Psychology 174
19. Jung On Religion Vs. Psychology 183
20. Jung Writes On Dogmatism 202
21. The Mental Technology Of Self-Witnessing 205
22. Regeneration Self-Witnessing Methodology 207
23. Self-witnessing What We Do In Talking 212
24. We Are Never Alone: The Vertical Community 216

Theistic Psychology - Expanding The Narrative Series—Volume 4
Correspondences, Synchronicity, And Self-Witnessing

25. Self-Witnessing The Threefold Self: Affective, Cognitive, Sensorimotor..218
26. Sudden Memory And The Method Of Discourse Thinking.............223
27. Our Evils Cannot Be Removed 234
28. Metanoid Self-Witnessing Or Being An Audience To Yourself 237
29. Macro-Behaviors Are Regenerated By Means Of Micro-Behaviors 243
30. Examples From The Daily Round Archives 249
31. Swedenborg On Self-witnessing And Regeneration....................257
32. The Daily Round Archives Classification Scheme (DRA)..............264
33. Summary And Overview 279

List Of Sections For All 12 Volumes..293
Other Books by Leon James................................ Error! Bookmark not defined.
About the Author 321
End Of Volume 4 324

Preface To The Series

*I am not what has happened to me. I am what I choose to become.
~Carl Jung*

Man was not born for his own sake, but for the sake of others; that is, so that he should not live for himself alone, but for others. Otherwise no society could hold together, nor could there be any good in it. ~Swedenborg, TCR 406

In this book with multiple volumes I strive to show that individuation is regeneration and that it is the true purpose and direction of living our immortal life.

God creates every individual for a unique purpose, a unique destiny, and a unique biography that is immortal and endless into eternity.

The journey of our life is from birth to psychological maturity, and then to an afterlife society in mental eternity. There exist numberless afterlife societies given that every human being who has ever been born ends up in one of the afterlife societies in eternity.

These afterlife societies in mental eternity arrange themselves relative to each other in the anatomical shape of a male and female human body, externally and internally. This universal totality of the human race is so arranged with numberless afterlife societies in mental eternity. The afterlife societies that are composed of positive or altruistic personality structures arrange themselves into an anatomical cluster that is called the *Grand Human* (or the "*Greatest Man*").

But the afterlife societies that are composed of negative or ego-love personality structures arrange themselves into an anatomical cluster that is called the *Grand Monster*. The Grand Human societies are called heaven in composite, but the Grand Monster societies are called hell.

God creates every individual with unique traits and potentials that are specifically needed in one of the afterlife societies in the Grand Human. Every individual is born to end up in one of the Grand Human afterlife societies in which the individual happily lives forever with his or her conjugial partner and soulmate.

The journey to there is involved and there are many distractors and psychological pitfalls on the way. The risk is that we may develop a negative personality that cannot thrive in an altruistic or positive afterlife society.

Afterlife societies organize themselves according to the personality of the individuals. The personality structure that we are born with is inherited from our parents and family genetic line. Since the historic Fall of Consciousness the inherited personality has evolved into a negative structure that is harmful to society and to the individual.

Our inherited negative personality is dominated by ego-loves and selfishness. *Self-love is to love self only, and to love others only when this is of benefit to the self.* When we reach adulthood the ego-based personality must be regenerated or transformed into a positive mutual love personality structure. This means that mutual love replaces self-love as the dominant motivator in the personality.

Mutual love or altruism is to love others as much as self or more than self, and to love God more than anything.

The process of transforming our personality structure from negative to positive is very involved and takes years to complete. This process is called *regeneration* and is a necessary component of individuation.

It is wise and prudent to learn about the details of that journey and to make sure we are adequately prepared for it in order to be able to settle in one of the positive afterlife societies. They are called "heavenly" because the people who live in that mental sphere are even more considerate of others as they are considerate of themselves. *This is called being in mutual love.*

The people who live together in mutual love have a happy life and create with each other an eternal conjugial heaven.

The journey to a heavenly afterlife society is called individuation, or, to individuate.

Carl Jung (1875-1961) made *individuation* to be the center of his influential *depth psychology*. Emanuel Swedenborg (1688-1772) made *regeneration* the center of his psychology. Regeneration is the central psychological process that is described within the verses of *Sacred Scripture*.

Every name, object, number, plant, or animal that are mentioned in the literal sense of the verses serve as external natural representations or symbols of interior psychological states that belong to our inherited personality structure. God discusses our inherited personality and how we are to cooperate with God in its regeneration.

In order for an individual to reach the destined heavenly afterlife society in the Grand Human, the inherited personality inclinations must be regenerated.

Individuation and regeneration are the same psychological process that moves the individual from birth to a specific anatomical location in the Grand Human.

"Theistic psychology" is the knowledge that we acquire from God's *Word* about regeneration or individuation, and specifically, about how we are to cooperate with God in this journey from birth to a destined heavenly afterlife society in mental eternity. It is not an automatic inevitable process. God gives the individual the freedom and ability to interfere with this unique destiny. Hence it is wise for us to study the psychological message about regeneration that God wants us to know about.

It is sad and disturbing to think about what happens when we do not reach that destined afterlife society, and yet we must consider the issue for our own eternal welfare. Our destined afterlife society is called "heaven" and our alternate afterlife society is called "hell". Everyone knows enough about heaven and hell to realize that we want to avoid hell at all cost. It is an awful experience and leads to the systematic de-humanization and de-individuation of the person. Eventually nothing is left of the personality that is human and intelligent.

And so this is the purpose of my book, namely, to assist readers in constructing a rational common sense psychology of our individual journey from birth to eternity, and especially, to help people to understand how we need to cooperate with God in order to insure that we actually will arrive to our destiny in one of the heavenly afterlife societies.

We need to know what are the psychological danger points that have power to attract us away and distract us from our real journey and destination.

Both Jung and Swedenborg discovered and described many of these psychological danger points. They each made their relationship to God to be the center of their understanding of what is individuation or regeneration. Jung gives back to the modern intellect the idea of *archetypes* as psychological forces or influences operating in our personality inclinations. This was well known to the ancient cultures as shown by Jung's carefully documented research on symbolism in ancient religions and in Gnostic alchemy and ancient astrology.

Swedenborg gives the modern intellect the rational and empirical proof of the existence of afterlife societies, and especially, how every individual personality, from birth onward, is unconsciously in connection with one or more of the afterlife societies.

We are never alone.

We could not survive an instant without being interconnected with afterlife societies, which in their turn are interconnected with each other as the *Grand Human* and its hell version called the *Grand Monster*. The Grand Human and the Grand Monster are inverse mirror images of each other and are united by radical opposition to each other.

God wills that everything created be united and unified as a whole with everything else. This is the Divine Human psychic force that drives individuation and regeneration.

This book shows how the daily process of individuation is to liberate and activate more and more of the unique potentials that God implants in the individual's soul and personality inclinations at birth.

This may sound paradoxical, but *the more we individuate the more we are immersed in the sphere of collective consciousness.*

Conscious access to the mental sphere of the Grand Human's collective consciousness gives the individual the potential to be quasi-omniscient and quasi-omnipresent in the afterlife of mental eternity.

When we start our journey of individuation, our individual consciousness is restricted to sensory things that we experience through our sensory organs and the sensations to which they correspond in the mind and personality. As we become psychologically mature we experience individuation as becoming actualized and integrated into a social structure such as a career and various personal accomplishments that are valued by society.

But even with these external activities and experiences, there is also an unshakable feeling of inner need or lack, an internal sub-conscious urge to seek our true reality that is beyond the social and societal accomplishments on this earth.

This feeling from within is the call.

God calls every adult human being to prepare for and partake in the psychic "*feast*" that is the heavenly life. God's Word contains the psychology of regeneration that is communicated within the meaning of each verse. The literal meaning of the text describes various historical events, and what happened in the lives of various personages and nations. It also describes God's promises of physical rewards to those who follow the Commandments, and describes threats of physical punishment for those who abuse other people and live contrary to the Commandments.

But beneath the Divine history, we find theistic psychology.

This book provides you with Swedenborg's method of correspondences and with Jung's method of symbolism to help you pull off the historical cover of the literal verses of *Sacred Scripture*, and thereby to gain full access to the psychological message they contain.

You will make the happy discovery that this knowledge is inborn with every individual, but remains hidden in the sub-conscious until we bring it out explicitly into our conscious.

Leon James
Kailua, 2018

> *Psychology did not exist in earlier days, people thought naively, and when they sank into themselves they saw the inside of their own body.* ~Carl Jung, Modern Psychology, p. 224

> *The higher or spiritual region of the human mind is a heaven in miniature, while the lower or natural region is a world in miniature, and for this reason man was called by the ancients a microcosm [a little world], and he may also be called a microuranos [a little heaven].* ~Swedenborg, True Christianity, TCR 604

****
Volume 4
Section 1
****

1. Selecting Our Afterlife Society

Regeneration is the anatomical procedure that God provides to the individual in order to be dis-joined from all evil afterlife societies. This involves the killing of selfhood and its evils. In actual cases, the killing of the individual's selfish loves in the personality is achieved when engaging in spiritual warfare against those societies in hell from which the individual is to be freed and anatomically excised by God's mental surgery in the flesh of the spiritual body that is the individual's mind. God regenerates the personality from self-love to mutual love. The regenerated personality is capable of living in the mental regions called heaven in eternity.

Regeneration must be gradual because if God excised all of it at once we would experience losing all our delights and happiness of life. It would be like dying. Hence God uses a gradual process that involves the gradual removal of the things we love and that give us pleasure and delight. As selfish loves are removed mutual loves take place in the personality. The process proceeds effectively to the extent that the individual is willing to resist the pleasures and delights that temptations occasion in daily life.

God manages events in order to bring to the individual's consciousness a particular temptation that is familiar to the individual through lifestyle habits. Now the spiritual warfare begins. It is called spiritual because it involves the individual's beliefs and knowledge of God. God through conscience says, *"Don't do it. I'll give you better delights."*, while the self playing the devil says, *"Oh, Go ahead, Do it. It's so bad that it's good"*.

Consummating selfish loves brings great delight. It is hard to resist the temptation to just give in and enjoy. The enjoyments of selfhood include wanting to be the greatest, wanting to be adored by everyone as a god, enjoying enemies treated cruelly, becoming rich by deception, exercising total power over someone, treating some people with disrespect and disregard, etc. etc. God brings relationships that provide the individual with opportunities to apply their principles of mutual love. In this way, God gradually changes the lifestyle practices of the person from inconsiderate to considerate, and from loving self to loving others in all relationships and interactions.

****

Volume 4
Section 2

****

2. Lifestyles In The Afterlife of Mental Eternity

Swedenborg writes:

> The case is the very same with men, as to their souls, which are constantly bound to some society of spirits and of angels. They too have a situation in the kingdom of the Lord according to the nature of their life, and according to their state. It matters not that they are distant from each other on earth even though it were many thousands of miles-still they can be together in the same society-those who live in charity in an angelic society, and those who live in hatred and such evils in an infernal society. In like manner it matters not that there be many together on earth in one place, for still they

are all distinct in accordance with the nature of their life and of their state, and each one may be in a different society.

Men who are distant from each other some hundreds or thousands of miles, when they appear to the internal sense may be so near each other that some of them may touch, according to their situation. Thus if there were a number of persons on earth whose spiritual sight was opened, they might be together and converse together, though one was in India and another in Europe, which also has been shown me. Thus are all men on earth, both generally and individually, most closely present to the Lord, and under His view and providence. ~Swedenborg, Heavenly Secrets, AC 1277

The case of Emanuel Swedenborg (1688-1772) is unique in the history of science and psychology. He was at the height of his brilliant career in Sweden as a respected government engineer and administrator of Sweden's steel production. He was known throughout Europe as an innovator and inventor and publisher of scientific works. As well, as a member of the legislature in the House of Lords, Swedenborg was the architect for Swedish money reform and industrial development.

Then at age 57 Swedenborg receives a personal visit from God who sends him on a special mission for which God had prepared Swedenborg since childhood. Swedenborg was now to come into dual consciousness, which is being fully conscious in both his natural mind and his spiritual mind. Ordinarily, when we resurrect from the dying process, everyone comes into the consciousness of the spiritual mind and loses consciousness of the natural mind. As a unique new phenomenon under the immediate direction of God, Swedenborg was continuing his life as a scientist and legislator in his natural mind, and simultaneously he was conscious in his spiritual mind and was exploring the world of the afterlife.

He was able to write down detailed notes through his natural mind what he was observing in the afterlife world through hjis spiritual mind. Swedenborg is the only scientist in the history of science who was given this opportunity of bringing scientific observations to the afterlife world. For

Theistic Psychology - Expanding The Narrative Series—Volume 4
Correspondences, Synchronicity, And Self-Witnessing

27 years continuously every day he was conscious in both worlds. He published his ethnographic notes in about 30 books that have been read and translated in many languages over the past 250 years. I discuss findings from the *Swedenborg Reports* throughout this book, as well as in my other books listed at the end of the volume.

I reproduce below some selections from Swedenborg's writings that deal specifically with details of the lives of people in the afterlife. These selections indicate that the afterlife begins a few hours following the death of our physical body on earth, which I call our *physical body*. We "*resuscitate*" or awaken in our afterlife body with which we were born. It is composed of mental substance from God, specifically, love-substance and truth-substance that emanate or flow into the spiritual world of humanity.

Human minds are made of mental substance, not of nothing, since it is a logical contradiction to say that something that exists is made of out of nothing, which does not exist. Our mind at birth is embodied in this afterlife body, which is made of mental substance and exists in the spiritual world. The afterlife world of eternity is nothing else than the spiritual world of eternity.

Our spiritual world is called "in eternity" because as we all know there is no fixed space or time in our spiritual world. Think of your dreams. All events appear to take place on earth with space, time, buildings, plants, etc. this is the appearance. You can change appearances at will. You can make more buildings or more ice cream just as easily. You can cross a thousand miles in an eye blink. A world that is not physical, thus not in time and space and energy, is the spiritual world. Hence it is called the spiritual world of eternity (no-time).

But there is only one possible eternity. Hence the spiritual world, the spiritual world, the afterlife world, the psychic world, the immanent world, and so on, *are all the same world*. This is the biggest discovery I have made since beginning to study Swedenborg for the past 37 years, and more recently studying Jung.

To continue with the content of the selections below, they further indicate that the afterlife world or spiritual world of eternity is made of living mental substance that is human and omnipresent (since there is no space). The spiritual world is an anatomical structure in the shape of the human body, both external and all its internal constructions. So you can see in Swedenborg's notes where he was exploring on a particular "mental trip", as for example "located in the province of the right eye", or "in the province of the gall bladder", or "in the region of the reproductive organs", and so on.

Perhaps the most amazing detail to me is the fact that afterlife societies are totally telepathic and collective. What one individual thinks and feels is instantaneously communicated to every other individual. In heavenly societies there is from this an increase of love and happiness as a collective, and also as an individual. Both are constantly enriched and deepened by a steady stream of new arrivals to each society. One by one people come into the afterlife from the endless number of inhabited planets in the physical universe when each individual is detached from his or her physical body on the planet.

Each afterlife society has a unique character that is composed of the collective consciousness that is produced by the sharing of each with all. This unique identifying collective consciousness may be called the afterlife society's *archetype*, a word that Jung coined for his greatest discovery in the collective unconscious of eternity.

The collective consciousness of each archetype society is so pervasive that it involves all three systems of the mental or spiritual body: affective, cognitive, and sensorimotor. The collectivity of the affective system comes from the sharing of their ruling love and its associated emotions and affections. The collectivity of the cognitive system comes from the sharing of their thoughts and associated principles of thinking and reasoning. The collectivity of the sensorimotor system comes from the sharing of their cardiac and pulmonary motion. In other words they breathe in unison and their heart pulse is synchronized.

To me it's fascinating to find out that the afterlife societies have cities, avenues, houses, and gardens, just like the cities on earth but more beautiful and sumptuous. These cities in the spiritual world of eternity are constructed out of mental substance, similar what we can do with our mind in our dreams while we are asleep.

Such is the marvelous nature of mental substance that it obeys the human will and thinking, so that we can construct whatever shape or size of housing that we desire, but not like the proverbial castle in the sky, which in daily speech is invoked with some negativity or disapproval, not withstanding that castles made of mental substance are more permanent, real, and sumptuous than the castles on the ground made out of stones and wood.

Furthermore, the people in these cities, who are called angel couples, have a system of government, have books and records, and various occupations or useful activities that they perform on a daily basis. I for one wondered greatly when I first read these details many years ago. All sorts of objections ran through my mind. These obscurities of my comprehension were caused by my false assumptions and ideas of what heaven might be like.

But gradually with more study of the Swedenborg Reports, I began to comprehend in a more rational or spiritual manner what these details meant.

The idea that I am a living person necessarily implies that I am active, that I do and perform things that my love or intention desires and my intelligence pursues workable plans that my sensorimotor system can execute and perform. This activity produces experiences, which gives us content about the world and other people. *This content of our experiencing is what we call consciousness.*

It became clear to me that there is no content without social life and daily activities. And these goings on must have a stage or place. Hence we have the cities on our planet for our physical bodys. Our natural mind in our spiritual body in eternity receives all its sensory input from our physical body on earth. We all believe that we live on earth, and that the physical body is alive and is us.

We grow up through experiences with other people through our physical bodys, and construct for ourselves a personality that is activated anatomically by loves in the affective system that are conjoined with thoughts in our cognitive system. These loves are not in us but all around us. We pick and choose which loves we allow entry into our personality.

After we lose our physical body we become fully conscious in our spiritual mind and the our sensory input is from the mental environment, not the physical as before in our natural mind. Now in our spiritual mind we can live our life with others who are also in the afterlife. But what kind of social life would be possible that could give us content of experiencing and consciousness?

It makes sense therefore to use the same technique that we use in our dreams. We essentially re-create the natural world around us when we are awake, though there are significant differences that are illuminated by the work of Jung and Swedenborg. Hence it is that the afterlife of eternity in heaven has a similar outward appearance of life as we have in the world of our physical body, though it is more sumptuous and grand.

Loves and thoughts are not created by individuals who select them from the mental environment that contains all of humanity's thoughts and all of humanity's loves. Each love that we admit from the mental environment selects from the same environment the thoughts and beliefs that are supportive of the love. Now we have in our personality that love conjoined with those thoughts. The offspring of this mental marriage is sensorimotor action that runs interactions and produces our experiencing through mental content.

The loves and thoughts that are in the mental environment are omnipresent since there is no space in the spiritual world of substance. We therefore each have continuous access to anything we want to know or anything there is to know. And likewise, we can have any feeling or emotion we want because all possible feelings and emotions are omnipresent and available to each human being from birth to eternal immortality.

And yet, and yet, how limited we appear to ourselves. How ignorant, and with such want of information, and hardships in learning and acquiring knowledge and expertise. *Why don't we just take from what's there that we can reach?*

Ah, there is the issue! What we can reach. It seems to us subjectively in our individual consciousness that everything is covered over and in order to get to see anything we must work hard to uncover bits and pieces here and there. We are facing reality with a veil over our eyes, or with very dark shades, or with an opaque wall right in front of our nose.

> *When something slips out of our consciousness it does not cease to exist...It is simply out of sight. Thus part of the unconscious consists of multitudes of temporarily obscured thoughts, impressions and images that, in spite of being lost, continue to influence our conscious minds.*
> ~Carl Jung, Man and His Symbols, p. 18

In other words, *God makes our mind to hide omnipresence.* Life, with its experiencing of content, then becomes the unveiling of omnipresence, which gets us closer and closer to what omnipresence is, namely, God's actual omnipresence. Soon we come to the realization that indeed we are not alone.

First, God's human mind is co-present in our mind and plays a directive and determinative role in what happens in our own mind as a unique individual. Second, *all human beings are co-present to each other* as collective consciousness, which is a mental state whereby each experiences what all the others are experiencing.

This means that our mind is born into collective consciousness. Jung realized that the collective unconscious is endless. Everything belonging to humanity was in it. Swedenborg discovered that this collective unconscious is the same as the collective consciousness of those who live in the eternal afterlife societies.

To put in my own way, we are unconscious of the "collective unconscious" throughout the time that our natural mind is still tied to the sensory input of the physical body on earth. We start our afterlife in our spiritual mind while the natural mind grows inactive. Now in our spiritual mind we are conscious in collective consciousness, which was and is the "collective unconscious" for the natural mind. Clearly, our mental functioning in the two minds is distinctly different.

The interior organs within the spiritual mind is called the celestial mind. Swedenborg interviewed many of the people who enjoy celestial consciousness. They are called the "highest angels". They live in married pairs with each other's soulmates. A husband's mind in celestial consciousness is totally integrated with his wife's mind. They are mentally conjoined so that the husband operates as the pair's cognitive system and the wife operates as the pair's affective system. Outwardly they act as one.

Swedenborg reports that when a "conjugial pair" approaches from a distance one can see only one angel walking, but when they come near they appear as husband and wife beautifully and becomingly appareled with garments and jeweled accessories.

Swedenborg's observations in dual consciousness fully confirm all the mental facts that I have just described in a summary. Now I'd like to give you the opportunity and delight of looking through some selections I take from the *Swedenborg Reports* regarding what's it's like to live in the afterlife. Each of us will soon be doing that, sooner or later.

I have selected general details but you can easily check out the specific details by looking up Swedenborg's book titled *Heaven and Hell* (1758), which is available free on the Web on many sites and in books, both print and digital. See for example the Web site *Sacred Texts*:
http://www.sacred-texts.com/swd/index.htm

In the selections below "angels" refer to the people who live in the positive or mutual-love regions of the spiritual world. "Devils" and "genii" are people who live in the negative self-love regions of the spiritual world. The angelic societies can be found at three levels of functioning, namely, those in the center region who exist in celestial consciousness, which is the highest and closest to God. The people in the middle level function in spiritual consciousness. The people in heaven in the lowest level at the circumference, function in spiritual-natural consciousness.

Levels of consciousness are determined by the loves in their personality. Mutual love is to love others as much or more than self, and to love God more than anything. The people who come into the afterlife having a mutual-love-based personality join and live in one of the three heavens. The people who come into the afterlife having a self-love-based personality live in one of the three corresponding hells.

The least severe hell societies are located near the top, and they are the less offensive and painful to endure. The personalities of the people who congregate there are based on the love and enjoyment of *the natural world* as giving them the deepest satisfaction in being alive. They elevate this physical delight to be greater than the mental delight of loving others and treating them with thoughtfulness.

The love of the physical world includes the delight in power, in riches, in receiving honors, and in being a celebrity. When people make these to be their greatest delight and satisfaction they are unwilling to undergo regeneration, which requires them to learn to love others more than self. This makes no sense to them and they reject it.

The personality of the people in the next lower or intermediate hells is based on love of self or egotism as being the deepest and greatest delight of living. The love of self is to love oneself more than anything else so that it becomes the source of their deepest delight. The love of self includes the delight of dominating and controlling others and the pleasure of tormenting those who oppose them or favor others over them.

Variations in the love of self are endless. They include practicing the classic "vices" such as greed, envy, adultery, promiscuity, cruelty, absence of compassion, deadened conscience, winning at any cost to others, and many more that introduce mental and social plagues into society and producing conflict, discrimination, prejudice, injustice, war, mental sickness and mental neuroses and dysfunctions.

The lowest hell is the worst of the hells and is populated by people who love to profane God and the holy things of *Sacred Scripture*. They also hate children to extremes, and the chastity of married love, going into a frenzy of insanity when these things are mentioned in their presence. These people live in unspeakable states of perversion, debasing themselves and their victims to sub-human savagery and insanity.

People in hell are constantly presented with the opportunity to exit that negative mental zone and to enter the positive zones of heaven and mutual love. However, they fly into an apoplectic frenzy when these ideas are just mentioned to them, and when they actually approach that zone they feel a loss of all ability to sensate and to think, falling down as if lifeless. Hence it is that no one ever leaves the hells that they join soon after resuscitation into the afterlife. Hell and heaven are forever!

It is important in my view that Swedenborg has confirmed by mental observation that the afterlife societies in both positive and negative mental states are populated by choice and not by punishment, as is believed by many. This belief is based on the literal meaning of *Sacred Scripture*, which states that hell is punishment for sins, and heaven is a reward for keeping the commandments.

But other parts of *Sacred Scripture* declare that God does not punish because He is pure love and love does not desire to punish. Further, God forgives from that love or mercy. So we need to reconcile the apparent contradiction by considering that God in *Sacred Scripture* speaks simultaneously to the natural mind and to the spiritual mind.

To the natural mind God says, keep My commandments or you'll suffer punishment in this world and in the afterlife. But to the spiritual mind God says that breaking the commandments brings its own punishment due to negative consequences of unhealthy and mentally harmful lifestyle practices. Swedenborg's observations of thousands of people in the afterlife societies confirms this deeper interpretation.

And now, to Swedenborg, in his own words.

Swedenborg writes:

[There Are Three Heavens]

In every angel and also in every man there is an inmost or highest degree, or an inmost or highest something, into which the Divine of the Lord primarily or proximately flows, and from which it disposes the other interiors in him that follow in accordance with the degrees of order.

This inmost or highest degree may be called the entrance of the Lord to the angel [inhabitant of one of the heavens] or man [=while still attached to an physical body on earth], and His veriest dwelling-place in them. It is by virtue of this inmost or highest that a man [human being] is a man [human], and is distinguished from irrational animals, for these do not have it.

From this it is that man, unlike the animals, is capable, in respect to all his interiors which pertain to his mind and disposition, of being raised up by the Lord to Himself, of believing in the Lord, of being moved by love to the Lord, and thereby beholding Him, and of receiving intelligence and wisdom, and speaking from reason.

Also, it is by virtue of this that he [a human being] lives to eternity. But what is arranged and provided by the Lord in this inmost does not distinctly flow into the perception of any angel, because it is above his thought and transcends his wisdom. HH 39

[Collective Societies]

The Heavens Consist Of Innumerable Societies. The angels of each heaven are not together in one place [appearance of location], but are divided into larger and smaller societies in accordance with the differences of good of love [mutual love] and of faith [genuine truths] in which they are, those who are in like good [=love] forming a single society. Goods in the heavens are in infinite variety, and each angel is as it were his [or her] own good. HH 41

Moreover, the angelic societies in the heavens are at a distance from each other [in appearance] as their goods [loves] differ in general and in particular. For in the spiritual world the only ground of [appearance of] distance is difference in the state of interiors [mental functions], thus in the heavens difference in the states of love, those who differ much being far apart [in appearance], and those who differ but little being but little apart, and likeness causing them to be together [co-present to each other as collective consciousness]. HH 42

Like are drawn spontaneously as it were to their like; for with their like they are as if with their own and at home, but with others they are as if with strangers and abroad; also when with their like they are in their freedom [of decision and choice], and consequently in every delight of life. HH 44

All the societies of heaven have [telepathic] communication with one another, though not by open interaction; for few go out of their own society into another, since going out of their own society is like going away from themselves or from their own life, and passing into another life which is less congenial.

But all the societies [telepathically] communicate by an extension of the sphere that goes forth from the life of each. This sphere of the life is the sphere of the affections of love and faith. This sphere extends itself far and wide into the surrounding societies, and farther and wider in proportion as the affections are the more interior and perfect. In the measure of that extension do the angels have intelligence and wisdom. Those that are in the inmost heaven and in the middle of it have extension into the entire heavens; thus there is a [telepathic mental] sharing of all in heaven with each one, and of each one with all. HH 49

It has been said above that in the heavens there are larger and smaller societies. The larger consist of myriads of angels, the smaller of some thousands, and the least of some hundreds. There are also some that dwell apart, house by house as it were, and family by family. Although these live in this scattered way, they are arranged in order like those who live in societies, the wiser in the middle and the more simple in the borders. Such are more closely under the Divine auspices of the Lord, and are the best of the angels. HH 50

[There Are Three Heavens]

All Heaven In The Aggregate Reflects A Single Man [of both sexes]. That heaven in its whole complex reflects a single man is an Arcanum [secret] hitherto unknown in the world [natural mind], but fully recognized in the heavens [spiritual mind]. To know this and the specific and particular things relating to it is the chief thing in the intelligence of the angels there, and on it many things depend which without it as their general principle would not enter distinctly and clearly into the ideas of their minds.

Knowing that all the heavens with their societies reflect a single man they call heaven the Greatest Man and the Divine Man;--Divine because it is the Divine of the Lord that makes heaven. HH 59

I have been taught from heaven that the most ancient men on our earth, who were celestial men, thought from correspondences themselves, the natural things of the world before their eyes serving them as means of thinking in this way; and that they could be in fellowship with angels and talk with them because they so thought, and that thus through them heaven was conjoined to the world.

For this reason that period was called the Golden Age, of which it is said by ancient writers that the inhabitants of heaven dwelt with men and associated with them as friends with friends. But after this there followed a period when men thought, not from correspondences themselves, but from a knowledge of correspondences, and there was then also a conjunction of heaven with man, but less intimate. This period was called the Silver Age.

After this there followed men who had a knowledge of correspondences but did not think from that knowledge, because they were in natural good, and not, like those before them in spiritual good. This period was called the Copper Age. After this man gradually became external, and finally corporeal, and then the knowledge of correspondences was wholly lost, and with it a knowledge of heaven and of the many things pertaining to heaven.

It was from correspondence that these ages were named from gold, silver, and copper, and for the reason that from correspondence gold signifies celestial good in which were the most ancient people, silver spiritual good in which were the ancient people that followed, and copper natural good in which were the next posterity; while iron, from which the last age takes its name, signifies hard truth apart from good. HH 115

As angels have no idea derived from time, such as men in the world have, so neither do they have any idea about time and what pertains to it. They do not even know what is meant by the terms of time, such as year, month, week, day, hour, today, to-morrow, yesterday. When angels hear these terms used by man [natural mind] (for angels are always associated with man by the Lord) in place of them they perceive state and what pertains to states. Thus the natural thought of man is turned into spiritual thought with angels. This is why times in the Word signify states, and the terms of time, as enumerated above, signify corresponding spiritual things. HH 165

.
.

[Clothes in Heaven]

The Garments With Which Angels Appear Clothed.
Since angels are men [human beings], and live among themselves as men [people] do on the earth [through their physical body], they have garments and dwellings and other such things, with the difference, however, that as they are in a more perfect state all things with them are in greater perfection. For as angelic wisdom [of the spiritual and celestial

mind] surpasses human wisdom [of the natural mind] to such a degree as to be called ineffable [not comprehensible], so is it with all things that are perceived and seen by angels, inasmuch as all things perceived and seen by them correspond to their wisdom. HH 177

That the garments of angels do not merely appear as garments, but are real garments, is evident from the fact that angels both see them and feel them, that they have many garments, and that they put them off and put them on, that they care for those that are not in use, and put them on again when they need them. That they are clothed with a variety of garments I have seen a thousand times. When I asked where they got their garments, they said from the Lord, and that they receive them as gifts, and sometimes they are clothed with them unconsciously. They said also that their garments are changed in accordance with their changes of state, that in the first and second state their garments are shining and glistening white, and in the third and fourth state a little less bright; and this likewise from correspondence, because their changes of state have respect to intelligence and wisdom.

I have talked after their death with some people who during their earthly lives had renounced the world and devoted themselves to a virtually solitary life, wanting to make time for devout meditation by withdrawing their thoughts from worldly matters. They believed that this was the way to follow the path to heaven. In the other life, though, they are gloomy in spirit. They avoid others who are not like themselves and they resent the fact that they are not allotted more happiness than others. They believe they deserve it and do not care about other people, and they avoid the responsibilities of thoughtful behavior that are the means to union with heaven. They covet heaven more than others do; but when they are brought up to where angels are, they cause anxieties that upset the happiness of the angels. So they part company; and once they have parted, they betake themselves to lonely places where they lead the same kind of life they had led in the world.

[What Personality We Need For Heaven]

The only way we can be formed for heaven is through the [natural] world. That is the ultimate goal by which every affection must be defined. Unless affection manifests itself or flows into action, which happens in sizeable communities, it is stifled, ultimately to the point that we no longer focus on our neighbor at all, but only on ourselves.

We can see from this that the life of thoughtfulness toward our neighbor-behaving fairly and uprightly in all our deeds and in all our responsibilities-leads to heaven, but not a life of piety apart from this active life. This means that the practice of thoughtfulness and the benefits that ensue from this kind of life can occur only to the extent that we are involved in our occupations, and that they cannot occur to the extent that we withdraw from those occupations.

But let me say something about this from experience. Many people who devoted their energies to business and trade in the world, many who became rich, are in heaven. There are not so many, though, who made a name for themselves and became rich in public office. This is because these latter were led into love for themselves and the world by the profits and the positions they were given because of their administration of justice and morality and of profits and positions. This in turn led them to deflect their thoughts and affections from heaven and direct them toward themselves; for to the extent that we love ourselves and the world and focus on ourselves and the world exclusively, we estrange ourselves from the Divine and move away from heaven.

Thoughtfulness toward our neighbor is doing what is good, fair, and upright in all our deeds and in all our responsibilities. So thoughtfulness toward our neighbor extends to every least thing we think and intend and do. Without a life of thoughtfulness, a life of piety is of no use, but with it, it is immensely productive. HH 360

As the whole heaven is distinguished into [afterlife] societies according to affections that are of love, and as all wisdom and intelligence is according to affections, therefore each society has distinctive breathing, different from that of any other society, and similarly, distinctive cardiac pulsation. Owing to this, no one from one society can enter another society remote from it, nor can any one from a higher heaven descend into a lower one, or any one from a lower ascend into a higher, for in that case his heart beats with difficulty and his lungs feel compressed; least of all, can any one from hell ascend into heaven: any one venturing to do so begins to struggle for breath like some one in the death agony, or like a fish taken out of water into the air. D Wis 7

[Palaces, Streets, And Government In Heaven]

Whenever I have talked with angels face to face, I have been with them in their abodes. These abodes are precisely like abodes on the earth which we call houses, but more beautiful. In them there are chambers, parlors, and bedrooms in great number; there are also courts, and there are gardens and flower beds and lawns round about. Where they live together their houses are near each other, arranged one next to the other in the form of a city, with avenues, streets, and public squares, exactly like cities on the earth. I have been permitted to pass through them, looking about on every side, and sometimes entering the houses. This occurred when my inner sight was opened, and I was fully awake. HH 184

I have seen palaces in heaven of such magnificence as cannot be described. Above they glittered as if made of pure gold, and below as if made of precious stones, some more splendid than others. It was the same within. Both words and knowledge are inadequate to describe the decorations that adorned the rooms.

On the side looking to the south there were parks, where, too, everything shone, in some places the leaves glistening as if made of silver, and fruit as if made of gold; while the flowers in their beds formed rainbows with their colors. Beyond the borders, where the view terminated, were seen other palaces. Such is the architecture of heaven that you would say that art there is in its art; and no wonder, because the art itself is from heaven.

The angels [people who dwell in a heavenly afterlife society] said that such things and innumerable others still more perfect are presented before their eyes by the Lord; and yet these things are more pleasing to their minds than to their eyes, because in everyone of them they see a correspondence, and through the correspondences what is Divine. HH 185

Government in the Lord's celestial kingdom is called righteousness because all in that kingdom are in the good of love to the Lord from the Lord, and whatever is from that good is called righteous. Government there belongs to the Lord alone. He leads them and teaches them in the affairs of life. The truths that are called truths of judgment are written on their hearts; everyone knows them, perceives them, and sees them; and in consequence matters of judgment there never come into question, but only matters of righteousness, which belong to the life. About these matters the less wise consult the more wise, and these consult the Lord and receive answers. Their heaven, that is, their inmost joy, is to live rightly from the Lord. HH 214

In the Lord's spiritual kingdom the government is called judgment; because those in that kingdom are in spiritual good, which is the good of charity towards the neighbor, and that good in its essence is truth; and truth pertains to judgment, as good pertains to righteousness. These, too, are led by the Lord, but mediately; and in consequence they have governors, few or many according to the need of the society in which they are. They also have laws according to which they live together. The governors administer all things in accordance with the laws, which they understand because they are wise, and in doubtful matters they are enlightened by the Lord. HH 215

The Power Of The Angels [inhabitants] Of Heaven. That the angels possess power cannot be comprehended by those who know nothing about the spiritual world and its influx into the natural world. Such think that angels can have no power because they are spiritual and are even so pure and unsubstantial that no eye can see them. But those who look more interiorly into the causes of things take a different view.

Such know that all the power that a man [people still connected to their physical bodys] *has is from his understanding and will (for apart from these he is powerless to move a particle of his body), and his understanding and will are his spiritual man* [mind]. *This moves the body* [physical body] *and its members at its pleasure; for whatever it thinks the mouth and tongue speak, and whatever it wills the body does; and it bestows its strength at pleasure.*

As man's will and understanding are ruled by the Lord through angels and spirits [vertical community], *so also are all things of his body* [physical body], *because these are from the will and understanding; and if you will believe it, without influx from heaven man cannot even move a step.*

That this is so has been shown me by much experience. Angels have been permitted to move my steps, my actions, and my tongue and speech, as they pleased, and this by influx into my will and thought; and I have learned thereby that of myself I could do nothing.

I was afterwards told by them that every man is so ruled, and that he can know this from the doctrine of the church and from the Word, for he prays that God may send His angels to lead him, direct his steps, teach him, and inspire in him what to think and what to say, and other like things; although he says and believes otherwise when he is thinking by himself apart from doctrine. All this has been said to make known what power angels have with man. HH 228

It is a notable fact that the writings in the heavens flow naturally from their very thoughts, and this so easily that the thought puts itself forth, as it were, and the hand never hesitates in the choice of a word, because both the words they speak and those they write correspond to the ideas of their thought; and all correspondence is natural and spontaneous. There are also writings in the heavens that exist without the aid of the hand, from mere correspondence with the thoughts; but these are not permanent. HH 262

[Children In the Afterlife]

As soon as little children are resuscitated, which takes place immediately after death, they are taken into heaven and confided to angel women who in the life of the body tenderly loved little children and at the same time loved God.

Because these during their life in the world loved all children with a kind of motherly tenderness, they receive them as their own; while the children, from an implanted instinct, love them as their own mothers. There are as many children in each one's care as she desires from a spiritual parental affection.

This heaven appears in front before the forehead, directly in the line or radius in which the angels look to the Lord. It is so situated because all little children are under the immediate auspices of the Lord; and the heaven of innocence, which is the third heaven, flows into them. HH 332

[Marriage In the Afterlife]

Marriage in heaven is a conjunction of two into one mind. It must first be explained what this conjunction is. The mind consists of two parts, one called the understanding and the other the will. When these two parts act as one they are called one mind. In heaven the husband acts the part called the understanding and the wife acts the part called the will. When this conjunction, which belongs to man's interiors, descends into the lower parts pertaining to the body, it is perceived and felt as love, and this love is marriage love. This shows that marriage love has its origin in the conjunction of two into one mind. This in heaven is called cohabitation; and the two are not called two but one. So in heaven a married pair is spoken of, not as two, but as one angel. HH 367

I heard an angel describing true marriage love and its heavenly delights in this manner: That it is the Lord's Divine in the heavens, which is Divine good and Divine truth so united in two persons, that they are not as two but as one. He said that in heaven the two consorts are marriage love, since everyone is his own good and his own truth in respect both to mind and to body [physical body], the body being an image of the mind because it is formed after its likeness.

From this he drew the conclusion that the Divine is imaged in the two that are in true marriage love; and as the Divine is so imaged so is heaven, because the entire heaven is Divine good and Divine truth going forth from the Lord; and this is why all things of heaven are inscribed on marriage love with more blessings and delights than it is possible to number. He expressed the number by a term that involved myriads of myriads. HH 374

Everyone knows that a married pair who love each other are interiorly united, and that the essential of marriage is the union of dispositions and minds. And from this it can be seen that such as their essential dispositions or minds are, such is their union and such their love for each other. HH 375

[Selfish Traits And Infernal Fire]

The mind is formed solely out of truths and goods, for all things in the universe have relation to good and truth and to their conjunction; consequently such as the truths and goods are out of which the minds are formed, exactly such is the union of minds; and consequently the most perfect union is the union of minds that are formed out of genuine truths and goods. Let it be known that no two things mutually love each other more than truth and good do; and therefore it is from that love that true marriage love descends. Falsity and evil also love each other, but this love is afterwards changed into hell. HH 375

The interiors pertaining to the thoughts and affections of those who love themselves above all things are turned towards themselves and the world, and thus are turned away from the Lord and from heaven; and consequently they are obsessed with evils of every kind, and the Divine cannot flow in; for if it does flow in it is instantly submerged in thoughts of self, and is defiled, and is also mingled with the evils that flow from what is their own.

This is why all such in the other life look backwards away from the Lord, and towards the densely dark body that is there in the place of the sun of the world, and is diametrically opposite to the sun of heaven, which is the Lord. "Thick darkness" signifies evil, and the "sun of the world" [physical] the love of self.

The evils of those who are in the love of self are, in general, contempt of others, envy, enmity against all who do not favor them, and consequent hostility, hatred of various kinds, revenge, cunning, deceit, unmercifulness, and cruelty; and in respect to religious matters there is not merely a contempt for the Divine and for Divine things, which are the truths and goods of the church, but also hostility to them.

When man becomes a spirit this hostility is turned into hatred; and then he not only cannot endure to hear these truths and goods mentioned, he even burns with hatred against all who acknowledge and worship the Divine. I once talked with a certain spirit who in the world had been a man in authority, and had loved self to an unusual degree; and when he simply heard some one mention the Divine, and especially when he heard him mention the Lord, he was so excited by hatred arising from anger as to burn with the desire to kill; and when the reins of his love were loosened he wished to be the devil himself, that from his love of self he might continually infest heaven.... HH 561-562

Since infernal fire means every lust for doing evil that flows forth from the love of self, this fire means also such torment as exists in the hells. For the lust from that love is a lust for injuring others who do not honor, venerate and worship oneself; and in proportion to the anger thereby excited, and the hatred and revenge from that anger, is there a lust for venting one's rage upon them.

When such lust is active in everyone in a society, and is restrained by no external bond, such as the fear of the law, and of the loss of reputation, honor, gain, and life, everyone from the impulse of his own evil rushes upon another; and so far as he prevails subjugates the rest and subjects them to his dominion, and vents his rage with delight upon those who do not submit themselves.

This delight is so intimately united with the delight of bearing rule that they exist in the same measure, since the delight of doing harm is contained in all enmity, envy, hatred, and revenge, which as said above, are the evils of that love. All the hells are such societies, and in consequence everyone there bears hatred in his heart against others, and from hatred bursts forth into cruelty so far as he has power. These cruelties and their torments are also meant by infernal fire, since they are the effects of lusts. HH 573

Those are the worst of all who have been in evils from love of self and at the same time inwardly in themselves have acted from deceit; for deceit penetrates more deeply into the thoughts and intentions than other evils, and infects them with poison and thus wholly destroys the spiritual life of man. Most of these spirits are in the hells behind the back, and are called genii; and there they delight to make themselves invisible, and to flutter about others like phantoms secretly infusing evil into them, which they spread around like the poison of a viper. These are more direfully tormented than others.

But those who are not deceitful, and who have not been so filled with malignant craftiness, and yet are in the evils derived from the love of self, are also in the hells behind, but in those less deep. On the other hand, those that have been in evils from the love of the world are in the hells in front, and are called spirits. These spirits are not such forms of evil, that is, of hatred and revenge, as those are who are in evils from the love of self; and therefore do not have such malice and cunning; and in consequence their hells are milder. HH 578

[Afterlife Hell Societies]

I have also been permitted to look into the hells [people who inhabit negative afterlife societies] and to see what they are within; for when the Lord wills, the sight of a spirit or angel from above may penetrate into the lowest depths beneath and explore their character, notwithstanding the coverings. In this way I have been permitted to look into them. Some of the hells appeared to the view like caverns and dens in rocks extending inward and then downward into an abyss, either obliquely or vertically.

Some of the hells appeared to the view like the dens and caves of wild beasts in forests; some like the hollow caverns and passages that are seen in mines, with caverns extending towards the lower regions. Most of the hells are threefold, the upper one appearing within to be in dense darkness, because inhabited by those who are in the falsities of evil; while the lower ones appear fiery, because inhabited by those who are in evils themselves, dense darkness corresponding to the falsities of evil, and fire to evils themselves. Those that have acted interiorly from evil are in the deeper hells, and those that have acted exteriorly from evil, that is, from the falsities of evil, are in the hells that are less deep.

Some hells present an appearance like the ruins of houses and cities after conflagrations, in which infernal spirits dwell and hide themselves. In the milder hells there is an appearance of rude huts, in some cases contiguous in the form of a city with lanes and streets, and within the houses are infernal spirits engaged in unceasing quarrels, enmities, fightings, and brutalities; while in the streets and lanes robberies and depredations are committed. In some of the hells there are nothing but brothels, disgusting to the sight and filled with every kind of filth and excrement.

Again, there are dark forests, in which infernal spirits roam like wild beasts and where, too, there are underground dens into which those flee who are pursued by others. There are also deserts, where all is barren and sandy, and where in some places there are ragged rocks in which there are caverns, and in some places huts. Into these desert places those are cast out from the hells who have suffered every extremity of punishment, especially those who in the world have been more cunning than others in undertaking and contriving intrigues and deceits. Such a life is their final lot. HH 586

What has been said in this work about heaven, the world of spirits, and hell, will be obscure to those who have no interest in learning about spiritual truths, but will be clear to those who have such an interest, and especially to those who have an affection for truth for the sake of truth, that is, who love truth because it is truth; for whatever is then loved enters with light into the mind's thought, especially truth that is loved, because all truth is in light. HH 603 ~Swedenborg, Heaven and Hell

----

****

Volume 4
Section 3

****

3. Free Full Text Access To Swedenborg's Writings

You can search and read the Writings of Swedenborg at this Web site:
http://www.eswedenborg.com/

The following titles to Swedenborg's Writings are links to full text copies of each work. These are made available by Sacred-Texts Web site: http://www.sacred-texts.com/index.htm.

SPIRITUAL DIARY [1747-65]

ARCANA COELESTIA [1749-56]

APOCALYPSE EXPLAINED [1757-9]

LAST JUDGMENT POSTHUMOUS [1757-9]

LAST JUDGMENT [1758]

LAST JUDGMENT CONTINUED [1758]

HEAVEN AND HELL [1758]

WHITE HORSE [1758]

THE NEW JERUSALEM AND ITS HEAVENLY DOCTRINE [1758]

EARTHS IN THE UNIVERSE [1758]

ATHANASIAN CREED [1759]

DE DOMINO [1760]

PROPHETS AND PSALMS [1761]

DE VERBO [1762]

DIVINE LOVE [1762-3]

DIVINE WISDOM [1762-3]

DIVINE LOVE AND WISDOM [1763]

DOCTRINE OF FAITH [1763]

DOCTRINE OF LIFE [1763]

DOCTRINE OF SACRED SCRIPTURES [1763]

DOCTRINE OF THE LORD [1763]

DIVINE PROVIDENCE [1764]

APOCALYPSE REVEALED [1766]

CHARITY [1766]

DE CONJUGIO [1766]

CONJUGIAL LOVE [1768]

GOD THE SAVIOR [1768]

CANONS [1769]

BRIEF EXPOSITION [1769]

INTERACTION OF THE SOUL AND BODY [1769]

TRUE CHRISTIAN RELIGION [1771]

CORONIS [1771]

INVITATION TO THE NEW CHURCH [1771]

The following is an authoritative and detailed biography of Swedenborg:

Dr. R. L. Tafel, *Documents Concerning the Life and Character of Emanuel Swedenborg* (1877)

Full text available here:
https://archive.org/stream/documentsconcern21tafe/documentsconcern21tafe_djvu.txt
And also here:
https://archive.org/details/documentsconcern00tafe

Online biographies and commentary works based on the Writings of Emanuel Swedenborg are available full text here:
http://www.swedenborgstudy.com/books.htm
Or here:
https://web.archive.org/web/20170314104308/http://www.swedenborgstudy.com/books.htm

****
Volume 4
Section 4
****

4. Jung's Psychology Of The Collective Unconscious

Jung writes:
> We analyze dreams not in order to learn about particular matters, but to learn about the relationship of the unconscious to these matters, namely, to learn whether certain conscious developments coincide with the collective unconscious, or what the reasons are for certain disturbances in the conscious. ~Carl Jung, Visions Seminar, Pages 1356

> The idea of 'instinct' is of course nothing more than a collective term for all kinds of organic and psychic factors whose nature is for the most part unknown. …

... The ways that lead to conscious realization are many, but they follow definite laws. In general, the change begins with the onset of the second half of life. The middle period of life is a time of enormous mental importance....

... Every man carries within him the eternal image of woman, not the image of this or that particular woman, but a definite feminine image. This image is fundamentally unconscious, an hereditary factor of primordial origin engraved in the living organic system of the man, an imprint or 'archetype" of all the ancestral experiences of the female, a deposit, as it were, of all the impressions ever made by woman-in short, an inherited system of psychic adaptation. Even if no women existed, it would still be possible, at any given time, to deduce from this unconscious image exactly how a woman would have to be constituted psychically. The same is true of the woman: she too has her inborn image of man.

Actually, we know from experience that it would be more accurate to describe it as an image of men, whereas in the case of the man it is rather the image of woman. Since this image is unconscious, it is always unconsciously projected upon the person of the beloved, and is one of the chief reasons for passionate attraction or aversion. I have called this image the "anima," and I find the scholastic question Habet mulier animam? especially interesting, since in my view it is an intelligent one inasmuch as the doubt seems justified.

Woman has no anima, no soul, but she has an animus. The anima has an erotic, emotional character, the animus a rationalizing one. Hence most of what men say about feminine eroticism, and particularly about the emotional life of women, is derived from their own anima projections and distorted accordingly. On the other hand, the astonishing assumptions and fantasies that women make about men come from the activity of the animus, who produces an inexhaustible supply of illogical arguments and false explanations.

Anima and animus are both characterized by an extraordinary many-sidedness. In a marriage it is always the contained who projects this image upon the container, while the latter is only partially able to project his unconscious image upon his partner. The more unified and simple this

partner is, the less complete the projection. In which case, this highly fascinating image hangs as it were in mid air, as though waiting to be filled out by a living person. ~Carl Jung, Marriage as a Mental Relationship, in The Development of Personality (1954/1991), Volume 17 of The Collected Works of C.G. Jung
[see copy in: articles-books/marriage books/Jung article]

+++

It was the anticipatory quality in dreams that was first valued by antiquity and they played an important role in the ritual of many religions. It is impossible to put the conscious before the unconscious, for the latter exists before and after consciousness.

In childhood we are still contained in it and our consciousness slowly emerges from it as islands that gradually join together and form a continent. It is as if our consciousness were a continent, an island or even a ship on the great sea of the unconscious.

The subject of the unconscious has been occupying philosophers for some time back and there are thousands of examples on every side that show how consciousness is fed from the unconscious; we are only able to speak if ideas flow to us from the unconscious part of the psyche, which is the mother of consciousness.

So we cannot judge dreams from the conscious point of view, but can only think of them as complementary to consciousness. Dreams answer the questions of our conscious. It is a primeval belief that questions can be put to the Gods and answered by dreams.

We are not far from the truth, in fact we are very near to primeval truth, when we think of our dreams as answers to questions, which we have asked and which we have not asked. ~Carl Jung, ETH Lectures, 23 November 1934

+++

Without personal life, without the here and now, we cannot attain to the supra-personal. Personal life must first be fulfilled in order that the process of the supra-personal side of the psyche can be introduced. ~Carl Jung, The Psychology of Kundalini Yoga, Page 66

+++

Individuation is not that you become an ego—you would then become an individualist. You know, an individualist is a man who did not succeed in individuating; he is a philosophically distilled egotist. ~Carl Jung, The Psychology of Kundalini Yoga, Pages 39-40

+++

If you succeed in remembering yourself, if you succeed in making a difference between yourself and that outburst of passion, then you discover the self; you begin to individuate. ~~Carl Jung, The Psychology of Kundalini Yoga, Pages 39-40

+++

In contrast to the meditation found in yoga practice, the psychoanalytic aim is to observe the shadowy presentation — whether in the form of images or of feelings — that are spontaneously evolved in the unconscious psyche and appear without his bidding to the man who looks within. In this way we find once more things that we have repressed or forgotten. Painful though it may be, this is in itself a gain — for what is inferior or even worthless belongs to me as my Shadow and gives me substance and mass. How can I be substantial if I fail to cast a Shadow? I must have a dark side also if I am to be whole; and inasmuch as I become conscious of my Shadow I also remember that I am a human being like any other. ~Carl Jung; Modern Man in Search of a Soul; Page 35

+++

People will do anything, no matter how absurd, in order to avoid facing their own souls. They will practice Indian yoga and all its exercises, observe a strict regimen of diet, learn theosophy by heart, or mechanically repeat mystic text from the literature of the whole world - all because they cannot get on with themselves and have not slightest faith that anything useful could ever come out of their own souls. Thus the soul has been turned into a Nazareth Gradually from which nothing good can come. Therefore let us fetch it from the four corners of the earth - the more far-fetched and bizarre it is the better. ~ Carl Jung, Psychology and Alchemy, Page 99

Many people are familiar with the phrase the "*collective unconscious*" that was introduced in the work of world-renowned psychiatrist Carl Jung in the 20th century. As a mini review of how Jung's concept is described in popular literature, let's take a look at a few selected paragraphs from *Wikipedia*. They will show how Jung's collective unconscious has entered into popular consciousness and understanding.

From Wikipedia: (2016)

> **Collective unconscious** (German: kollektives Unbewusstes), a term coined by Carl Jung, refers to structures of the unconscious mind which are shared among beings of the same species. According to Jung, the human collective unconscious is populated by instincts and by archetypes: universal symbols such as the Great Mother, the Wise Old Man, the Shadow, the Tower, Water, the Tree of Life, and many more.
>
> Jung considered the collective unconscious to underpin and surround the unconscious mind, distinguishing it from the personal unconscious of Freudian psychoanalysis. He argued that the collective unconscious had profound influence on the lives of individuals, who lived out its symbols and clothed them in meaning through their experiences. The psychotherapeutic practice of analytical psychology revolves around examining the patient's relationship to the collective unconscious.
>
> The name "collective unconscious" first appeared in Jung's 1916 essay, "The Structure of the Unconscious". This essay distinguishes between the

"personal", Freudian unconscious, filled with sexual fantasies and repressed images, and the "collective" unconscious encompassing the soul of humanity at large. ...

Jung explains a few years later:

> *My thesis then, is as follows: in addition to our immediate consciousness, which is of a thoroughly personal nature ... there exists a second psychic system of a collective, universal, and impersonal nature which is identical in all individuals. This collective unconscious does not develop individually but is inherited. It consists of pre-existent forms, the archetypes, which can only become conscious secondarily and which give definite form to certain psychic contents. ~Carl Jung, The Concept of the Collective Unconscious, 1936*

As modern humans go through their process of individuation, moving out of the collective unconscious into mature selves, they establish a persona—which can be understood simply as that small portion of the collective psyche which they embody, perform, and identify with.

The collective unconscious exerts overwhelming influence on the minds of individuals. These effects of course vary widely, since they involve virtually every emotion and situation. At times, the collective unconscious can terrify, but it can also heal. ~Wikipedia, 2016

These selections anticipate some of Jung's most striking ideas that I discuss in this book. In what follows I will discuss Jung's striking propositions.

Proposition 1. In addition to our familiar "individual consciousness" or everyday awareness, there is a second mental system that is unknown to the individual and may be called "the collective unconscious".

Proposition 2. The collective unconscious is inherited and is the same for all individuals. It contains the mental life of the whole human race. Our own mental life experiences add themselves to the collective unconscious, and will therefore be inherited by future individuals.

Proposition 3. The content of the collective unconscious is spiritual, not natural like the content of our individual consciousness or awareness in daily life. Spiritual content includes instincts, archetypes, and universal symbols in literature and dreams, such as the Great Mother, the Wise Old Man, the Shadow, the Tower, Water, the Tree of Life, etc. These are mental metaphors for different types of mental activities that are going on constantly in the human mind. We are not aware of these ongoing activities in our mind.

Proposition 4. As the collective unconscious is part of the human mind, it must have an anatomical component or substance. In other words, the entire human race is connected anatomically through the inherited collective unconscious. Through that anatomical connection every human being has mental access to every other individual that has ever been born.

Proposition 5. The mental activity that is forever going on in the collective unconscious has a strong influence on our conscious growth and development. The mental growth process of "individuation" or "regeneration" is guided by particular organic components of the collective unconscious that the individual mind absorbs for consummation as mental food. This reception from the collective unconscious shapes our developing
.

The details of this interaction can be known by studying the correspondences between mental and natural activity. These include symbols, dreams, legends, and spiritual ideas that are expressed metaphorically throughout the *Sacred Scripture* texts of all the major religions in history. Jungian psychotherapy known as "analytical psychology" involves giving the patient a clearer understanding of how mental forces in the collective unconscious influence the patient's emotions and relationships.

****

Great art has always derived its fruitfulness from the myth, from the unconscious process of symbolization. ~Carl Jung

5. The Collective Unconscious

I will now expand a little each of the numbered items listed above. I will use what I know from the Swedenborg Reports as background knowledge.

Jung's Proposition 1. In addition to our familiar "individual consciousness" or everyday awareness, there is a second mental system that is unknown to the individual and may be called "the collective unconscious".

In order to understand this fully we need to know that the mind is not just in the brain but also in every part of the body. This means that the mind and the body have the same shape and completely overlap each other, both outside and in all its internal organs.

It's amazing to me that this basic fact is almost completely unknown today in the modern world. Ask people to make a sketch or drawing of the mind. See if you can find even one person who will draw the human body. And to go even further, the body takes its shape from the mind, and not the other way around.

The next idea is to understand what the mind-body is made of. Unless we know this, we know and believe nothing. To understand this we need to know that God created two worlds, the physical world of matter, time, and space, and the spiritual world of the mind which is not matter, not time, not space, but consciousness and truths which are made of mental substance.

We are born in both worlds simultaneously with two functionally connected bodies, one in each world. The physical body is a model of the mental or spiritual body, which is our mind. We live in the spiritual world with our mental or spiritual body. We are consciously aware of the physical world through the sense organs of the physical body.

The physical body is temporary and will be separated from our spiritual body by the dying process. At that point we are no longer conscious of anything in the physical world, but continue our immortal life in our mental or spiritual body. We can now see and interact with everyone else who has passed through the dying procedure since the beginning of the human race on all the inhabited planets.

Now we can finally understand Jung's statement that there is "second psychic system" that he called the collective unconscious.

The collective unconscious refers prior to death to what becomes the collective conscious after death.

In other words, right now as you are reading this, you can abstractly think that there is a mental life that you are not aware of. You cannot consciously access that portion of your mind even though you know it is within you. That inaccessible portion of your own mind is called the collective unconscious. Now you can still abstractly think about what that collective unconscious is like. But you already know that you will be able to access that portion of your mind immediately following the two-day dying resuscitation procedure that cuts off all access to the physical world that you enjoyed while you were connected to your temporary physical physical body on earth.

Now you can see how it is true that "*The collective unconscious prior to death becomes the collective conscious after death.*" This statement becomes even clearer when you consider that the spiritual world is a telepathic medium. Mental things do not have physical space or quantitative limits. Think about your dreams and your imagination. You are spontaneously capable of creating or removing space or size or number. It will be amazing to experience consciousness in the spiritual world after death. We will then still be mental beings as we are now, but now we are restricted and imprisoned in the sensory organs of our earth-bound physical body.

This is why time and space are no longer separators in the collective consciousness of the afterlife. We now have passed through the gates of death and are freed from our former limitations. No time or space can separate individuals. We now have access to anyone who ever lived and has passed through death. There is only one spiritual world for humanity.

> *Jung's Proposition* 2. The collective unconscious is inherited and is the same for all individuals. It contains the mental life of the whole human race. Our own mental life experiences add themselves to the collective unconscious, and will therefore be inherited by future individuals.

To make this clearer, keep in mind that the spiritual world is made of mental substance. Something cannot exist in nothing. The physical world is constructed of a limited number of chemical elements that God created within a framework of time and space. Similarly, God constructed the spiritual world with a limited number of spiritual substances within a framework apart from time and space. This framework is called "eternity".

So we are born into the spiritual world eternity with a permanent spiritual body called the mind or individual. This immortal spiritual body is made of spiritual substance called love-substance and its associated truth-substance. God created the spiritual world of eternity from the living and immortal substance that is God's Human mind. Remember that if you accept the idea of creation by God you also accept its logical implications.

So if God created the universe what was the construction material given that nothing existed yet. For many generations tradition gives the answer that God created the world out of nothing. But the modern mind sees this as illogical, and therefore needs another type of answer, namely, that everything is created from things that are uncreate in God.

In other words, there are two kinds of things that are part of our reality. These are created things and uncreate things. Clearly, God had to use uncreate things in order to create the physical and spiritual worlds.

So now you understand how it is the case that you were born into the spiritual world of eternity with an immortal spiritual body that is made of God's human love-substance and its associated truth-substance. And you also understand that you were unconscious of this spiritual world of eternity prior to the death of your temporary physical body.

Jung's Proposition 3. The content of the collective unconscious is spiritual, not natural like the content of our individual consciousness or awareness in daily life. Spiritual content includes instincts, archetypes, and universal symbols in literature and dreams, such as the Great Mother, the Wise Old Man, the Shadow, the Tower, Water, the Tree of Life, etc. These are metaphors for different types of mental activities that are going on constantly in the human mind. We are not aware of these ongoing activities in our mind.

It is startling to learn that so much more is going on in our mind than what we are conscious of. It makes sense to think that the consciousness that we have in the afterlife of eternity is higher and more complex than the consciousness we have now being attached to our temporary physical body. We may call this level of rationality our "natural consciousness". This is what we are aware of in our daily lives.

The higher consciousness that we have in the afterlife of eternity may be called spiritual consciousness. When separated from our temporary physical body at its "death", our consciousness is no longer restricted and limited to material ideas that apply to the physical world. Suddenly we become aware of a superior rationality with more complex and exquisite meanings of spiritual truths about reality, God, love, intelligence, society, flowers, animals, etc.

A still higher level of rationality and thinking is called celestial consciousness. Here we are practically omniscient in the sense that anything we think of and want to know more about it is instantly available in our awareness. There is no feeling of active learning or research. These are instantaneous. At the celestial level of consciousness we live with others in eternity who are also in their celestial consciousness.

Now what to me is startling to no end is that all three levels of human consciousness are already complete in our mental anatomy. *What we aspire to in knowledge, wisdom, and higher consciousness is something that we have already functioning in us.* The problem is not one of "learning, growing, and developing" but one of accessing

we have access to each other's celestial consciousness. We then are immersed in a collective consciousness of the ultimate human level. This is what every human being is born to achieve. Every individual is given at birth a genetic potentials packet of human potentials that enable the individual to undergo regeneration in adulthood. This refers to the daily self-modification efforts we perform in order to resist our selfish loves and adopt mutual love.

All celestial consciousness is immersed in mutual love, and where there is no mutual love there can be no celestial consciousness. Mutual love means that one loves others more than self. Mutual love rejects doing things for self-interest, self-justification and self-centered intentions.

Mutual love rejects selfish emotions such as anger, resentment, deception, unfairness, hatred, hostility, disrespect, inconsiderateness, prejudice, discrimination, criminality, violence, unhealthy lifestyle, laziness or lack of ambition, and other such tendencies that we inherit, acquire, and practice in lifestyle.

So regeneration or individuation is the continued mental development of the mind that alters our basic personality from self-love to mutual love. The further we go into this phase the more we enter celestial consciousness.

> *Jung's Proposition 4. As the collective unconscious is part of the human mind, it must have an anatomical component or substance. In other words, the entire human race is connected anatomically through the inherited collective unconscious. Through that anatomical connection every human being has mental access to every other individual that has ever been born.*

So many of spiritual propositions that come to our awareness are amazing and startling. But Proposition 4 must be one of the most startling of all. It contains the spiritual idea that the minds of human beings are anatomically interconnected. We are born with our mind into the afterlife world of eternity. We don't go anywhere at "death" when we are separated from our temporary physical physical body. We are already there from birth. Nothing of our mind can exist in the physical physical body, and our mind was never "out there" in the physical world.

A logical consequence of our anatomical connectedness is that whatever mental activity is going on with one individual reverberates and communicates itself to all other individuals through that common human anatomy. *Consider this awesome fact*: what you have on your mind, the things you think of, communicates itself to all other individuals in the universe regardless of place or phase of growth.

This communication pattern may be called our "community" in order to distinguish it from our horizontal community such as we have here through our physical body. Our natural consciousness with our temporary physical body is influenced through our geographic and physical connection to horizontal communities in the form of geographic location, century, culture, lifestyle, and tradition. In contrast, our spiritual consciousness with our immortal spiritual body is influenced through our vertical communities in the form of anatomical overlap as determined by compatible and similar personalities.

> *Jung's Proposition 5. The mental activity that is forever going on in the collective unconscious has a strong influence on our conscious growth and development. The mental growth process of "individuation" or "regeneration" is guided by particular organic components of the collective unconscious that the individual mind absorbs for consummation as mental food. This reception from the collective unconscious shapes our developing .*
>
> *The details of this interaction can be known by studying the correspondences between mental and natural activity. These include symbols, dreams, legends, and spiritual ideas that are expressed metaphorically throughout the Sacred Scripture texts of all the major religions in history. Jungian psychotherapy known as "analytical psychology" involves giving the patient a clearer understanding of how mental forces in the collective unconscious influence the patient's emotions and relationships.*

Jung talks about "psychic forces" in the collective unconscious that influence our mind and . What are these forces? Where do they come from? You need to know this in order to have a realistic idea about the spiritual world of eternity.

The idea of psychic forces in the spiritual world of human beings implies that these forces are living, immortal, and human. Everything in the spiritual world, and everything in our mind, is living, immortal, and human. This is by definition since only human things can exist in a human spiritual world. This is similar to understanding that only physical things can exist in a physical world. Only mental things can exist in the spiritual world. Hence "psychic forces" refer to the mental forces in people's mind and their consciousness.

For instance, the desire to speak to and hug a good friend is a psychic force in the mind of the individual. The motivational "force" leads you to pick up the phone in order to communicate with the friend. Love is the strongest "psychic force" in the spiritual world of eternity. What is new and amazing in this regard is that the love and motivation of *other people* who live in our collective unconscious have the telepathic power to influence us here while we still are attached to our temporary physical body. This is big news!

Jung discovered that there are people living in our collective unconscious. He talked to some of them. Swedenborg interviewed thousands of people who are living their immortal lives in the spiritual world of eternity. He called the "spiritual world of eternity" and he explained that it is a spiritual world constructed out of love-substance and its truth-substance from the substantial human mind of God.

.

****
Volume 4
Section 6
****

6. Jung On The Thoughts In Our Mind

Jung writes:
> Thoughts are real, they are the consciousness. People can't see that. Einstein could not. ~Carl Jung, J.E.T., p. 90 ff
>
> For the understanding of the unconscious we must see our thoughts as events, as phenomena. We must have perfect objectivity. ~Carl Jung, 1925 Seminar, p. 103
>
> In the process of directed thinking, thoughts are handled as tools, they are made to serve the purposes of the thinker; while in passive thinking thoughts are like individuals going about on their own as it were. ~Carl Jung, 1925 Seminar, p. 28
>
> He [Elijah] said I treated thoughts as if I generated them myself, but, according to his views, thoughts were like animals in a forest, or people in a room, or birds in the air. ~Carl Jung, 1925 Seminar, p. 103
>
> Of course it is quite useful to us to have the idea that our thoughts are free expressions of our intentional thinking, otherwise we would never be free from the magic circle of nature. ~Carl Jung, 1925 Seminar, p. 82
>
> Today we have lost to a great extent this sense of the immanence of thought, as one might put it, and have instead the illusion of making our thoughts ourselves. ~Carl Jung, 1925 Seminar, Page 82
>
> While I am writing this I observe a little demon trying to abscond my words and even my thoughts and turning them over into the rapidly flowing river of images, surging from the mists of the past, portraits of a little boy, bewildered and wondering at an incomprehensibly beautiful and hideously profane and deceitful world. ~Carl Jung, Letters Vol. II, Page 408

Whole numbers may well be the discovery of God's "primal thoughts," as for instance the significant number four, which has distinctive qualities. ~Carl Jung, Letters Vol. II, Pages 301-302

After all, man cannot dissect God's primal thoughts. ~Carl Jung, Letters Vol. II, Pages 301-302

I find that all my thoughts circle round God like the planets round the sun, and are as irresistibly attracted by him. I would feel it the most heinous sin were I to offer any resistance to this compelling force. I feel it is God's will that I should exercise the gift of thinking that has been vouchsafed me. ~Carl Jung, Letters Vol. II, Pages 235-238

I confess I am afraid of a long drawn-out suffering. It seems to me as if I am ready to die, although as it looks to me some powerful thoughts are still flickering like lightnings in a summer night. Yet they are not mine, they belong to God, as everything else which bears mentioning. ~Carl Jung, Letters Vol. 1, Pages 449-450

Just as conscious contents can vanish into the unconscious, other contents can also arise from it. Besides a majority of mere recollections, really new thoughts and creative ideas can appear which have never been conscious before. They grow up from the dark depths like a lotus. ~Carl Jung, Man and His Symbols, Page 37

Then there are philosophical dreams which think for us and in which we get the thoughts that we should have had during the day. ~Carl Jung, ETH Lecture XI 5 July 1934, Page 135

If Neumann recommends the "inner voice" as the criterion of ethical behaviour instead of the Christian conscience, this is in complete agreement with the Eastern view that in everybody's heart there dwells a judge who knows all his evil thoughts. ~Carl Jung, Letters Vol. 1, Pages 518-522

It seems to me as if I am ready to die, although as it looks to me some powerful thoughts are still flickering like lightnings in a summer night. Yet they are not mine, they belong to God, as everything else which bears mentioning. ~Carl Jung, Letters Vol. 1, Pages 449-450

Before my illness I had often asked myself if I were permitted to publish or even speak of my secret knowledge. I later set it all down in Aion. I realized it was my duty to communicate these thoughts, yet I doubted whether I was allowed to give expression to them. During my illness I received confirmation and I now knew that everything had meaning and that everything was perfect. ~Carl Jung, Jung–White Letters, p. 103

A certain line of thought, for instance, is developed through a series of dreams; and I discover that I am the duplicate of my unconscious anticipation of myself; at the same moment I am filled with a sense of purpose as if a secret arrangement of my fate existed. ~Carl Jung, ETH Lecture 26th Jan 1940

Then thoughts come to me, as for instance that consciousness is only an organ for perceiving the fourth dimension, i .e., the all-pervasive meaning, and itself produces no real ideas. ~Carl Jung, Letters Vol. II, Pages 17-18

Just as conscious contents can vanish into the unconscious, other contents can also arise from it. Besides a majority of mere recollections, really new thoughts and creative ideas can appear which have never been conscious before. They grow up from the dark depths like a lotus. ~Carl Jung, Man and His Symbols, Page 37

Then there are philosophical dreams which think for us and in which we get the thoughts that we should have had during the day. ~Carl Jung, ETH Lecture XI 5July1934, Page 135

I must learn that the dregs of my thought, my dreams, are the speech of my soul. I must carry them in my heart, and go back and forth over them in my mind, like the words of the person dearest to me. Dreams are the guiding words of the soul. ~Carl Jung, The Red Book, Page 232

The ego is an illusion which ends with death but the karma remains, it is given another ego in the next illusion. ~Carl Jung, ETH Lecture, Vol. 3, Page 17

+++

We spoke of the beginning of the "Fundamentum" in the last lecture and come today to the sentence: "And the other things on the face of the earth were created for man's sake." This sentence states that not only man but everything on the earth was created. The universe did not simply happen, but was created for the purpose of serving man. This gives man a central significance in creation; he is, so to speak, the summit of creation, the reason that it exists. Man thus acquires a dignity which natural science would never accord him.

From the point of view of natural science everything happened, it found itself, science does not concede any purpose behind creation or that man is in any way its goal. Natural science simply ridicules the old point of view. ~Carl Jung, Lecture IX 19th January, 1940. ETH Lectures, Pages 217-223.

+++

Materialism only began to exist after the beginning the Christian era, when matter really became matter.. Matter became de-spiritualised, and so suffered a de-valuation, which caused the psyche to move up towards the spirit.. The psychical standpoint, that man is in the centre only appeared gradually. The psychical man of antiquity was not the centre of the world, for the centre was in the phenomenal world, the world which was animated and filled by the gods. ~Carl Jung, ETH, 12/6/1940 (compilation from a lecture concerning the beginnings of alchemy.)

+++

Jung treated a man who spent the whole day with people. Jung told him he could never develop that way, everyday he must spend one hour of concentration upon himself to learn what he was inside. The man said he could spend an hour a day playing the piano with his wife. Jung said that would not do, he must be quite alone, without his piano or his wife. "But then I would get quite melancholy!" the man protested.

"Exactly," said Jung. "It is very depressing to be by yourself. But how do you think I can stand you? It is a test to stand yourself. If you can stand yourself, then the world might be able to stand you, but certainly nobody can stand you otherwise. It is like someone who is unwashed."
~Carl Jung, Visions Seminars, Vol. 1, p. 369

+++

Miss Hannah: Was it the self sleeping?

Dr. Jung: Of course, the self is then asleep. And in which stage is the self asleep and the ego conscious?

Here, of course, in this conscious world where we are all reasonable and respectable people, adapted individuals as one says. Everything runs smoothly; we are going to have lunch, we have appointments, we are perfectly normal citizens of certain states. We are under certain obligations and cannot run away easily without getting neurotic; we have to look after our duties. So we are all in the roots, we are upon our root support. ("Root support" is the literal translation of muladhara.) We are in our roots right in this world—when you buy your ticket from the streetcar conductor, for instance, or for the theater, or pay the waiter—that is reality as you touch it. And then the self is asleep, which means that all things concerning the gods are asleep.

Now, after this startling statement we have to find out whether such an interpretation is really justifiable. I am by no means sure. I am even convinced that Professor Hauer would not agree with me right on the spot. In these matters one needs a great deal of psychology in order to make it palatable to the Western mind. If we do not try hard and dare to commit many errors in assimilating it to our Western mentality, we simply get poisoned. For these symbols have a terribly clinging tendency. They catch the unconscious somehow and cling to us. But they are a foreign body in our system—corpus alienum—and they inhibit the natural growth and development of our own psychology. It is like a secondary growth or a poison. Therefore one has to make almost heroic attempts to master these things, to do something against those symbols in order to deprive them of their influence. Perhaps you cannot fully realize what I say, but take it as a hypothesis. It is more than a hypothesis, it is even a truth. I have seen too often how dangerous their influence may be.

If we assume that muladhara, being the roots, is the earth upon which we stand, it necessarily must be our conscious world, because here we are, standing upon this earth, and here are the four corners of this earth. We are in the earth mandala. And whatever we say of muladhara is true of this world. It is a place where mankind is a victim of impulses, instincts, unconsciousness, of participation mystique, where we are in a dark and unconscious place. We are hapless victims of circumstances, our reason practically can do very little. Yes, when times are quiet, if there is no important mental storm, we can do something with the help of technique. But then comes a storm, say, a war or a revolution, and the whole thing is destroyed and we are nowhere.

Moreover, when we are in this three-dimensional space, talking sense and doing apparently meaningful things, we are non-individual—we are just fish in the sea. Only at times have we an inkling of the next Chakra. Something works in certain people on Sunday mornings, or perhaps one day in the year, say Good Friday—they feel a gentle urge to go to church.

Many people instead have an urge to go to the mountains, into nature, where they have another sort of emotion. Now, that is a faint stirring of the sleeping beauty; something which is not to be accounted for starts in the unconscious. Some strange urge underneath forces them to do something which is not just the ordinary thing. So we may assume that the place where the self, the mental non-ego, is asleep is the most banal place in the world—a railway station, a theater, the family, the professional situation— there the gods are sleeping; there we are just reasonable, or as unreasonable, as unconscious animals. And this is muladhara.

If that is so, then the next Chakra, svadhisthana must be the unconscious, symbolized by the sea, and in the sea is a huge leviathan which threatens one with annihilation. Moreover, we must remember that men have made these symbols. Tantric yoga in its old form is surely the work of men, so we can expect a good deal of masculine psychology.

Therefore no wonder that in the second Chakra is the great half-moon, which is of course a female symbol. Also, the whole thing is in the form of the Padma or lotus, and the lotus is the yoni. (Padma is simply the hieratic name, the metaphor for the yoni, the female organ.) ~Carl Jung; Kundalini Yoga

Here is a summary, in his own words, of what Jung says about thoughts.

> Thoughts are real, they are the consciousness. We must see our thoughts as events, as phenomena. We must have perfect objectivity. In directed thinking, thoughts are made to serve the purposes of the thinker; while in passive thinking thoughts are going about on their own. Thoughts [are] as if I generated them myself, but, thoughts [are] like animals in a forest, or people in a room, or birds in the air. It is quite useful to us to have the idea that our thoughts are free expressions of our intentional thinking. [We do not see] the immanence of thought, and have instead the illusion of making our thoughts ourselves. ~Carl Jung (as quoted above)

.
.

From here we can see that Jung realized that thoughts are omnipresent or "immanent" in the spiritual world. It also shows that Jung realized that thoughts were not "generated" by the thinker, as is commonly believed. Instead, thoughts are immanent and they come into our conscious mind and we do not know from where. The thoughts just appear.

Swedenborg proved by empirical observations many times confirmed that thoughts are telepathically communicated to all individuals. To me this is equivalent to saying that thoughts are omnipresent. This follows logically since there is no space in the spiritual world. I conclude therefore that everything in the spiritual world is omnipresent, which means that God creates us in such a way that every human being has access to the thoughts of all other human beings. Jung was also aware of this when he wrote more than once that the psychic world has no size but is endless. He asserted that the Self of every human being is located in the collective unconscious of humanity that has no limits.

Philosophers, psychologists, and psycholinguists have been debating were thoughts come from, but were unable to give a satisfactory answer according to their own reckoning. Thanks to the pioneering work of Jung and Swedenborg we now can know where thoughts come from. The answer is that they don't come from anywhere. They are always there!

Thoughts are omnipresent and without time limitations. The spiritual world is called the spiritual world of eternity because there is no time and space in the spiritual world. Where there is no time there is eternity, a word that means apart from time and space.

We come back to the question of why are we not aware that all thoughts are present all the time?

The reason we are not aware is because our awareness or consciousness is made to face an opaque, dark, and impenetrable wall or veil. Jung and Swedenborg discovered ways of lifting the veil here and there, or finding windows in the wall through which we can have a glimpse of the world of eternity, that is apart from time and space. This is what we call the afterlife world of eternity, which is the same as the spiritual world of eternity, as discussed throughout this book.

As you are reading this the meanings and thoughts are operating in our mental or spiritual body, which is the body we have now and in the afterlife. Nothing of the meaning is located in the brain of your physical body whose biomedical sensory organs are communicated to your mental or spiritual body. Your spiritual body is looking through the eyes of the physical body. Some people think that this would mean that we are inside the physical body and looking out. This idea is physical and therefore impossible since a spiritual body cannot exist in a physical atmosphere of time and place.

Hence it is that our consciousness and knowledge are limited or restricted to the physical conditions. There is nothing mental in this. And because our spiritual body in eternity sees and touches and hears and tastes through the physical body on earth, we are under the powerful illusion that we are on earth and that we are the physical body. But as soon as the physical body becomes what is called a "corpse" the spiritual body can no longer access or be aware of the physical world. At that point our sensory input is from the spiritual world of eternity. Now at last we can see, hear, taste, touch with our mental or spiritual body, without the interference or restrictive medium of the physical body.

Both Jung and Swedenborg found methodical ways of exploring the spiritual world of eternity for decades of their activity on earth with their physical body. Jung travelled into the collective unconscious of the psychic world through the use of mental vehicles and systems of thinking that he collected from dreams and symbolism in religion and art. Swedenborg travelled into the spiritual world of the afterlife in eternity and explored the afterlife communities and societies that gather there.

I still need to explain how each person selects thoughts from the universe of all thoughts that are co-present in his or her mind. Only God has the infinite ability, intelligence, and wisdom to perceive, manage, and order all the thoughts of the mental universe. Swedenborg asserts that God wills to arrange all thoughts in the universe into the human form, both externally and internally.

But finite human minds cannot view the entirety of thoughts, and can only be aware of an infinitesimal bit of the totality. The mechanism that God makes available to our spiritual body may be called the *dynamics of love*. I use this expression in the sense that love in the spiritual world corresponds to gravity and energy in the physical world. Love is the energy and power that operates the spiritual world of substance in eternity.

For instance, when the first phase of the afterlife-changes is completed, we enter the second phase, which is deeper into the personality and more definitive. Love is the deepest structure of our affective system in the mental or spiritual body. Love in our spiritual body in eternity corresponds to blood in the physical body on earth. It is well known that the heart signifies love. This knowledge comes from correspondences that we discover between our spiritual body functions and our physical body functions in the physical body.

Every personality is ordered and restricted according to the ruling love of the person, which is at the very center and root of the personality. The ruling love arranges all loves underneath it, and permits only those loves in the personality that agree with the ruling love.

The dynamics of love creates the psychology of archetypes.

He who wishes to take the Kingdom of Heaven by storm, to conquer and eradicate evil by force, is already in the hands of evil. Carl Jung, Conversations with C.G. Jung, p. 47

The Kingdom of Heaven is a primordial condition like Paradise, but it is later in time and cannot be reached by regressing, only be going forward. We do not know whether our present order is final. At another level a new creative solution may be required. Carl Jung, Conversations with C.G. Jung, p. 39

He said "My kingdom is not of this world." But "kingdom" it was, all the same. Carl Jung, C.G. Jung Speaking, p. 97

Social welfare has replaced the kingdom of God. Carl Jung, Letters Vol. 1, p. 534-537

"Therefore strive first to know yourselves, because ye are the city and the city is the kingdom." Oxyrhynchus Papyrus 654; Cited by Carl Jung; Letters Vol. 1, p. 523-524

To reach the Kingdom of God is the last stage in a Christian meditation, but our Buddhist text, unlike Christian- ity, goes a step beyond the saintly multitude. Carl Jung, Modern Psychology, p. 22

Transitions between the aeons always seem to have been melancholy and despairing times, as for instance the collapse of the Old Kingdom in Egypt ("The Dialogue of a World; Weary Man with His Soul") between Taurus and Aries, or the melancholy of the Augustinian age between Aries and Pisces. Carl Jung, Letters Vol. II, p. 229-230

These [UFO] symbolisms, which are cropping up everywhere nowadays, paint a picture of the end of time with its eschatological conceptions: destruction of the world, coming of the Kingdom of Heaven or of the world redeemer. Carl Jung, Letters Vol. II, p. 476-477

The author shows an amazingly sympathetic knowledge of the introvert of the thinking type, and hardly less for the other types. . . . Jung has revealed the inner kingdom of the soul marvelously well and has made the signal discovery of the value of phantasy. His book has a manifold reach and grasp, and many reviews with quite different subject matter could be written about it." Sonu Shamdasani, Introduction 1925 Seminar, p. xi

The Kingdom of Heaven is within ourselves. It is our innermost nature and something between ourselves. The Kingdom of Heaven is between people like cement. Carl Jung, Visions Seminar, Page 444.

To reach the Kingdom of God is the last stage in a Christian meditation, but our Buddhist text, unlike Christian-ity, goes a step beyond the saintly multitude. Carl Jung, Modern Psychology, p. 22

****

Volume 4
Section 7

****

7. The Archetypes of Afterlife Societies

Swedenborg made repeated ethnographic observations of afterlife societies that are distributed everywhere in the spiritual world of eternity, and are arranged relative to each other by the geography and physiology of body anatomy. Swedenborg discovered that each afterlife society is distinguished from other societies by what the ruling love is in which are all its members. This is the archetype of that society.

Each afterlife society in eternity lives in its own archetype. Hence what Jung called an archetype is the same as what Swedenborg called ruling love in the personality. Mental symbolism in dreams, art, myth, and religion are ordered by groupings of humanity's ruling loves that are called mental archetypes.

Archetypes are loves, and loves are made of mental substance and formed into the human form. God "plants" or forms these loves inside the personality of every human being. The distribution of human loves is the distribution of mental archetypes that create the distribution of afterlife societies in the Grand Human and Grand Monster, as I discuss elsewhere in this book.

In order to understand the mind we need to understand what part of our mind is the "collective unconscious" and what part is the "conscious" with which we are familiar in daily life.

We need to know that the collective unconscious refers to our perspective in natural-consciousness when we are thinking about something mental or spiritual. We are then always thinking about everything using only material ideas and their thoughts. In this naturalized mental state we make sense of the "collective unconscious" as something in our mind that is not part of us, or even hostile and mean to us.

The idea of the negative psychic power and the invisibility of the collective unconscious, incites in us feelings of anxiety, terror, and dread. Some of Jung's descriptions throughout his work of the collective unconscious are indeed scary and anxiety provoking. One of the best known is titled *The Red Book*. If you do an internet search of that title you will witness the enormous general interest that the ideas of Jung's Red Book have elicited in people today.

But all this is like a heavy black curtain on a stage. It is designed to lift or part asunder giving sight to what it was hiding. The idea of the "collective unconscious" is a heavy black curtain blocking our awareness of Consciousness.

Another confusing aspect when trying to understand the collective unconscious is this: Jung wrote that he met his departed parents in the collective unconscious. He also reports that all our ancestors all the way back to the beginning are in the collective unconscious. This is confusing because the collective unconscious is in the mind of every individual. How then can all those ancestors be in the mind of each individual?

This puzzle gets unconfused when you consider that every human individual has a mental life and that the location of this mental activity is the spiritual world of eternity. But logically we know that there is only one eternity. Therefore when we say the afterlife of eternity, or the spiritual world of eternity, or the afterlife world of eternity, or the spiritual world of eternity – it is the same reference because of "eternity".

This is one of the most amazing discoveries I have made in my career of nearly 60 years as a psychologist. The discovery that the world of the afterlife is the same as the spiritual world is astonishing! Think of the implications. For instance, first, that we are born into eternity with our immortal mental or spiritual body. Second, since eternity is the afterlife in which we exist after death, then it follows that we are born into the afterlife of eternity where we still are and always will be.

Just think! You are now in the afterlife of eternity! Your thoughts and feelings are activities of your immortal spiritual body that is located in the spiritual world of eternity. But there is only one spiritual world in which every human being is and remains forever. Hence it follows that all the people who ever lived are in the afterlife of eternity, which is our spiritual world, the one we are familiar now.

So all humanity passes on at death into the same spiritual world as they were in from birth. This means that there is really no "passing" int the afterlife, as the common expressions says. The spiritual reality is that we are already in the afterlife.

But there is a change at "death". Prior to death our awareness of Consciousness was very limited. Our awareness was determined by the sensory input of our physical physical body. At death we are separated from our physical physical body and lose all input from the natural world. Now at last our sensory input comes from the mental or spiritual body's sensory organs. We can now detect what is going on in the afterlife world.

Now we can see all the other humanity that ever lived attached to an physical body on earth and entered the afterlife world through death. Everybody we ever heard of from antiquity is there, accessible to see, hear, or touch.

****
Volume 4
Section 8
****

8. Dual Consciousness And The Unity Of Opposites

There is no consciousness without discrimination of opposites.
~Carl Jung, Mental Aspects of the Mother Archetype, CW 9i, par. 178

There are many so-called "opposites" that I discuss throughout the book. Here are some of them as I try to reconstruct it from memory:

(1) semantic opposites, reflecting the unity of emotional meaning
(2) individual and collective consciousness, as the balance of subjective and objective
(3) collective unconscious and collective consciousness, being each other's front view and back view
(4) waking consciousness and dreaming consciousness, dependent on each other like cerebrum and cerebellum
(5) higher consciousness before the Fall and lower consciousness after the Fall, one succeeding the other
(6) restricted individual consciousness while attached to the physical body on earth and individual consciousness in the spiritual body in eternity
(7) Grand Human and Grand Monster, form contrastive personalities in part and in whole
(5) part and whole, in which the smallest is a model of the whole
(4) male and female, as the unity between truth and love substance
(6) wife and husband, as the oneminded couple in conjugial love
(7) natural and spiritual mind, anatomically conjoined in the spiritual body

(8) spiritual world and physical world, united as cause and effect
(9) material ideas and non-material ideas, conjoined by correspondences
(10) literal meaning of God's Word and spiritual meaning, conjoined by symbolism
(11) mutual love and self-love, the psychodynamic theme of regeneration
(12) can you find some others?

It is clear just from this list that God creates opposites as a strategy for balancing two mental operations so that they may work together in our personality. Jung discovered that the yin/yang symbol signifies the union of opposites in the human mind. Swedenborg discovered by empirical observation that every afterlife society in the heavenly regions has a connection by correspondence with a particular afterlife society in the hell regions. Jung observed that consciousness itself depends on "discrimination of opposites". Swedenborg showed that there is consciousness ceases without sensory-motor input.

When Jung discovered archetypes he was violently attacked by the shadow archetypes of darkness but he was protected by the archetypes of light with whom he felt safe and cared for. Archetypes are mental soul-like forces that live in the personality of human being. They are created there by God who uses them as mental management tools to guide and instruct the individual. Through the mental forces of archetypes God can produce all the mental states that assist people in undergoing regeneration of personality.

And for those who are not yet undergoing regeneration or are unwilling to do so, God provides sub-conscious mental urges, attractions, and aversions that unconsciously lead the individual to less extreme and less hurtful modes of expression and lifestyle habits. God moderates the extremism of selfish personalities through fear and negative consequences. God encourages more positive ways of interacting with others through rewards and success.

> *There is no form of human tragedy that does not in some measure proceed from conflict between the ego and the unconscious. ~Carl Jung, Analytical Psychology and Weltanschauung, CW 8, par. 706*

The "ego" is our individual consciousness by itself. Our ego's relationship to the collective unconscious is that of oppositional conflict. Since the Fall of consciousness the ego of every individual may be called the "Fallen ego" because it is born with an inherited mental wall between individual consciousness and collective consciousness. What before the Fall was the collective consciousness, after the Fall became the collective unconscious. The anatomical Fall in consciousness in the history of this earth refers to this seeming disappearance behind a mental wall of collective consciousness. Now a new psychology began and has evolved.

> *The repressed content must be made conscious so as to produce a tension of opposites, without which no forward movement is possible. ~Carl Jung, The Problem of the Attitude-Type, CW 7, par. 78*

"Mental movement" is the process of maturing and becoming more capable individuals. Jung observed that this movement proceeds by means of apparent opposites in the personality. "Repressed content" is the aversion that we feel in our individual consciousness for anything that threatens the current mental supremacy of self, which is "What I want". Jung observed in his psychotherapy work that ego fights against personality change through the negative subjective experience of conflict and avoidance. The unconscious fights the ego in order to enter or penetrate individual consciousness. Jung observed that there is no "forward movement" in therapy without experiencing this conflict.

In this all important mental conflict or mental warfare, God uses archetypes of mutual love to defeat the archetypes of self-love. As Jung puts it, "*all consciousness, perhaps without being aware of it, seeks its unconscious opposite*". But the conflict must be conscious to the individual. God cannot exchange destructive self-love with enhancing mutual love in our personality without our agreement and conscious cooperation. If it the change in personality were to be hidden and unconscious, it would not work and there would be no "forward movement" which results in "stagnation and ossification". Our ego would reject the mutual love that God is promoting. Mental conflict between personality opposites is a necessary experience.

Jung saw the therapist's work as assisting the individual in allowing or agreeing to such experience of conflict. One strategy he used was the now well-known dream analysis techniques that he taught his patients. Another strategy, not as well known, was to recommend patients to get in touch with their childhood idea of God and return to that innocent and accepting relationship. Jung's idea was picked up by water signifies natural truth, wine signifies spiritual truth, fire signifies love, Sarah signifies intellectual truth, the number 12 signifies the complete complex of faith and worship, 40 signifies temptations.

According to Jung "*Life is born only of the spark of opposites*". Mental health and individuation are outcomes of the individual's war against egoism or egotism. Regeneration consists of two steps that follow each other in order to make forward progression.

One step is to face the enemy of our happiness in eternity. It is ego. The personality of ego is the embodiment of the symbol: "*me first; then maybe you or maybe not, depending on how I like it*". No society or group can survive if people are egotistical, supporting only what is good for themselves.

So the first phase in mental "forward movement" is to confront the psychic forces that are threatening to ego. The greater the tension in this confrontation, the more effective it will be as a change factor, and the more permanent the change with little regression.

Today Jungian therapists or analysts recognize the importance of assisting individuals in discovering then incorporating mental forces in their that are unconscious and need to be made conscious. This incorporation or psychodynamic resolution is what Jung called the "united personality".

> *The united personality will never quite lose the painful sense of innate discord. Complete redemption from the sufferings of this world is and must remain an illusion. Christ's earthly life likewise ended, not in complacent bliss, but on the cross.* ~Carl Jung, The Psychology of the Transference, CW 16, par. 400

What Jung called *"the painful sense of innate discord"*, Swedenborg called the experience of *"spiritual temptations"*. God brings these temptations to the regenerating individual by means of the archetypes of afterlife societies. God brings various afterlife societies into telepathic "communication" with the individual's consciousness as a method for assisting the individual in forward movement in the regeneration process, a systematic personality modification process that takes years and decades.

Jung says that "complete redemption" from selfish and mean personality traits cannot be achieved, and he points to the biography of Jesus Christ that is described in the *New Testament* as ending "on the cross". Swedenborg explains that the "death" on the cross was the final and ultimate temptation in the regeneration of Jesus. Swedenborg explains that God as Jesus caused himself to acquire a physical body on earth for the purpose of regenerating that physical body from the inherited traits of selfism that was passed down the genetic line for many generations.

The personality that needs regeneration is not the physical body since it has no personality or mind, being made of inert chemical and electrical material. It is the natural mind in the spiritual body in eternity that inherits the personality traits. So it is the natural mind that has a Fallen consciousness and contains the collective unconscious. It is the natural mind that struggles against the personality changes and needs to be retrained by temptations and regeneration.

Swedenborg explains that God regenerated the inherited natural mind of Jesus through a series of temptations of which the physical body's "death" on the cross was the last and the most serious. Some of the other temptations are described in the *New Testament*. Throughout these mental temptations, and especially the final temptation on the cross, the physical body of Jesus was transformed into a "*glory body*", which Swedenborg explains is immortal and omnipresent in the spiritual world of eternity.

As a result of the new presence of this Glory Body in the spiritual world of eternity, the natural mind of any individual is capable of perceiving, acknowledging, and relating to this Glory Body. This final result turns out to be the purpose of God acquiring an ordinary physical body on earth. God's plan all along since the beginning of creation was that at some particular point in creation there shall be the new natural presence of God's non-material Glory Body.

Now that the Glory Body is visible to the natural mind it can serve to assist anyone in the regeneration process of the natural mind. The natural mind in the living spiritual body in eternity controls the inert physical body on earth. Regeneration of the natural mind in eternity takes place by managing one's physical body's relationship to other physical bodys on earth. The relationship is through the physical bodys not from the physical bodys, but from the person's natural mind in eternity that controls the physical body on earth.

Jung frequently uses the "Christ" archetype as God and mere human opposites that are reconciled and unified in the archetype image of God-Man. Swedenborg demonstrates that the *Book of Genesis* in the *Old Testament* describes the details of the regeneration of the physical body into the Glory Body that took place thousands of years after the Book of Genesis was dictated to Moses by God or the "Holy spirit" of God.

This is truly an awesome and amazing demonstration. You'll find it in Swedenborg's 12-volume Series called *Heavenly Secrets* (also known as the Latin title of "*Arcana Coelestia*"), and is available full text on the Web. The details are not in the literal sense but in the mental sense in which names like Abraham, Sarah, Jacob, Joseph, Samson, David, etc. are all shown to symbolize particular mental states and personality traits.

Regeneration is the process of reconciling opposites in one's personality. Individuation is the restoration of balance through the opposites. When we face the excruciating egotism and selfishness in our personality we are giving ourselves the occasion for rejecting what is selfish and adopting what is altruistic. Jung points out that heaven cannot exist without hell, and Swedenborg in his dual consciousness confirms this through his explorations of heaven and hell. Good cannot be known unless evil is known. Truth cannot be known unless falsified truth is known.

Note however that to "know" evils and their falsified truths is not to embrace them nor to accept them. Our balance in opposites here is between the truths that are derived from God's Word, especially in the psychological meaning, and the falsified truths or hypotheses that are derived from self-intelligence apart from God's Word.

****

Volume 4
Section 9

****

9. Explanation Of Key Concepts Used In Theistic Psychology

AFTERLIFE, DYING, DEATH

The expression "death" or "dying" originates in the erroneous belief that we are on earth, that we are in the physical body, and that the physical body is living, sensing, thinking, and feeling. Hence also, it is believed that the physical body can "die".

Similarly, the word "afterlife" is based on the erroneous belief that there is death and dying of the physical body and that there is a life "after" death, though people don't know about the immortal spiritual body with which we are born into eternity. Hence many people assume that the "afterlife" takes place in the physical world with a new physical body.

But other people know from the psychological meaning of *Sacred Scripture* that there are two worlds, one physical, and the other "spiritual" or "psychic". They understand that life after death takes place in a separate world called the "spiritual world", which is in the afterlife of eternity. For instance, "heaven" and "hell" are mental "places" or psychological states in the spiritual world of eternity in which people live in the afterlife when they lose connection with the physical body on earth and become active in mental eternity with their spiritual body.

People are not aware that the spiritual world of the afterlife and the mental world of eternity are the same. *You are now in the afterlife world of eternity because you are born into the mental world and you are a mental being.* You are not here on this earth and there is nothing about you that is physical.

There is only one mental world of eternity and all human beings are born into it.

It is not known that everyone in the afterlife speaks the same universal language that is inborn and is activated when we are disconnected from the physical body on earth. Because there is only one universal language used by all human beings we have the happy opportunity in the afterlife of meeting with and interacting with any human being that has ever been born and was connected temporarily to a physical body on one of the numberless earths in the physical universe. Every human being lives in one of the *Grand Human* afterlife societies, or else in one of the *Grand Monster* afterlife societies.

Life in an afterlife society consists of a "*collective psycho-culture*" that is particular and different for each society. Each individual consciousness is immersed in the collective consciousness of that society so that there is a continuous sharing of psychological states between all individuals. Each individual remains unique and does not merge in the collective.

This is because every individual is anatomically unique and reacts to or receives the collective influence in a unique way. The sharing results in an enrichment of individual life or individuation. Everyone in a collective afterlife society becomes more and more an individual with unique potentials and influence or use to others.

ARCHEYTPES AND THE SOUL

God creates the unique soul of each individual. The soul is perfect and is called the "*Temple of God*" that is located within the mind of human beings. The mind is not perfect but has the capacity to individuate endlessly and thus to become more and more perfect as it grows and develops to eternity. This process is called individuation. See the entry on *Individuation*.

The soul has access to the endless pool of archetypes in the collective conscious of humanity. Archetypes are psychic power packs made of mental substance. This substance is omnipresent and is available to the soul for constructing a unique personality with consciousness.

Once we are born the soul activates these implanted psychological archetypes in the spiritual body, different ones for different purposes. The soul activates the psychic forces in our personality in such a way that our personality can be an image and embodiment of the unique soul.

The soul is a psychic organ that operates at a higher human level than the conscious and unconscious mind. The soul is above consciousness in existence. The soul does not possess consciousness but can produce consciousness in the mind that is below and outside itself. The soul interacts with God directly, while the mind interacts with God through the mediation of the soul.

Archetypes came into existence with creation. Since they are omnipresent, every individual mind contains them. This explains what Jung observed that archetypes are known to every generation of humans since the beginning and they are present in dreams, fairy tales, myths, and intuitive artistic creations. All archetypes exist in the collective conscious. They become activated in our personality to assist the process of individuation. See the entry on *Individuation*.

Archetypes are active or inactive. Their pattern of psychic activity in any one personality is motivated and managed to assist the process of individuation. This is the process of interacting with the objective collective conscious and establishing there psychic roots that expand the psychic territory that can be encompassed by or incorporated into one's subjective individual consciousness.

BORN INTO MENTAL ETERNITY: SPIRITUAL BODY, PHYSICAL BODY

God created two worlds, one world with physical matter and in time, and the other world with mental substance and in eternity (or apart from time).

Mental substance is in God's mind, and therefore it is living, human, and eternal. Human beings are born in mental eternity with an immortal spiritual body that is made of mental substance. All mental operations, including our mind, our personality, and our consciousness, operate in the spiritual body.

God temporarily connects our immortal spiritual body to a physical body on earth that is inert and is not capable of having sensations, feelings, or thoughts. Instead, the physical body reacts by correspondence to our thoughts and intentions in the spiritual body. In this way we can develop a natural mind that thinks with material ideas that are adaptive to the conditions on earth.

The purpose of having a body on earth is to be able to temporarily enjoy sensory input from the physical world. Our natural mind uses this sensory input to form material ideas with which to think, solve problems, and become an intelligent adult. After regeneration, this adult natural mind becomes the basis for our spiritual mind and personality in eternity.

All sensory input to our natural mind comes from the physical body. We are therefore not aware of the environment of our spiritual body in mental eternity, and therefore we are not conscious of the presence of other people there.

We have the powerful illusion that we are on earth and that we are the physical body.

This illusion is lifted when we lose contact with the physical body through the "dying-resuscitation" process. *After resuscitation our sensory input is from the environment of the spiritual body in mental eternity.* Hence we can then see everyone else who has undergone the dying process and lives in the afterlife of mental eternity.

The afterlife is called "mental eternity" because everything there is made of mental substance from God's mind.

After resuscitation we begin to explore some of the numberless afterlife societies that form themselves through the law of mental attraction. People who have compatible s and similar loves are spontaneously attracted to each other and collect together to form afterlife societies. We then enter one of these societies that is populated by people with a similar character to ours.

Some of the afterlife societies are called "heavenly" and others are called "hellish". In general, heavenly personalities and societies are formed by people who have acquired mutual love after regeneration of the natural mind. Hellish personalities and societies are formed by people who have not undergone regeneration of the natural mind, so that they have retained inherited that is based on self-love and the love of the world for the sake of self.

COLLECTIVE CONSCIOUS AND THE COLLECTIVE UNCONSCIOUS

The cumulative and endless process of life is unique for each human individual. Not only is the totality unique but every part of it is also unique. Hence no part of individual consciousness can be the same for two individuals. This total subjectivity of individual consciousness would prevent the existence of social and community life, and therefore it needs to be balanced objectively by collective consciousness. This is an intersubjective experience of collectivity, like telepathic sharing of thoughts and emotions.

CONSCIOUSNESS

**Individual consciousness is the awareness of experiencing.

**Collective consciousness is the shared pool of all human capacities.

**Dual consciousness is the awareness of experiencing simultaneously in natural and spiritual consciousness.

**Natural consciousness is the awareness of experiencing in our natural mind, which receives all its sensory input from the physical body and world, and consequently thinks with material ideas.

Spiritual consciousness is the awareness of experiencing in our spiritual mind, which receives all its sensory input from the spiritual body in the psychic world, and consequently thinks with non-material ideas. The psychic world is non-material and psychological, made of mental substance.

**Rational consciousness is the awareness of experiencing in our rational mind, which receives its sensory input from both the natural mind and the spiritual mind, and therefore can think with non-material ideas as well as material ideas.

FAMILY SPIRITS

We all know what thinking is. It defines what it is to be a human being. One of the most amazing realizations of my long career as a psychology professor is my discovery that *thinking is actually collective, and it only appears to us as being individual and private*.

I felt the need to coin a new phrase, *"vertical community"*, which contrasts with our "horizontal community" that everyone is a member of, like citizenship, culture, language, lifestyle habits, religion. Our horizontal community is visible to us.

And yet we are also in a vertical community since birth. By "vertical" I mean to indicate that the community is *internal in our mind* relative to the horizontal community, which is external and involving the physical body.

We begin our afterlife immediately following the two-day dying-resuscitation procedure. We are then active in our immortal spiritual body, which is where the operations of our mind take place since birth. The people who are in our vertical community is determined by compatibility of personality.

Since we inherit our basic we have an automatic connection with those in the afterlife of eternity who have a similar to the one we inherited.

We may call them our *"family spirits"*, which is a common expression that has been used for millennia. People in the afterlife spontaneously gather and socialize only with those people who have a compatible or similar . This means that there is an overlap in what they love and what they prefer to believe.

Besides the inherited family spirits our vertical community includes many afterlife societies with whom God temporarily connects individuals during regeneration. God makes use of these specific connections or links to guide the individual through the process of temptations that must be endured and fought during regeneration.

HEAVEN AND HELL

These are anatomically defined mental states that are present in every individual mind. The societies in the afterlife are arranged relative to each other in the form of the human body. This may be called their "psycho-geographic location". The "heavenly" societies are based on mutual love personalities, while the "hellish" societies are based on self-love personalities. The heavenly afterlife societies are in the body of the *Grand Human*. The hellish afterlife societies are in the body of the *Grand Monster*.

INDIVIDUATION

Individuation refers to the process of entering and rejoining the collective consciousness. Through our birth as an individual we become detached from the collective consciousness. The collective consciousness is the consciousness of the *Grand Human*.

Our individual consciousness and life originates in the collective consciousness. When we are born our individual consciousness is formed by being anatomically ripped away from the collective consciousness. When we individuate after being born we are on the journey back to the collective consciousness, though we must wait until adulthood before we can progress.

The more we individuate the closer we get back to the collective consciousness, though we never reach it to achieve a merger.

Individuation is the process of personality growth through the gradual release of innate potentials from the unconscious into the conscious. Innate potentials or "remains" provide the context for experiencing heaven in eternity. Every individual is born for others and performs uses for them through these *remains*.

Individuation is related to regeneration. When we are unwilling to undergo regeneration in adult life we are continuing on the path of de-individuation. Regeneration requires that we be willing to undergo personality change from self-compulsion.

See the entry on "Regeneration And Personality".

INFINITY, GOD

There can be only one infinity.

There cannot be two infinities because then neither would be infinity.

God alone is infinity. God is called the Being of Life or *Esse* ("what is"),

Every part and attribute of God is infinite and eternally existing. They have no beginning and no end. These include life, immortality, consciousness, awareness, intelligence, good and truth, love and wisdom, rationality, virtue, an infinite variety of heavenly loves and affections, compassion and the ability to be affected by the suffering of others, infinite inventiveness, artfulness, grace, beauty, conjugial love, friendship, striving for achievement, freedom, desire to give to others what one has, and so on. These properties define what is human.

We can name and comprehend many of God's eternal attributes because God creates human beings with finite versions of capacities that exist in God. These are God's human capacities and attributes, and God anatomically implants them in our mind, giving us the freedom of choice of emulating them or acting contrary to them.

Divine infinity cannot be given away in whole or in part. Infinite things in God make one distinctly. Life, love, consciousness, intelligence, and wisdom are in God infinite and eternal. *They are uncreate, having always existed.*

God is the original and infinite Human.

God is omnipresent, and therefore *all that exists is an image of the human.* This can be seen more clearly if you remove from your thinking the idea of "image" as a visual representation. This clearly is not the case because forks, cats, and mountains do not physically look like humans. But they possess human characteristics.

For instance, forks are manufactured objects that serve a use. The construction of a fork involves intelligence, intent, goal, and use. These are human attributes. A mountain has a top, which may be called its "head", a middle portion that may be called the "torso and hip", and a bottom portion that may be called "legs or feet". These are of course human attributes. And we love cats because they are so "human-like" in their affection, emotion, attention, fears, comfort, play, freedom, and so on. These are human attributes.

The most complete collection of God's human attributes is implanted in human creation. Human beings receive life, love, consciousness, and intelligence from God, but these remain God's life, love, consciousness, and intelligence that are now in created and finite human beings. Each individual receives a finited and unique form of life, love, consciousness, and intelligence.

The finite cannot be in the infinite since all things in the infinite are infinite in part and in whole. Nothing finite can therefore exist in God. *But the infinite can be within the finite because size or quantity does not apply to the infinite.* Hence God's infinite and eternal life, love, or consciousness can be in finite human minds, though they do not belong to the human being.

All finite mental things can contain the infinite because mental things are not in physical space and in material quantity of things.

Consider for instance one of your thoughts. The more you think about it the more new things seem to be contained in it, things you did not know about before. All this is contained in a single thought, and much more than we can imagine.

God's infinity is reflected in everything that exists. Consider for instance uniqueness, or the fact that every human mind is unique to eternity. No two objects can ever be identical. Nothing ever repeats. Everything is unique. This reflects God's infinity, which is in everything that exists.

God created physical space and time while being apart from space and time. God could not create space and time within space and time. Nothing of life, love, consciousness, or intelligence can exist in physical matter or space. Hence the physical body on earth is inert and cannot have sensations, life, love, consciousness, or intelligence.

MENTAL SUBSTANCE:
LOVE AND TRUTH

From the mental environment of the afterlife world of eternity, our spiritual body captures or receives love-substance in the affective system, and truth-substance in the cognitive system. This is God's love-substance and its truth-substance that fills the sphere of the entire mental world of eternity.

You are in that world right now. Thinking and feeling is possible only in the mental world

Love-substance is active in our affective system in the form of feelings, intentions, emotions, strivings, urges, pleasures, and enjoyments. Truth-substance is active in our cognitive system in the form of thinking, knowing, learning, reasoning, and perceiving.

Our mind therefore is an anatomical organ in the spiritual body that feels and thinks by means of the love-substance and truth-substance that the mind captures or receives from the mental environment of eternity. You are in that mental environment right now.

Every individual receives love and truth substance in a unique way. No two minds receive love and truth in exactly the same way. Hence every person has unique thoughts and feelings.

God is present in our mind through the love-substance and its truth-substance, which is God's love-substance and truth-substance that exist eternally and infinitely in God's mind. There was no other substance that God could use to create the two worlds. Since the world cannot be created from nothing, therefore God used mental substance from God's mind.

The idea of mind as mental substance is a non-material idea. Substance is the stuff that is necessary to create anything. The material world was created through the mental substance from the mental world. The process of creation from mental substance goes through multiple and graduated steps. The human mind is the first step of externalization or separation from God's infinite mind. The last of the steps is the material world and its objects.

NDE / DYING-RESUSCITATION PROCESS

A near death experience is a psychological state of awareness that mimics the dying-resuscitation process, which is the state everyone passes through when undergoing the two-day process that separate the spiritual body in eternity from the physical body on earth.
NDE mimics the dying process but is not the same since all NDEs are the experiences of people who did not actually die.
The near-death experience is a biological and universal event available to everyone. It functions as a "life-changing" experience that impresses the person so strongly as to encourage the motivation for regeneration. Everything in the person's psychology changes: attitude toward the afterlife, relationship to God, modifying lifestyle habits, general outlook on the purpose and opportunity of life.

MENTAL ANATOMY

Human beings are mental beings. The mind is the real person. Our mind is our unique personality, consciousness, and identity.

Our mind operates anatomically in our immortal spiritual body, which is the embodiment of our mind from birth.

Human beings are born with an immortal spiritual body that is made of God's mental substance. We are mental beings, and we are born into mental eternity with our immortal spiritual body within which we have our mental operations.

At birth, our immortal spiritual body in mental eternity is temporarily afforded connection with an inert physical body on earth. No mental operations are possible in inert physical things. The physical body on earth is functionally connected to our spiritual body in mental eternity. The physical body on earth reacts to every intention and emotion in our spiritual body. In this way we can develop a natural mind that thinks with material ideas and is suitably adaptive to the material environment of the physical body.

We need a natural mind in order to manage successfully our life while connected to the physical body. After we are disconnected from the physical body, our natural mind becomes inactive since it no longer has sensory input from earth. Yet the natural mind retains its function as an anatomical covering of the interior spiritual mind.

In other words, the personality of our natural mind forms a basis and containant for the personality of our spiritual mind. One is within the other, and they must be in such an organic relationship in order for them to function, each in their own world. This is the reason God provides us with a physical body on earth, namely to allow us the experience of developing an adult natural mind. This natural mind is needed to form the basis for the spiritual mind that we use in the afterlife of eternity.

Our natural mind in our spiritual body in eternity receives all its sensory input from the physical body on earth. This leads to the powerful illusion that we are the physical body and that we live on earth. This illusion vanishes when we lose connection with the physical body at the time of its so-called "death".

Table of the Anatomical Levels of a Human Being

Name	Discrete Layer	Description
CELESTIAL MENTAL BODY	4	Celestial—interior rational
	5	Celestial--external-rational
	6	Celestial--interior-material
RATIONAL MENTAL BODY	7i	Rational—interior or celestial
	7e	Rational—external or materialized
MATERIAL MENTAL BODY	8	Material--abstract
	9	Material--corporeal
	10	"Spiritual body"
PHYSICAL BODY	11	"Limbus"
	12	Physical body

The 12 Layers of Mental Anatomy
in successive order

1 Spiritual Sun
2 souls at conception
3 souls at birth
-----
4 celestial-rational (third heaven)
5 spiritual-rational (second heaven)
6 spiritual-natural (first heaven)
7i natural-rational, interior-natural

7e natural-rational, external-natural
8 abstracted materialism, sensual
9 concrete materialism, corporeal
10 spiritual body
11 limbus covering
-----
12 physical body

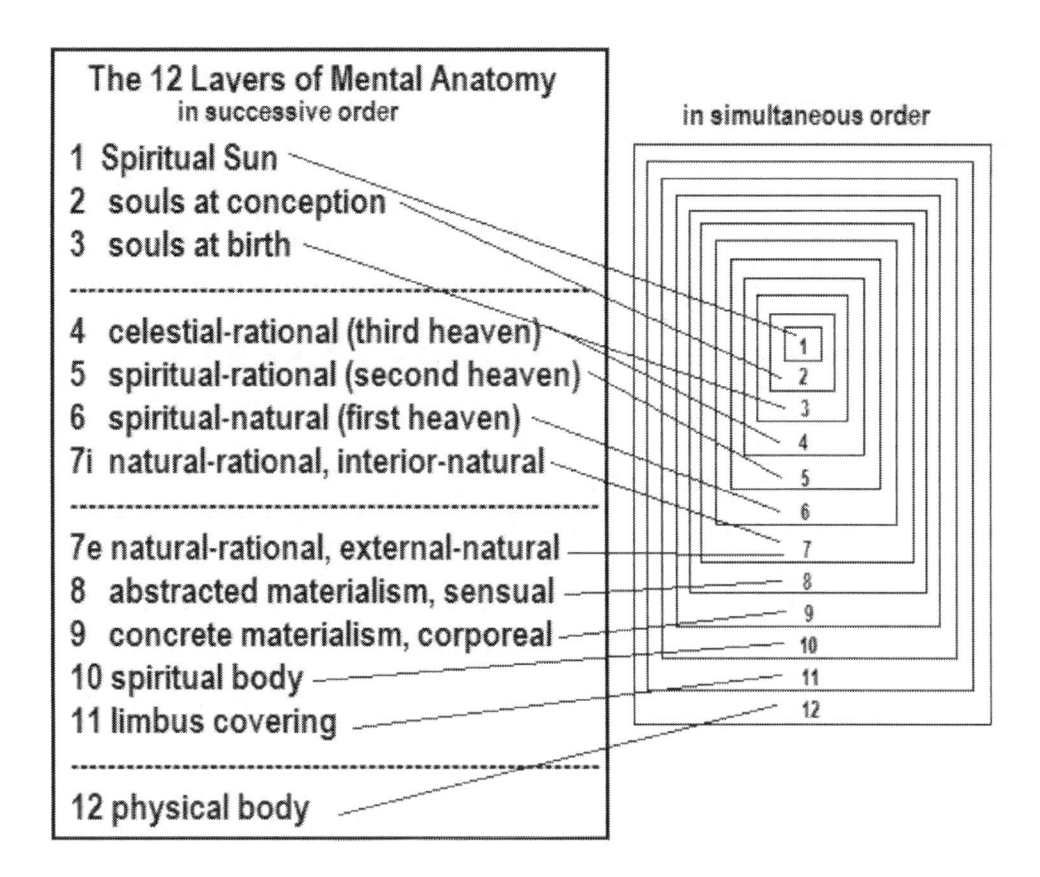

in simultaneous order

PERSONALITY, SYMBOLISM, AND TALKING WITH GOD

Consider what would happen if God prevented bad things from happening to people. What kind of society would that make? An individual would grow up to be without discipline and without the motivation to consider consequences of their actions or thoughts. As adults they would continue a lifestyle that is grossly excessive, irresponsible, selfish and cruel to others.

In the afterlife people explore, seek, and settle in one of the afterlife societies that is most compatible with their own. Other societies don't feel right and there arises psychological conflict that is not tolerated in a telepathic collective environment. All afterlife societies are in collective consciousness, both in the heavenly *Grand Human* and the hellish *Grand Monster*.

So now we're stuck! We're stuck with our personality such as it is. It is not in a regenerated state, which means that the ruling archetype in the personality is the self or ego. Only regeneration can remove self-love from dominance. The natural mind must be regenerated in order to remove self-love and install mutual love, which is altruistic.

All afterlife societies consist only of personalities in whom altruistic or mutual love is dominant. Hence those in whom self-love is dominant cannot settle in the heavenly Grand Human afterlife societies. This means settling in one of the hellish Grand Monster societies that has a compatible personality.

These societies are called "hellish" or "hell" because a community of selfish people creates a social psychological environment that feels like hell to the people there. Nor is there an exit possible because whatever other society is explored feels much worse than one's own hell.

So God would not want to prevent bad things from happening to good or to bad people. God always manages in such a way as to give each particular individual the maximum possible opportunities to choose to go along with regeneration. Hence God manages to prevent all bad things that do not contribute to the person's willingness or psychological readiness to undergo regeneration. Only those bad things happen to a person that contribute to his or her willingness or psychological preparedness to undergo regeneration.

Regeneration is necessary because it is the voluntary removal of one's selfish loves, one by one in daily struggles for many years.

This sounds so bad as to be repelling or prohibitive. That extreme negative appearance is caused by the fear we have of losing any love. It is built into our anatomy. No love wants to end. All loves want to be consummated and experience the delights thereof. This is life itself.

So loves furiously resist attacks that threaten its life. And regeneration threatens the life of all of them because they are all dependent on the ruling love, which is self-love. Our inherited personality has self-love installed at the very top. As we grow into an adult personality, self-love arranges and organizes all loves into a hierarchy that is obedient to itself only.

Other loves that are ruled by altruism and mutual love are banished to the unconscious and never allowed back. More and more as the adult personality ages self-love is fully established in every motive and every intention. Such a personality is anatomically deeply rooted in the afterlife society to which they are headed where others similar to them live in eternity.

God creates every individual with a unique and a unique collection of human potentials to be unpacked progressively through the individuation process that God provides. God never "leaves" the individual from conception, to gestation, to birth, to growth, to the afterlife, to eternity. God is present throughout. Biography wouldn't work by itself. God arranges the life details of every individual from conception to eternity.

God does all these amazing things for each of us. How amazing it is then to meet God, one on one. This is possible because (a) God is present in our mind and personality because God is a mental or spiritual being, like we are; (b) God is human, being the original and infinite human; and (c) God has a perfect love and caring for every individual that God creates, and God is longing with human feelings to meet in consciousness with every person.

Once we know this about God we feel an inner urge or desire to meet God one-on-one.

God provides three channels of communication for us to use. The first channel is the literal meaning of the verses of *Sacred Scripture*. Here we can meet the living God that interacts with our mind in two places. One is the natural mind in which we think with material ideas, and the other is the rational mind in which we think with non-material ideas.

So as we read a verse or chapter of *Sacred Scripture* we tap into the online mental channel or chat room that contains messages from God expressed in material ideas and addressed to our natural mind. Simultaneously, each material idea implies a non-material idea when you reflect on Why is God telling me this detail, or What does God want me to know about myself by telling me this detail.

So we interact with God with both our natural mind and our rational mind. God mentions many details in the literal text of *Sacred Scripture* that involve physical things such as objects, places, names, animals, numbers, fruits and crops, wars, miracles, punishments, rewards, etc. This is the channel with which God addresses our natural mind. The events and stories that are unfolded are given as a guide that we can use to form our daily morality and social personality.

We can reflect on how every detail that God mentions involving a material object or event is a correspondence to a psychological detail about our personality. This is the second channel of communication that God provides.

So we first practice for a while receiving communication from God through the two channels that God provides through *Sacred Scripture.* Then at some point, we are sufficiently prepared to meet God in dialog using the third channel. Now at last we meet, O God!

The third channel uses mostly non-material ideas. Talking to God is the activity of our *rational* mind. Before this, we experienced in our natural mind listening to God and reading or saying prayers to God. Now we are talking to God. It is a dialog. The person and God take turns talking. But it's not necessarily verbal. We don't hear anything. We don't see a video or picture.

Talking to God occurs above the senses and apart from the senses. It takes place telepathically by an exchange of conscious ideas in our rational mind.

Talking to God is a rational experience. For instance, when we reflect on a dream that we had we understand the dream rationally when we perceive its symbolism. This points our thinking to a relationship of correspondence that exists between some detail in our and some detail of the physical events and scenes in the dream.

An interesting little book published posthumously by Swedenborg's family contains a collection of daily notes that Swedenborg wrote about his dreams during the initial months at age 57 when his dual consciousness began. He went through an initial psychologically challenging phase as he struggled to adjust to being conscious simultaneously in both worlds. He carried out his daily work obligations even as he was trying to manage his interactions with those who were in the afterlife.

One world was material and his natural mind managed that part. The other world was non-material and his rational mind managed it. Through his natural mind, Swedenborg kept daily detailed notes with his physical body. Later these were published in a collection of 24 volumes translated into English. They are available free on the Web today.

During the adjustment months during which Swedenborg kept his "dream diary" he came to realize there is a direct connection of correspondence that existed between what was going on in his personality and what was going on in the dreams that he had.

Two centuries later Jung re-discovered that same connection of correspondence, which he called "*symbolism*". Jung was a psychiatrist and so he applied his momentous discovery to his therapy. Dream analysis since then has become known to millions of Jung followers, as it becomes evident when searching the web.

Symbolism involves thinking with immaterial-ideas. The physical symbol or visual object represents or points to the . For instance, the number "1", which is a material idea, represents or points to God's "unity" and "omnipresence", which are non-material ideas. The number "2" represents "*conjunction*". Every time this number appears in *Sacred Scripture* God is implying something about the psychological process of conjunction. For example, a husband and wife in heavenly afterlife societies are conjoined into one mind. Also, loving and obeying God's stated order in our daily thinking and acting is a state of conjunction with God.

As another example, every time *Sacred Scripture* mentions a species of animal, God is implying or pointing the correspondence of that species with our. Thus, when God mentions a viper hurting people, the statement is about our intentions to betray others in our daily dealings and relationships. We are the viper!

And similarly, when we are willing to undergo regeneration God compares us to a lamb, an eagle, or horse. But when not willing, God compares our to a scorpion, a pig, or snake. Over the centuries people have kept track of the human personality that corresponds to various types of animals. Jung calls them archetypes..

PSYCHOLOGY

Contemporary psychology gives material explanations for non-material phenomena. For instance, it defines experience and consciousness as physically sourced and measurable events.

Theistic psychology gives non-material explanations for non-material phenomena. For instance, it defines experience and consciousness as mentally sourced and cannot be measured.

Psychological states are non-physical events in the psychic world of mental eternity, which is constructed with mental substance that is sourced in God's mental activity. Mental substance is human, living, immortal, and uncreate or infinite. God creates the two worlds out of the 'stuff' of mental substance.

REGENERATION OF PERSONALITY

The mental process of cooperation with God in the construction of a new personality that replaces the inherited personality ruled by the love of self, which is the hatred of anyone who won't serve them.

The new *regenerating personality* progresses by persistent striving to acquire and practice the following *psychological competencies*:

1. Loving God and acknowledging God's Word as the source of all spiritual truth
2. Being loving and loyal to one's spouse, willing to become one-minded
3. Being in mutual love to society and its people
4. Respecting the human rights of everyone as being God given
5. Wanting to do what is right and just in every situation
6. Showing generosity in helping others who are in need
7. Showing compassion when seeing others who are suffering
8. Feeling delight in being useful to society and to people
9. Looking forward to the afterlife and preparing for it by regeneration
10. Maintaining a constant aversion for departing from any of these items

We prepare for the afterlife of eternity by striving every day to acquire a personality that is based on *mutual love and love of God*. Only such a personality can breathe and survive in a heavenly mental sphere. Our personality needs to be compatible and agreeable to the inhabitants of the heavenly cities in which we wish to settle.

Everyone after the two-day dying-resuscitation process begins the life of eternity in his or her spiritual body. Our explorations then begin in search of an afterlife society in which we want to settle. We feel compelled from within to leave a society that is not in accord with our basic personality, which consists of what we enjoy and what we hate, and what we believe and how we speak with others.

Every afterlife society is made up of people who have compatible personalities. Other people may visit for a while but cannot settle there.

You can see from this that it is the personality factors that determine our final destination in eternity. Hence you can see why the central and only issue in theistic psychology is the psychology of regeneration.

No other topic can be of greater critical importance to every individual.

It might be worth your while to reflect for a few days on the list of personality competencies that appear just above. Each item is critical and essential. No item can be left out. If one item falls, all the other items fall.

Our personality inclinations are an anatomical organ in our immortal spiritual body. There is an external portion and an internal portion. The external personality thinks with material ideas and intentions. The interior personality thinks with non-material ideas and intentions. In other words, we use our external personality for our daily social interactions, and we use our interior personality for regeneration.

The list of regenerating personality competencies discussed just above must first be acquired in our interior personality, and afterward we compel our external personality to also act accordingly.

The process of regeneration depends on overcoming spiritual temptations by applying non-material thinking to some dilemma or situation using non-material ideas such as mutual love and afterlife societies.

We are extremely vulnerable in psychological states of spiritual temptation. The more we enjoy an activity that is from self-love, the more painful seems to be the necessity of giving up the enjoyment. The state of compelling ourselves to give up a deeply loved selfish enjoyment is experienced as a tearing apart, as if skin or bone was being ripped off.

Selfish loves form a central part of our inherited anatomy and when these loves are denied and removed we feel deep mental pain and intense psychological distress during the process of regeneration. God supervises this psychological process in its smallest detail and is closely present in our mind mitigating the overwhelming emotional process.

We are to think of it as the process of salvation, namely:

- of recovery from inherited hell,
- of recapturing the Garden of Eden or reception of love and wisdom,
- of being lifted up to above our present fallen consciousness,
- of replacing the collective unconscious with collective consciousness,
- of the restoration of true individuation,
- of becoming an angel couple in eternal conjugial love.

Regeneration to be successful depends on our willingness to engage God through a daily talking relationship on a personal level. Through this inner dialog we acquire the ability to receive non–material ideas into our day-to-day thinking. For this to occur God must become visible to the natural mind. Through the Incarnation Event, God's physical body was made Divine Human, which in *Sacred Scripture* is called "being glorified". God's glorified physical body is infinite and omnipresent in the natural mind and in the spiritual mind.

As a result, any individual can mentally see God with the interior personality and start a daily personal talking relationship with God.

Through this daily and personal relationship with God our motivational structure is empowered to act in obedience to what is just and right. This process of denying ourselves selfish delights must go on every day for many years. But eventually the old personality of self-love is replaced with the new personality of mutual love. This new personality can live in heaven in the afterlife of eternity. This personality switchover is called "*salvation*" because through it we can avoid a life of eternal suffering in hell.

It is eternal because our ruling self-love defeats our longing for relief. By staying in hell with others who are like us we are able to enjoy both the delights of insanity when we have the upper hand over others, and the sufferings of insanity when the others have the upper hand. This alternation of mental state keeps people in hell, forever denying themselves the desire to leave by giving up self-love and its delights.

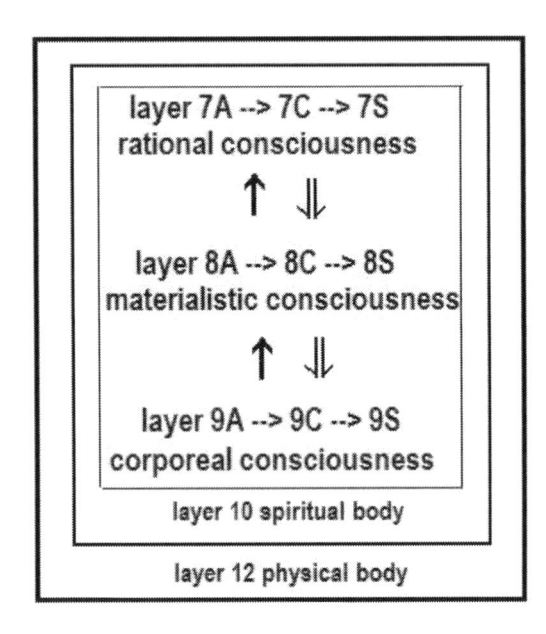

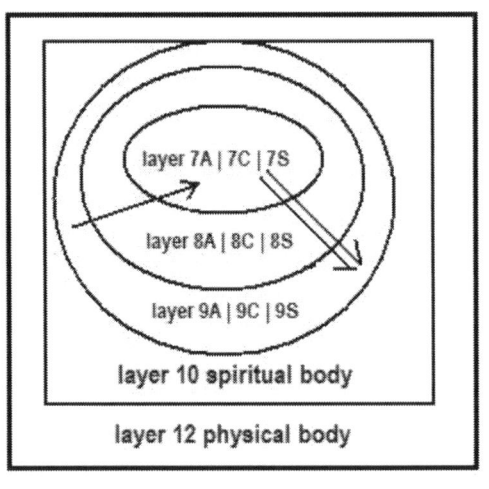

```
layer 7A --> 7C --> 7S
rational consciousness
      ↑  ⇓
layer 8A --> 8C --> 8S
materialistic consciousness
      ↑  ⇓
layer 9A --> 9C --> 9S
corporeal consciousness
layer 10 spiritual body
layer 12 physical body
```

```
layer 7A | 7C | 7S
layer 8A | 8C | 8S
layer 9A | 9C | 9S
layer 10 spiritual body
layer 12 physical body
```

↑ maturation by age   ⇓ mental regeneration

Maturation and Regeneration of the Natural Mind
Sequential and Simultaneous View

Those who are willing to undergo regeneration, first acquire the teachings of God in *Sacred Scripture* regarding regeneration. This information is contained in the psychological meaning of each verse. It is also contained in the literal sense of selected verses. Second, God manages to put the individual in situations of temptation when he or she experiences a strong urge to act or think in a selfish way. Third, the tempted person uses God's teaching to fight and counteract the urge. At that point God removes the temptation, weakening the selfish love. The person then experiences deep relief and thankful closeness to God.

This process proceeds for several years, even decades. All along, the person is regenerating with a new positive personality that can live in the afterlife of eternity with others who are like-minded and who form with each other heavenly afterlife societies in eternity. The unregenerate personality in the afterlife joins others of like-minded selfish and cruel people and they form hellish afterlife societies in eternity.

THEISTIC ANIMISM

Everything that is alive has an immortal soul in mental eternity. God creates human souls, animal souls, and plant souls. Archetypes are living organic forms or psychological entities that the soul uses to create a personality or unique individual being. A plant on earth is the embodiment in physical matter of a plant soul that exists in mental eternity. Human souls use human archetypes to form a mental embodiment of themselves as an individual personality. Objects made of inert matter are not living and do not have a soul. They disintegrate and disappear in time and place.

THEISTIC PSYCHOLOGY

God's teaching about the psychology of regeneration. This teaching is found in the psychological meaning of every verse of *Sacred Scripture* in all religions that receive *Sacred Scriptures* from God. The psychological meaning is given for the use of one's regeneration of personality. This book in 5 Volumes is an explanation of the content of theistic psychology. My prior books on theistic psychology may also be of interest to readers.

The narrative for theistic psychology that I present in my most recent books is a synthesis of the work of Jung and Swedenborg. I present more specific details on theistic psychology in the subsequent volumes in this series.

USES:
SELFISH AND ALTRUISTIC

We inherit both selfish and altruistic traits. Spiritually considered, a person can be held morally responsible only for those traits that the person loves. *It is the individual's love that causes the trait to be "appropriated".*

We are spiritually responsible for all traits that we accept, love, and practice as a lifestyle habit.

Hence we are not spiritually responsible for the traits that we inherit but we do not love, accept, and practice from choice.

It is clear from self-observation and from observation of others that most people in adult life have come to accept and practice by choice various lifestyles that are motivated by selfish loves. Self-love has regard for self only, and has regard for others only to the extent that they receive support and favor from them. All others are despised and hated, and treated cruelly whenever the occasion allows it.

Self-love is the love of self and at the same time the hatred of others.

Psychologically those two (self-love and hatred of others) cannot be separated in the minds of those who are immersed in a life of self-love. The fact is that our entire generation is so deeply involved in social materialism and in mutual competition that most of us develop a personality that is dominated or ruled by inherited self-love. Furthermore, we practice and reinforce self-love as part of our socialization and education process.

Of course God is able to remove self-love from a newborn infant so that the child might grow up only with the love of altruistic uses that the child also inherits. Why not sift out the selfish and leave the altruistic? This would allow everyone to live in a heavenly afterlife society and be happy forever. Why not?

It's important that we have a rational answer, otherwise doubt and obscurity enters consciousness. This self-made cloud obscures the closeness and benign influence of God. We need therefore to figure out what the rational answer is. And it is this.

Consider what happens after God filters out from the infant's personality the inherited self-loves. Behold, there is nothing of life left to the infant! How could this be? It is because the parents, grandparents, and distant ancestors have led materialistic lifestyles in which self-love was the ruling love or chief archetype. All other loves that are contrary to self-love that may have been inherited, are removed to the distant circumference of the personality where they are inactive and sub-conscious.

So now what happens if you remove the ruling self-love with all the compatible loves that it has installed for itself in the personality structure – like weeds, thistles, and thorns in an unattended field?

There is nothing left! The entire personality of the individual shuts down. All sensations and experiences are inhibited. The person is then like in a coma, unable to perform psychological acts such as making a choice, wanting something, enjoying something, feeling affected by something, desiring something, etc. Just nothing. Not even like sleep, which is active and imaginative in dreaming.

You can easily see from this why God doesn't filter out the individual's evils and self-loves. God first allows the individual to grow up into an adult personality, and then God activates the adult individual's conscious attention to the afterlife and the critical need to prepare for it through undergoing regeneration of . The individual is then called a "seeker", that is, a seeker of truth, which involves learning to think with non-material ideas. Doing this will overcome the powerful illusion we have that we are on earth and that the physical body senses and thinks.

Our inherited personality since the historical Fall is based on self-love and the love of the world for the sake of self, which is to love oneself exclusively.

Self-love is destructive of community and society, which depend on people loving or respecting others at least as much as they respect themselves. Self-love prompts us to do helpful things under certain conditions in order to be accepted or in order to achieve some gain and social influence.

In the afterlife, self-love based personalities congregate together in afterlife societies that are populated with selfish people that create a hell society for each other. Self-love personalities can be regenerated into mutual love personalities when the individual is willing. This can be done over an extensive period of years.

The process of regeneration must be voluntary and involves as-of self effort while resisting temptations. God's Word informs us that regeneration must be undertaken while we are still connected to the physical body. In the afterlife no one is willing to depart from what they already are.

God creates every individual not for the sake of the individual, but for the sake of others. This is a fundamental fact of true reality and needs to be included in our thinking and reasoning about our selves, our personality and our relationship to others.

Everything we think and do is motivated either for the sake of self or for the sake of others.

While we grow up and develop an adult personality we are motivated most of all for the sake of self, and only secondarily for the sake of others. When we agree to undergo regeneration of personality, the situation starts to reverse itself, so that we end up doing and thinking more and more for the sake of others primarily, and only secondarily for the sake of self or not at all.

What we do or think for the sake of self or for the sake of others is called *uses,* that is, being motivated to be useful to others, to community, and to society.

For example, we learn to tie our shoes or brush our teeth for the sake of self. We learn to be loyal to friends and protective of family for their sake. Similarly, we learn to sing in a choir or to play on a team both for the sake of others and for the sake of self.

Each of us being unique provides unique uses to others and to society.

We acquire and practice uses that are selfish and uses that are altruistic. Selfish uses are the things we do for ourselves only. We exclude others except when it is of benefit to our selves. Loving oneself exclusively produces selfish uses and avoids altruistic uses, which are being useful to others as well as to self. Wanting to be useful to oneself alone is the hallmark of self-love.

We inherit self-love, which forms the very basis of our . In adulthood we can opt to undergo regeneration and alter our personality from being based on selfish uses to altruistic uses.

We do selfish uses when they are done exclusively for the sake of self only. When we are in the mental state of selfish love we hate the idea of doing something useful or good to someone without receiving something in return for oneself. But when we are regenerating we learn to love to do things for others that are useful to them. At the same time these things are often useful or beneficial to us.

Altruistic uses are produced by the motive to benefit others and self. But selfish uses are produced by the motive to benefit self only.

It is not generally known that the "*love of the world*" is part of the architecture of the love of self. The two loves coexist together and support one another. To be in the "love of the world" is to love power, riches, honor, glory, admiration, notoriety, etc. These are selfish loves and delights when they are done for the sake of self only.

One can also love power and riches not for the sake of self but for the sake of society and community. This is an altruistic love. People serving in public office may love power either for the sake of benefit to oneself, or else for the sake of being in a position to be useful to others. The love of the world for the sake of others is an altruistic love.

Patriotism and love of country are altruistic loves when the welfare of others is being considered and protected. But patriotism and "glory" that are sought for the sake of historical notoriety and celebrity status are selfish loves that seek to benefit self only.

The love of power and riches for the sake of self is selfish, but is altruistic when done for the sake of being of use to needy others. Honesty and integrity for the sake of justice and for what is right, is altruistic, but is selfish when being honest is merely for approval and profit. In other words, when no benefit to self is foreseen a selfish love gives up the intention of being honest.

In general most traits can be qualified as being done "*for the sake of self and one's own benefit*" or else "*for the sake of others and their benefit*". The first type is hellish, and the second type is heavenly. It is often not visible in any specific situation as to which of these two motives are actually involved in someone's actions, until you decide whether it is done for the sake of self only or for the sake of others as well as self.

We inherit a penchant or tendency for performing selfish uses, which are results that serve us and serve what we want to happen for our own benefit and comfort regardless of how it might affect various others.

You can observe this when children are playing together. Sometimes they are generous and want to share, but often they are selfish, jealous, and do not want to share, even bursting out in cries when they see another child being successful. These selfish traits are inherited. As we grow older we practice these selfish and self-serving traits and they become an integral part of our personality and lifestyle.

Hence it is necessary to undergo regeneration by which God removes the inherited and acquired selfish uses, replacing them with altruistic uses.

This new regenerated personality is capable of living and being happy in a heavenly afterlife society in eternity, and is accompanied by one's conjugial love mate. But the unregenerate personality is not capable of being happy in a society where everyone shuns selfish uses and is happy only when performing altruistic uses.

When we awaken in the afterlife following the two-day dying-resuscitation procedure, we begin exploring and searching for the right afterlife society in which to settle. People feel inexorably attracted from within towards certain explorations in which they soon find the society of their love, where they are recognized, welcomed, and accepted by those who live there.

If your personality is regenerate then your primary love is the love of altruistic uses. You settle in one of the numberless afterlife societies that are populated with people having such a regenerate personality. Together they form a pleasant and agreeable heavenly society made up of married conjugial pairs.

But if your personality is not regenerate then your primary love is the love of selfish uses. You then settle in one of the many afterlife societies that are populated by people who love themselves only, and love others to the extent that the others favor them and are willing to perform uses for their benefit. All others are hated and treated cruelly whenever they can.

Such societies are called hells. People in the afterlife cannot switch societies from hellish to heavenly, or vice versa, because when the other side is visited, the psychic sphere of mutual love envelops the visitor who is thrown into the agony of death when the selfish and altruistic loves strive to annihilate each other within the personality. They then quickly throw themselves back into their hell society where they feel revived.

They then take turns practicing on each other cruel and inhuman things from which they suffer terribly. They then get a big emotional relief when it's their turn to torment the others. This life of endless alternating states of suffering and of delight is the lot of those who live in a hellish afterlife society.

****
Volume 4
Section 10
****

Nobody has ever known what this primal matter is. The alchemists did not know, and nobody has found out what is really meant by it, because it is a substance in the unconscious which is needed for the incarnation of the god. ~Carl Jung, Zarathustra Seminar, p. 886

You see, it is as if the self were trying to manifest in space and time, but since it consists of so many elements that have neither space nor time qualities, it cannot bring them altogether into space and time. ~Carl Jung, Zarathustra Seminar, p. 977

And those efforts of the self to manifest in the empirical world result in man: he is the result of the attempt. So much of the self remains outside, it doesn't enter this three-dimensional empirical world. ~Carl Jung, Zarathustra Seminar, p. 977

---

10. Conclusions From What Precedes

So now we can conclude wonderful and awesome things from these non-material ideas, facts, and principles. I will list those that I discussed throughout the book:

1) Human beings are born into eternity and immortality.
2) The light of human life is the awareness of consciousness.
3) The awareness of consciousness is the experiencing of omnipresence.
4) Consciousness is the eternal and infinite mental activity of God.
5) Consciousness is substantive, infinite, eternal, uncreate, omnipresent, omniscient, omnipotent, and human.
6) God is the original human, infinite and omnipresent. Hence God is the Divine-Human.
7) Consciousness in God's eternal mind is the Divine marriage of love-substance and its truth-substance.
8) All things in the universe are created out of love-substance and its truth-substance. Love-substance is uncreate, living, human, and infinite. It is the construction material or stuff for all things that God creates.
9) Love-substance is infinite as a whole and in every part of it. Therefore no part of love-substance can be given to human beings. But the

human mind is so constructed that it can receive love-substance into the affective system, and its truth-substance into the cognitive system. This reception is by inflow or transfer from the mental environment that surrounds our spiritual body.

10) Once received into our spiritual body, love-substance with its truth-substance draws out and activates the unique human potentials in each individual's soul that God plants at birth as a personal gift to the individual.

11) God is omnipresent in every thing or place because these are all constructed out of love-substance and its truth-substance, which is infinite and remains in God as it cannot be displaced or given away to finite human beings.

12) God therefore is present in the mind of human beings through God's own mental substance of love-substance and its truth-substance.

13) God's presence in our mind must be acknowledged by talking to God on a daily basis about what is going on in our mind.

14) By maintaining a daily talking relationship with God we are able to undergo the anatomical process of regeneration of our inborn character and self-based . This requires that we gather non-material ideas or truths and use them to resist our selfish lifestyle.

15) The opposite of a selfish lifestyle is the life of altruism or mutual love. Selfish loves arise when we pervert the love-substance that we receive into our mind by misusing it for self-centered intentions and motives. To succeed in being regenerated we must first stop hurting others, whether in our mind or behavior. Second, we compel ourselves to think respectfully and act with consideration and generosity.

16) Regeneration is the process of cooperating with God in modifying our inherited self-love-based . God sets up situations where we are tempted to think and do the usual selfish thing. We compel ourselves as-of self to resist the temptation. God then makes it efficacious. In this way we eventually acquire a new personality that is based in mutual love, and therefore can live in heaven in eternity.

17) Following the two-day dying resuscitation procedure we become conscious in the afterlife world of mental eternity. This is a substantive world, more real and delightful than the physical world. Our sensory input is from the afterlife world where is our immortal spiritual body, and we are conscious in our spiritual mind that forms the interior portion of our spiritual body. We now can see all the people who are already in the afterlife, and we can interact with them using a universal thought-language that is inborn to all human beings.

18) Again God brings certain events into our experience in which we discover what is our ruling love that lies hidden in the personality. Once we know this, we are spontaneously attracted to one of the afterlife societies that matches our ruling love. We then enter it and remain a part of that society forever.

19) If our ruling love is self-love, as it was when we were born, we enter an afterlife society of self-love-based personalities. It is called hell. If our ruling love is mutual love, as it became after regeneration, we enter an afterlife society of mutual love-based personalities. It is called heaven.

20) All heavenly societies are made of married couples who are in "conjugial love", and willed themselves to become oneminded. All hell societies are made of infernal couples who are in hatred of each other and yet are compelled to live together. They have not been willing to undergo regeneration while still attached to the physical body. Hence they arrive into the afterlife with the same self-love-based personality that they inherited.

21) The afterlife societies arrange themselves relative to each other in the form of the human body, both externally and internally. The heavenly societies form a Grand Human Body, beautiful and perfect, but the hell societies form a Grand Monster Body, deformed and ugly. Every society in the Grand Human has a corresponding counterpart society in the Grand Monster.

Volume 4
Section 11

11. Synchronicity And Correspondences

Jung writes:
> *A man likes to believe that he is the master of his soul. But as long as he is unable to control his moods and emotions, or to be conscious of the myriad secret ways in which unconscious factors insinuate themselves into his arrangements and decisions, he is certainly not his own master...*
>
> *Modern man protects himself against seeing his own split state by a system of compartments. Certain areas of outer life and of his own behavior are kept, as it were, in separate drawers and are never confronted with one another. ~Carl Jung, Man And His Symbols*

Jung discovered the phenomenon of *synchronicity* by observing that two physical events in different places are related to each other and occur at the same time even though there is no apparent physical cause-effect relation between them. This implies that there exist non-physical cause-effect relations. Jung called them "*acausal*" in the sense of not being caused by physical events.

Consider for example a situation in which two old friends who have not been in communication with each other for many years, unexpectedly bump into each other at an airport and renew an old friendship. One can take the materialistic perspective and say that these are low probability events but still possible to occur by chance.

Or one can take the non-material or spiritual perspective, and say that the encounter event at the airport occurred from a non-physical cause, and that instead of a low probability of occurring it actually had a maximum probability or certainty of occurring. I believe this is what Jung had in mind when discussing synchronicity, namely when two events co-occur through "acausal" factors. There is a complex sequence of actions that led each of the two old friends to be at the same airport at the same time and in the same waiting room. The integration of the two independent sequences is achieved by the need each had in their biography to renew the old friendship. Through this concurrence each has access to new experiences that he or she needed to have for psychological development.

Swedenborg discovered the existence of "*laws of correspondence*" that govern the relation between two events: one physical and the other mental or spiritual. He states that these laws were familiar to the ancients from the study of their *Sacred Scripture*. Swedenborg convincingly proves that *Sacred Scripture* is written in a unique style that consists of two levels of meaning connected to each other by the laws of correspondence.

When reading *Sacred Scripture*, the literal meaning of each verse and phrase appears to us as referring to historical details of various individuals and nations in relation to God. The literal sense also gives us various specifications for how God wants us to worship and what lifestyle we are to maintain. This is the literal meaning.

Simultaneously, there is a psychological meaning to each verse and phrase and this is unrelated to the historical details. Swedenborg called this the "spiritual meaning" or the "internal meaning", which is to say, a *psychological meaning* having to do with our personality and its regeneration.

There is a relation of correspondence between the literal historical events mentioned in a verse and the psychological events that are implied from the details. We can derive the implied psychological event from the literal meaning of the verse by being familiar with the laws of correspondence and symbology.

The laws of correspondence that Swedenborg discovered within *Sacred Scripture* overlap with the laws of symbology that Jung discovered in the universal culture-free expressions that he found in dreams, religion, children's stories, and art. I was stunned when I discovered this relationship between *Sacred Scripture* and dreams or children's stories. It has many implications.

For instance, if you study the correspondences in *Sacred Scripture* you'll be able to interpret the symbolism in dreams. And I would say, vice versa. You can know a lot about *Sacred Scripture* if you learn the symbology of religious emblems such as the specific psychological functions of the mandala or the cross that Jung discusses at length in his works.

After considering the issue I can now offer an explanation for this mutual relationship between *Sacred Scripture* and our dreams and fantasies. When we are asleep, our awake-time cerebrum consciousness inhibits the sensory input that we receive from our physical body on earth. Our consciousness that is normally turned outward to our sensory organs and thus to the physical world, is now turned inward to our spiritual world of thoughts, feelings, and imagination. As a result of this switch in mental focus there is a lifting in some places of the dark veil that covers up the collective unconscious.

Now being asleep to the physical world, the cerebrum consciousness can see through windows in the endless wall, or through the tearing of the veil of the unconscious. At this point it is the cerebellum or "old brain" that is running the show while the cerebrum ("new brain") watches and remembers. The cerebellum old brain consciousness connects with our affective system, while our cerebrum new brain consciousness connects with our cognitive system.

The language of our affective system and old brain cerebellum is the language of love and spiritual reasoning with non-material ideas. The language of our cognitive system and new brain cerebrum is the language of natural reasoning with material ideas. Our natural reasoning makes use of concepts that are based exclusively on time, place, energy, number, and material objects.

For instance, in our natural reasoning we think of death as being asleep. Or we think of life after death as occurring in this physical world. Or we think of heaven as a reward for those who were obedient to God's commandments, and we think of hell as the opposite situation. And we think of hell as the pain of physical burning of the body or being pierced by a pitchfork. Or we think of morality and justice as the law and order that allows society to survive.

It's different altogether in our spiritual reasoning. We think of death as a transitional mental state that is followed by being conscious and active in the afterlife of eternity, which is a spiritual world in eternity, not a physical world in time. Or we think of life after death as occurring in the spiritual world of eternity, which is a spiritual world. Or we think of heaven as a choice that people make when they have a personality that focuses on obedience to God's commandments and mutual love and consideration for others.

This personality chooses the life of heaven where mutual love reigns in the mental atmosphere. And we think of hell as the mental torment of obsessive demands of the mind that cannot be satisfied. Or we think of morality and justice not only as the law and order that allows society to survive, but we also think of beauty of God's order everywhere and the decisiveness with which God manage and intervenes in all details of each event.

Natural thinking and spiritual thinking are therefore contrastive and distinct, like two dimensions vs. one dimension. Natural thinking is one-dimensional while spiritual thinking is two-dimensional. Natural thinking involves material ideas and principles that apply to things in time, place, and energy. Spiritual thinking involves the correspondence between natural events and spiritual or mental events. Spiritual thinking allows us to understand the causes of natural world events, and the dynamics of our natural mind, that is, its psychology.

Synchronicity is a concept in spiritual thinking. It has no meaning in natural thinking, which collapses two dimensions of reality into just one, thus denying the second one. The idea of correspondences also belongs to our spiritual thinking since it explicitly seeks to describe the causal relationship between any physical event and its mental cause, and this is a relationship of dependency called correspondence. The physical world of our physical body on earth is in the world of effects, while the spiritual body in eternity is in the world of causes.

Here in this spiritual idea you can see the grander meaning of human beings. God created everything in the physical universe to be of service or utility to human beings. Hence it is that *anything physical is an effect produced by something mental, which is its cause.* This deep secret was known to the ancients and can be seen embedded in the symbols and archetypes of today's religions of the East. We can also see it in our dreams in which we build physical looking castles out of our imagination.

The world of imagination is a substantial world, while the world on earth is a material world. The difference is that between the rigidity and limited quantity of matter to the fluidity and endlessness of mental substance. Spiritual thinking reveals that mental substance in God is the only eternal reality. Swedenborg described this eternal and infinite mental substance as love-substance and its truth-substance. Nothing existed at creation. Therefore the two worlds had to be constructed out of mental substance in God's human mind. Nothing else existed out of which it could be constructed.

This is the spiritual or spiritual meaning of the well-known verse in *Sacred Scripture* "*Let there be light. And there was light.*" (Genesis 1:3). In natural reasoning we think that the world was created out of nothing because to create something out of nothing is illogical. We know that God is never illogical, nor are the celestial societies in heaven. God is rational and as are regenerated people who think with God's rationality.

Logical thinking in our natural mind makes it evident to us that out of nothing, nothing is created.

The idea that "God speaks and it is". Certainly this is true. But we need to know that God creates all things by mediation and connection through other things, endlessly. Swedenborg showed that in God's management system of the world all things are woven together to form an overall entity. In God's construction system the whole is always in the image of the part, and vice versa.

We can have a material idea of this principle by considering how the largest and smallest things in the physical world are models of each other, when you consider how the structure of an atom in the space inside the molecule resembles that of a galaxy in outer space and with similar working energies that are proportional to size.

Swedenborg often asserted that nothing unconnected can exist. Creation involves the construction of something unique that is inserted within a matrix of other created things, in away that it unites with them in a form that corresponds with God's human mind through the Grand Human of afterlife societies in eternity. Creation is therefore continually going on. Creation is a process that never stops. And yet, we must add to this idea the notion that to omniscient God all things of the past, present, and endless future are already present.

In other words, all creation takes place in an instant in God's human mind, but then God appears to us as acting and participating sequentially through the history of nations and the biography of individuals. Both images are true. In non-material thinking there is no contradiction because the sequential operation is an appearance that God wills for us to think in order to accommodate the material logic of our natural mind.

It is believed by most that time passes; in actual fact, it stays where it is. ~Dogen, Zen Master, 1200-1253

The expression used in *Sacred Scripture,* "*Let there be light*" when viewed in non-material thinking, means that it is God's intention to create human beings out of God's own mental substance, which is eternal, infinite, human, and living. It is called love-substance with its truth-substance. Swedenborg also uses the "good" for love-substance, and "wisdom" for truth-substance. Our immortal spiritual body or mind is constructed out of God's exteriorized and finited form of that mental substance.

In *Sacred Scripture* it is told in material ideas that God "Then the Lord God formed man of dust from the ground, and breathed into his nostrils the breath of life; and man became a living being." (Genesis 2:7), which in its non-material or mental sense means that human consciousness is constructed from God's own consciousness or mental substance. "*Dust from the ground*" refers to the physical body on earth that is non-living and without consciousness or mind. The "breath" of the physical body on earth corresponds to the "mind" of the spiritual body that is in eternity.

Even though God constructs everything from God's own mental substance, nevertheless, God's substance remains God's and is not given away to the individual who is thus formed from it. This is the sense in which we can think that God is omnipresent consciously through God's own mental substance or mind out of which everything is constructed.

Comparing this to a material idea, think of our furniture that is made of wood. The origin of wood is tree growth. So wooden furniture is made of trees. But the contact of our furniture with the original trees is broken. The tree is not in the furniture. But it is contrastive with God's mental substance. The original contact with God's mental substance is not broken. That substance remains God's forever and cannot be given away to finite beings. That's because every part of God is God. IN other words, every part of the in finite is infinite. And the in fin ite cannot be given away to the finite.

Since human beings are constructed with God's consciousness or mental substance, it logically implies that God is human. Actually we can correctly think of God as the only true and original human. Human minds are constructed out of this Divine Human mental substance. Everything that God has created is human in one property or another. And in human beings God's humanness is most explicit and complete in creation. Everything created was for the sake of maintaining and fostering human beings.

God's motive is to create human beings who can reciprocate the love that God has for every individual.

This is God's desire from eternity to eternity. God longs for acknowledgment because in this acknowledgment God can gift human beings with grand capacities, the chief of which is immortal consciousness and its rational thinking that is designed to control all things that exist.

It makes sense therefore that God would want to unify the entire human race and to afford people an immortal existence in one anatomically unified spiritual world that is shared by all humanity past, present, and future. Everything that is individual human must unify through what is collective humanity. Individual consciousness is subjective and unique. It needs an objective context that is collective and unified.

Human beings are therefore created into dual consciousness: material and non-material. Consciousness with material ideas are operated by the exterior of the spiritual body and is called our lower natural mind. Consciousness with non-material ideas are operated by the interior of the spiritual body and is called our higher spiritual mind.

As I explain in an earlier Section, human beings prior to the historical Fall of humankind were in dual consciousness, but after the Fall, everyone has had a split-mind in the spiritual body and a split-brain in the physical body on earth whose anatomy corresponds to the spiritual body in eternity.

Volume 4
Section 12

12. Archetypes In Sacred Scripture

Jung writes:
> In those days I saw a compensatory principle that seemed to show a balance between the conscious and unconscious. But I saw later that the unconscious was balanced in itself. It is the yea and the nay.
>
> The unconscious is not at all exactly the opposite of the conscious. It may be irrationally different. You cannot deduce the unconscious from the conscious. The unconscious is balanced in itself, as is the conscious.
>
> When we meet an extravagant figure like Salome, we have a compensating figure in the unconscious. If there were only such an evil figure as Salome, the conscious would have to build up a fence to keep this back, an exaggerated, fanatical, moral attitude.
>
> But I had not this exaggerated moral attitude, so I suppose that Salome was compensated by Elijah. When Elijah told me he was always with Salome, I thought it was almost blasphemous for him to say this. I had the feeling of diving into an atmosphere that was cruel and full of blood. This atmosphere was around Salome, and to hear Elijah declare that he was always in that company shocked me profoundly.
>
> Elijah and Salome are together because they are pairs of opposites. Elijah is an important figure in man's unconscious, not in woman's. He is the man

with prestige, the man with a low threshold of consciousness or with remarkable intuition. In higher society he would be the wise man; compare Lao-tse.

He has the ability to get into touch with archetypes. He will be surrounded with mana, and will arouse other men because he touches the archetypes in others. He is fascinating and has a thrill about him. He is the wise man, the medicine man, the mana man.

Later on in evolution, this wise man becomes a spiritual image, a god, "the old one from the mountains" (compare Moses coming down from the mountain as lawgiver), the sorcerer of the tribe. He is the legislator.

Even Christ was in company with Moses and Elijah in his transfiguration. All great lawgivers and masters of the past, such as for example the Mahatmas of theosophical teaching, are thought of by theosophists as spiritual factors still in existence. Thus the Dalai Lama is supposed by theosophists to be such a figure.

In the history of Gnosis, this figure plays a great role, and every sect claims to have been founded by such a one. Christ is not quite suitable; he is too young to be the Mahatma. The great man has to be given another role. John the Baptist was the great wise man, teacher, and initiator, but he has been depotentiated.

The same archetype reappears in Goethe as Faust and as Zarathustra in Nietzsche, where Zarathustra came as a visitation. Nietzsche has been gripped by the sudden animation of the great wise man. This plays an important role in man's psychology, as I have said, but unfortunately a less important part than that played by the anima. ~Carl Jung, 1925 Seminar, p. 100-101

In other words, individual consciousness must be in balance with the collective consciousness that is now coming through from the collective unconscious. Jung is describing our natural mind with which we think with material ideas. From its perspective of materialism the collective consciousness appears as the collective unconscious. This is the case since the Fall of Consciousness and the resultant anatomical schism in our spiritual body between the lower external mind containing material ideas and the higher interior mind containing non-material ideas.

Jung came to the conclusion that the collective consciousness is independent of individual consciousness and possesses its own balance and objectivity. Hence it is also the case with the collective unconscious, since this is merely the other side view of the same thing. Jung is discussing the perspective in our natural mind that looks at the wall of consciousness in total incomprehension.

But Jung's work shows how our individual consciousness in our natural mind can learn to think with non-material ideas when applying symbolism and correspondences to the incoming content from the collective unconscious. Individuation is the process whereby more and more of the collective unconscious becomes the collective consciousness. This process progresses through regeneration, as I explain elsewhere.

Jung gives as an example the character image of *Salome* who is described in the *New Testament* of the *Bible*. The spiritual meaning of "Salome" is one of the *affective archetypes* in the collective consciousness whose qualities Jung describes as "*exaggerated, fanatical, moral attitude*". Jung says that his conscious thinking in the natural mind rejected "*such an evil figure*". Jung was "profoundly shocked" when a familiar and trusted psychic character in his unconscious mind named Elijah asserted that he was with Salome all the time.

Jung then came to the realization that "*Elijah and Salome are together because they are pairs of opposites*". Elijah represents the animus or male side of our personality, while Salome represents the anima or female side in our natural mind. Jung traces the mental evolution of the animus in a sequence: First, the "wise man" who has "remarkable intuition". Then, he is able to penetrate the collective unconscious and is able "to get in touch with archetypes" there. He is "surrounded by mana" which represents thinking with non-material ideas in which the archetypes are immersed.

The natural mind is "fascinated and thrilled" by the symbols that correspond to the non-material ideas. After that, the natural mind is able to receive in individual consciousness the supreme of all non-material ideas, namely the "*God-image*". With this supreme archetype in place, the natural mind incorporates and appropriates related archetypes that are called "*Moses, Christ, and the Mahatmas*".

Jung says that the key character of "*John the Baptist*" in the New Testament represents this central group of archetypes but has been "depotentiated", which means that this image has lost power in the materialism of the natural mind. Other archetypes in this group include Goethe's "Faust" character and Nietzsche's character of *"Zarathustra"*.

In our natural mind we take in characters in story and imagination that correspond by symbolism to specific archetypes that influence our mental make up, and even determine it. Jung had the courage to engage the characters of the collective unconscious that managed to come across the wall of the collective unconscious and straight into his individual consciousness. He wrote that at one point he thought he was going mad and would not be able to return to sanity and be Jung again. But a few weeks later he was back to being Jung again, which made him feel grateful and happy.

Jung discovered archetypes empirically by direct experience and observation when his natural mind receded a bit to the back and he saw the schism! Jung saw where the break in logic takes place when our individual consciousness contemplates the collective consciousness in the form of the collective unconscious. Jung may have had the vision of the celestial humanity that existed on this earth prior to the Fall of Consciousness.

Swedenborg had the opportunity of visiting with and interviewing some of those people prior to the Fall who had an physical body on earth thousands of years ago. Their physical body did not do the normal air breathing as we do now. They said they had "internal breathing" and did not use their lungs to inhale and expel air. Hence also they did not use a sonorous or vocal language, but used complex lip movements to communicate. In their heaven today they live in tribes and tents as with their physical bodys long ago.

They are married couples in conjugial love, who will to be oneminded anatomically and live their daily lives in mutual love with other couples who feel the utmost regard for each other and for all. Above all, they are united in their love and worship of God who sometimes appears to them as Divine Human and interacts with them.

This is amazing to me! Swedenborg says that God also appears to him from time to time as a Divine Human.

When we think with material ideas about the ideas that I am developing in this book we remain cold to it. It is "DOD", or dead on arrival. We have a collection of ideas that we put in one category in our mind that may be called "Read Later". I have such a category in an online magazine app that lets me add an item anytime I see something I might want to read some other time. And all the items I have put in there stay put, forever it seems. But I never get to read from that category! How could I? Every day there are more news articles than I can process. This is how we deal with non-material ideas. Either we reject them immediately, or later, by not getting back to them.

But many find themselves with a different type of response when first considering a non-material idea. They feel intrigued. They feel an attraction from within that feels liberating. It is a new experience in our natural mind to feel inwardly liberated, like a duck on a lake who never tried to lift off and fly, but one day did.

Jung was such a duck. He was accepted as a world renown psychologist of innovative and deep thinking. His non-material ideas spawned millions of Jungians, I suppose including myself. I believe that Jung's special and universal attraction is the elevation of consciousness that is felt by anyone who encounters non-material ideas without rejecting them.

It is widely believed that elevation of consciousness and reaching for closeness with God is a "mystical" experience that is above language and words, above logic, above rationality. But in fact the opposite is the case as demonstrated by Swedenborg and Jung. Non-material ideas such as the psychology of regeneration are pure theistic psychology and science. It requires the highest attainable rationality for the natural mind to be able to understand non-material ideas.

But it's important to consider Swedenborg's description of the rational in two forms, lower and higher. We use our rational thinking when we manage society and evaluate scientific proposals. This may be called the natural-rational mind. It consists of material ideas only. Then there is a higher rational that we use to manage our relationships to others and to God. This higher or more interior rational capacity may be called the spiritual-rational. It consists of non-material ideas only.

God is rationality itself. Human rationality originates or is sourced in God's rationality. The traditional idea of "mystical union" with God proposes the opposite direction. When we think with material ideas in our natural mind we believe that our own religion is better than the other religions. People who believe that another religion is better, move over to that religion. So our religion is always the best.

And for some people, our religion is the only true religion, and therefore all religions are false except our own. Such are the beliefs and opinions of the natural mind thinking with material ideas. The literal meaning of Scriptural verses defines all religions. Since the verses of revelation involve historical events and real people it is inevitable that each religion sees itself as the only true one.

But when we allow non-material ideas into this oversimplified mental package we experience an elevation of our understanding of religious belief systems. We first of all put in place the non-material idea that human beings have two minds and God's Word speaks to both minds simultaneously. The literal or historical meaning of the verses involves the physical body of the people talked about. Here God talks to the lower natural mind with material ideas such as nations, wars, kings, crops, rituals, punishments, rewards, and death. These are things that God gives us through the physical body.

Simultaneously God also talks to the higher spiritual mind using the language of non–material ideas. Every detail in the literal meaning that deals with various objects, characters, or numbers, stands for its corresponding mental objects and properties, such as personality, love, truth, intention, affection, feelings such as mental pain from regretting what one has done or considered, loyalty, selfishness, etc. These are non-material things and ideas. God talks to us with non –material ideas about the psychology of regeneration, which involves what we think, what we love, and how we feel.

So there is a perfect balance between God's speech to the natural mind and to the spiritual mind, in other words, God's message to individual consciousness and God's message to collective consciousness. God continuously enriches collective consciousness through the mental sense of *Sacred Scripture*.

For example, what the literal message calls the punishment of hell as burning in fire represents in the mental message mental torment and suffering. God instructs us that in the afterlife of eternity it is our personality that determines whether we live in the happiness of heaven or the torment of hell. It is not punishment for the bad things we did, nor rewards for the charitable things we did. Not punishment in hell, because God is pure love and compassion, feels for human beings, and cannot punish anyone. Not reward in heaven, because everything good we did was from God who did it, as we remain powerless to do any good from ourselves.

Therefore heaven and hell are not choices that God makes for us. We each make that choice through the personality that we have acquired and that reflects our lifestyle habits.

Such is the difference between the literal and spiritual message in each verse. Note that while there are conflicts between religions from the literal message that God gives to various nations through their *Scriptures*, there are no conflicts from the mental message. All people regardless of religion and culture must undergo regeneration in accordance with the psychology of the human mind.

When human beings become conscious in the afterlife they spontaneously begin to use a spiritual language that has nothing in common with the natural language that we were using through our physical bodys on earth. This universal language or communication system is the same for all regardless of prior religion, culture, historical epoch, or family history. People from other earths in the universe all speak this one language in the afterlife of eternity. This is substantially confirmed in the *Swedenborg Reports*.

I might mention here an article I wrote of a tentative study I did in which I compared samples of *Scriptures* recognized in the five major historical religions that are alive today. My preliminary results indicate that they are all written in dual style just like the *Old and New Testament*, as demonstrated by Swedenborg. The literal verses discuss objects, events, and characters in the context of a particular culture and race. The mental message discusses regeneration.

Note: The article is reproduced at the end of volume 11.

****

Volume 4
Section 13

****

13. Durkheim's Description of Collective Consciousness

Collective consciousness in Durkheimian social theory

Durkheim used the term in his books *The Division of Labour in Society* (1893), *Rules of the Sociological Method* (1895), *Suicide* (1897), and *The Elementary Forms of Religious Life* (1912). In *The Division of Labour*, Durkheim argued that in traditional/primitive societies (those based around clan, family or tribal relationships) totemic religion played an important role in uniting members through the creation of a common consciousness (*conscience collective* in the original French). In societies of this type, the contents of an individual's consciousness are largely shared in common with all other members of their society, creating a mechanical solidarity through mutual likeness.

> *The totality of beliefs and sentiments common to the average members of a society forms a determinate system with a life of its own. It can be termed the collective or creative consciousness.*
> ~ Emile Durkheim

In *Suicide*, Durkheim developed the concept of anomie to refer to the social rather than individual causes of suicide. This relates to the concept of collective consciousness, as if there is a lack of integration or solidarity in society then suicide rates will be higher.[8]

Collective consciousness or collective conscious (French: conscience collective) is the set of shared beliefs, ideas and moral attitudes which operate as a unifying force within society. The term was introduced by the French sociologist Émile Durkheim in his Division of Labour in Society in 1893.
https://en.wikipedia.org/wiki/Collective_consciousness

We experience collective consciousness in both the natural mind and the spiritual mind. In the natural mind collective consciousness may be called "intersubjectivity" and involves material ideas based on interaction with others through the physical body. Durkheim mentions shared beliefs and moral attitudes that "*operate as a unifying force within society*". As an example consider the common laughter of the audience during a comedy routine. Or the national grief people experience together during disasters. Or the holidays everyone is celebrating together and in similar ways and activities. These are experiences of intersubjectivity made possible by culture.

Culture is a process of maintaining intersubjectivity within a geo-political region.

Sharing the content of individual consciousness with other individuals in a group creates *group intersubjectivity*, from which emerges a natural collective consciousness that envelops each individual subjective consciousness and gives it a basis of objectivity.

In other words, collective consciousness is an objective environmental psychological medium in which are immersed the individual consciousness of each member or co-participant.

Individual consciousness is subjective and internal, and does not merge into collective consciousness, which is objective and external. The two remain anatomically distinct.

Sometimes you can hear someone say, *"We think alike. We each know what the other is thinking. We can finish each other's sentences."* This experience of natural onemindedness is produced by intersubjectivity.

Durkheim argues that worship rituals and spiritual doctrines in a "clan" or "tribe" create a "*common consciousness*" that is shared by the members. In this social psychological sense, culture and tradition in all societies contribute to the emergence of a national collective consciousness. The result is that social events influence individual consciousness in similar ways in all members.

To be affected similarly means that an event or idea will produce in all individuals emotions that are compatible, and it will produce overlapping *causal attributions*. These are ways in which people explain how an event happened. Sometimes this shared feeling is called solidarity. They will express compatible explanations and evaluations of the situation.

The awareness of compatibility in thinking and feeling produces attraction and bonding.

Individuals will show the same readiness for similar actions. They will enjoy the same events and outcomes. They will mutually like each other. They will have similar sentiments. According to Durkheim, this emergent collective consciousness and mentality gains a "life of its own".

In other words, collective consciousness within a group becomes objective because it is mutual and living. *Mutuality is the source of objectivity.* Thinking of myself in terms of how others think of me is called "being objective".

Individual consciousness remains subjective because it is experiential and interior. It does not have an external presence. And yet it is this subjective individual consciousness that enhances the objective collective consciousness through mutuality of relationship.

This occurs in all the different types of relationship that exist such as the relationship between marrieds, or being a member of a team or task force, or being among those who own a house, or those who live together as neighbors, and so on endlessly. In each of these types of relationship the way members strive to forge intersubjectivity determines the character of their collective consciousness.

There are cases where some individuals in the group feel divorced from the collective consciousness. Their thoughts and emotions are different from the group experience of the other individuals. They no longer feel at home in the group. Durkheim used the French word "anomie" to designate this phenomenon of estrangement from the group.

He argued that the experience of anomie encourages suicide as a solution for some individuals. Durkheim argued that at times when societies are in extreme conflict and there results a disintegration, suicide rates increase. And no doubt murder rates, thinking of the recurrent news of a fired and disenchanted employee going back to the workplace with a gun.

Durkheim is considered to be the founder of the field of modern sociology. Many of the topics that Durkheim discusses in his books have endured as research areas not only in sociology but in social psychology. One such topic is "solidarity". Durkheim was Jewish in Europe at the end of the 19th and first half the 20th centuries. This was a time of intense anti-Semitism and Durkheim was able to observe an increased feeling of solidarity among the Jewish population.

In other words, collective consciousness in a group sharpens and clarifies in view when members experience a joint threat or danger.

Like Jung and Swedenborg, Durkheim saw the reality of religious symbols and meanings. The three psychologists focused less on religion as on the symbols and meanings that belong to all religions. These archetypes recur universally despite the vast cultural differences in religious practices and beliefs.

Durkheim was sometimes criticized for going back to primitive "aboriginal" religions or "cults" as a source for better understanding the mentality of modern societies. Durkheim's response was that ancient religious institutions should not be considered "outdated" as a source of valid sociological and psychological information. He argued that if an institution such as a primitive religion survives and succeeds it must rest on social psychological forces that are valid, or else that religion could not survive.

Durkheim acknowledged that we need to go beyond the language of primitive symbols and how the faithful justify their ancient rituals, so that we may discover the parallel mental forces that are still active in modern societies.

Durkheim argued that there are permanent and universal mental forms of collective consciousness that become visible when studying the various individual expressions of these forms in particular religious practice and experience. We can recognize this same attitude in Jung's work one century later that uncovered collective symbols of humankind that he called "archetypes", which Jung related to mental forces that permanently exist in the collective unconscious of the psychic world.

Durkheim's research led him to the conclusion that individual consciousness or thinking is subjective but is dependent on "collective representations" that are objective and universal to all humanity. Durkheim's work is considered as the foundation of modern thinking in sociology.

Today, social scientists study the "social origin" of individual ideas and actions, and this later focus has somewhat obscured and replaced the earlier notion that individual ideas originate from the "collective consciousness" of humanity and its biology.

This may explain why it is not generally recognized that Durkheim's ideas have a close relationship to the ideas of Jung and Swedenborg.

> *Jung stressed the importance of individual rights in a person's relation to the state and society. He saw that the state was treated as "a quasi-animate personality from whom everything is expected" but that this personality was "only camouflage for those individuals who know how to manipulate it", and referred to the state as a form of slavery. He also thought that the state "swallowed up [people's] religious forces", and therefore that the state had "taken the place of God"—making it comparable to a religion in which "state slavery is a form of worship".*
>
> *Jung observed that "stage acts of [the] state" are comparable to religious displays: "Brass bands, flags, banners, parades and monster demonstrations are no different in principle from ecclesiastical processions, cannonades and fire to scare off demons". From Jung's perspective, this replacement of God with the state in a mass society leads to the dislocation of the religious drive and results in the same fanaticism of the church-states of the Dark Ages—wherein the more the state is 'worshipped', the more freedom and morality are suppressed; this ultimately leaves the individual psychically undeveloped with extreme feelings of marginalization. ~Wikipedia entry*

Jung writes:
> *Psychic contents that belong not to one individual but to a society, a people or the human race in general. The conscious personality is a more or less*

arbitrary segment of the collective psyche. It consists in a sum of psychic factors that are felt to be personal. ~Carl Jung, The Persona as a Segment of the Collective Psyche, CW 7, par. 244

Identification with the collective and voluntary segregation from it are alike synonymous with disease. ~Carl Jung, The Structure of the Unconscious, par. 485

A collective quality adheres not only to particular psychic elements or contents but to whole psychological functions. Thus the thinking function as a whole can have a collective quality, when it possesses general validity and accords with the laws of logic.

Similarly, the feeling function as a whole can be collective, when it is identical with the general feeling and accords with general expectations, the general moral consciousness, etc. In the same way, sensation and intuition are collective when they are at the same time characteristic of a large group. ~Carl Jung, Definitions, CW 6, par. 692

****

Volume 4
Section 14

****

14. Natural Psychology And Theistic Psychology

Some of the concepts and ideas in theistic psychology pose a problem to contemporary psychologists who are philosophically imbued with material ideas of the world. I'm thinking especially of the non-material idea of the *"vertical community"*. This expression refers to Swedenborg's most spectacular and important discovery about the human mind, namely, that every individual is permanently immersed in the telepathic psychic sphere of afterlife societies.

We are never alone since we are mental beings and therefore omnipresent in the mental world given that there is no space in the mental world. We know this from our dreams. There is an apparent space and there are apparent objects that resemble the natural world when we are awake. But these objects and spaces are not physical. They are constructed mentally from mental substance, which is the environment of the mental world of eternity where our mind is born embodied in a mental or spiritual body made of that substance.

Psychologists are trained to consider communication with "spirits" of the afterlife as a serious delusion and is associated with psychoses and schizophrenia, thus the most serious psychological problems there are. Hence to hear about Swedenborg's communication with "spirits" of the afterlife immediately strikes psychologists as abnormal and psychotic, in other words, not real but imagined. Some contemporary psychiatrists have written that Swedenborg was delusional and seriously psychotic. But these evaluations are spurious and inapplicable. I predict that they will soon be regarded as outdated and old-fashioned materialism.

The writings and lectures of psychologist Carl Jung (1875-1961) was the one great exception that reshaped the spectrum of psychology in the twentieth century. The ideas of Carl Jung, along with those of Emanuel Swedenborg (1688-1772), created an intellectual basis for the narrative of theistic psychology. I have created this narrative by synthesizing the ideas of Jung and Swedenborg.

Jung writes:
> It is certainly remarkable that my critics, with few exceptions, ignore the fact that, as a doctor and scientist, <u>I proceed from facts, which everyone is at liberty to verify</u>. Instead, they criticize me as if I were a philosopher, or a Gnostic with pretensions to supernatural knowledge.
>
> As a philosopher and speculating heretic I am, of course, easy prey. That is probably the reason why people prefer to ignore the facts I have discovered, or to deny them without scruple. But it is the facts that are of prime importance to me and not a provisional terminology or attempts at theoretical reflections. ~Carl Jung, Psychology and Religion, Forward to White's God and the Unconscious, p. 307

In other words, Jung describes his approach to psychology by saying:

- That he proceeds from facts, which everyone is at liberty to verify.
- That critics of his work prefer to ignore the facts he has discovered.
- That to him it is the facts that are of prime importance, and not how or whether they fit current theorizing.

Due to the dualist content of their work, both Jung (1875-1961) and Swedenborg (1688-1772) were scientists who became embroiled in the methodological controversy of whether to allow *non-material* ideas into scientific explanations. I consider their work foundational contributions to modern theistic psychology.

Swedenborg was a near contemporary of Descartes and Newton. Both of these historically famous writers, along with Darwin a little later, make mention of their faith in "God" or in the "Creator" of the natural world, its laws and phenomena. After this acknowledgement of a non-material idea, they entered the world of science with their material ideas. They presented their *non-theistic* theories of the universe and its laws.

All their definitions, explanations, and measurements consisted exclusively of material ideas.

It was notably different with Swedenborg who consistently maintained a *theistic* direction in all his scientific works and theories in physics, chemistry, metallurgy, biology, and psychology. And so while Newton was publishing his classic and influential *Principia* book in 1687, Swedenborg was publishing the theistic version of his own *Principia* book in 1734. Newton gave himself the job of explaining natural laws without account to God's role in them.

Newton's theory of nature and natural laws contain material ideas exclusively. The same is true with all the "moderns" in the history of psychology: Descartes, Kant, Darwin, Pavlov, Wundt, Freud, Ellis, Rogers, Skinner, Chomsky. They all exclude non-material ideas such as those introduced by Swedenborg and Jung, which include:

- an omnipresent God
- consciousness that is independent of the physical brain
- heaven and hell in eternity
- psychic world independent of the physical world
- independent psychic forces such as archetypes that are operating in the mind
- built in correspondences of physical and non-physical events
- symbolism that interacts with mental health and development
- psychological meaning hidden within the text of Sacred Scripture
- afterlife societies that are psycho-geographically arranged according to human anatomy
- inherited personality inclinations
- individuation and regeneration

Swedenborg saw his work as explaining in more detail, rather than just generally, *how God effects and manages the natural laws through the spiritual laws*. In other words, he defined all natural events and phenomena as being *effects* that are produced by spiritual events and phenomena that are their *causes*. All causes are in the mental or spiritual world, and all effects are in the natural or physical world. Swedenborg's proposals were entirely new in science, not seen before.

Descartes proposal is dualist in the sense that he constructed two distinct categories of reality, physical and mental. His dualist proposal was not adopted in the march of modernism in psychology. Descartes however did not present a coherent and justified embodiment for mental phenomena. Modern science rjects anything that does not have a physical embodiment.

In natural psychology the embodiment of all mental phenomena is a number or physical measurement. If a proposed psychological explanation cannot be embodied in a number, or derived from a series of numbers, then it is immediately rejected as unscientific. The idea of an independent psychic world is rejected as "unscientific".

An instance of this naturalistic orientation in the current intellectual climate is shown by the history of an article I've been trying to publish for the past five years that discusses Swedenborg's dual consciousness and his theistic approach to personality and behavior. After completing the multiple revisions that I was asked to do, the final decision by the editor was to reject my article.

After going through this process with three journals, I decided to give up the attempt, realizing more than ever, how deep is the fear in modern natural psychology of non-material ideas. This is equally true of those sectors in cognitive psychology and neuroscience that discuss dualism and consciousness exclusively with material ideas such as "emergent properties" of brain activity.

So now here I come in the twenty-first century, a contemporary professor of psychology with a proposal that is based almost entirely on non-material ideas. You can see these ideas exhibited in this book and in my other recent books. Since 1960 I have published many articles in traditional psychology journals. I wrote them in conformity with the rules and standards expected. But by 1981 my ideas were directly influenced by the study of Swedenborg's Writings. I started writing psychology with non-material ideas and principles, including placing God at the center of the new approach. That is when I started using the expression "*theistic psychology*" for the work I was doing. I then discovered that theistic psychology as I conceived it was unpublishable in any academic journal in psychology. As a result, all my books dealing with theistic psychology are self-published.

Despite this experience, I believe that the future of psychology is the re-alignment of natural psychology to become a correspondence science to theistic psychology. This requires the admission into psychology of non-material concepts, research, and theory. The psychology of Jung in the twentieth century is already a part of theistic psychology of the future. And so is the psychology of Swedenborg, which in my view has been for 250 years a part of the theistic psychology of the future.

I'd like to share with readers a brief Web information page that refers to a new book by Dr. Ian Thompson, a researcher in nuclear physics, and an expert on Swedenborg, and as well a longtime email correspondent with me.

"Beginning Theistic Science"

A book (just now published) to introduce possible connections of theism (from philosophy and religion) with physics and psychology (of science).

Theism is the belief that God is the creator and sustainer of the world, and hence of all life and activity within the world, yet in a way whereby the world is as if active from itself.

This contributes to the science and religion debate, as well as to contemporary conversations about mind and consciousness, especially since there is considerable doubt (especially in academia) that any such connections exist at all. The result will be judged by the plausibility of the detailed structure.

The book begins with a general discussion about the possibility of theistic science today, followed by a chapter on the historical background. There is then a set of chapters each discussing one of the basic premises of theism, and drawing out consequences for the structure of the created world. In Part III, each part in turn is identified in terms of what we think we know already, so giving consequences for the kinds of psychology and physics that should be used to describe the minds and materials we see around us.

For more about this book and its topics, see www.BeginningTheisticScience.com for sample chapters, reviews and ways to get it.

For discussions about this book go to blog.beginningtheisticscience.com

For discussions about the current website go to blog.theisticscience.org

----
.
Dr. Thompson's current site introduces the subject as follows:

Foundations of Theistic Science:
The Theory of Spirit, Mind and Nature from Theism.

Approaches through Physics, Biology,
Psychology, Philosophy, Spirituality, Religion, Theology

Basic Principles with Consequences for Nature,
Evolution, Mind, Bible Meanings and Dualism

http://www.theisticscience.org
.
.

I recommend Dr. Thompson's site to readers who are interested in the historical and philosophic context of Swedenborgian dualism, and how it is relevant to the sciences today.

Dr. Thompson is also the Webmaster for the theistic psychology site that presents my earlier work (theisticpsychology.org or at: https://web.archive.org/web/20171220225308/http://www.theisticpsychology.org:80/). You will find there my 18-volume series titled:

Theistic Psychology: The Scientific Knowledge of God Extracted From The Correspondential Sense Of Sacred Scripture.

Theistic Psychology - Expanding The Narrative Series—Volume 4
Correspondences, Synchronicity, And Self-Witnessing

The titles of the volumes reflect some of the content of theistic psychology as I envisioned it in 2004. Some volumes are not completed. I rely exclusively on Swedenborg and I do not mention Jung in that earlier series.

1. Introduction to Theistic Psychology
2. Q&A on Theistic Psychology
3. Levels of Thinking About Theistic Psychology
4. Derivation and Function of Scientific Revelations
5. Research Methods in Theistic Psychology
6. Personality Theory
7. Character Reformation
8. Learning and Cognition
9. Spiritual Development
10. Health Behaviors
11. The Marriage Relationship
12. The Heavenly and Hellish Traits
13. Religious Psychology
14. Prayer as Revelation from God
15. Rational Faith and Charity
16. Religious Mysticism
17. Religious Movements
18. Topical Index to All Sections and Reading List

I'd like to quote myself in a passage from Volume 2 of that series:

Q. What's the difference between religion and theistic psychology?

A. The difference is that between mystical and scientific. Mystical systems depend on blind faith or credulity and as a result, there are a variety of mystical systems, or religions, and each believes to have the real truth while thinking that the others do not. This is why religion depends on declared membership, on affirmations of a common creed, and dependence on the willingness to believe something that cannot be explained in a scientific manner. As a result, when we examine religions in a rational or scientific way, we cannot arrive at a conclusion since the creed or faith resists breakdown and rational analysis.

On the other hand theistic psychology is not a religion but a science. Theistic psychology contrasts with non-theistic psychology that automatically excludes God as an explanatory concept. Theistic psychology automatically includes God as a concept in all explanations about human behavior and dynamics. While religion depends on creed and faith, theistic psychology depends on rational and scientific explanations of the laws and mechanisms by which God causes every event and behavior to occur. Therefore theistic psychology advances by cumulative research and critical analysis of all models, theories, and data.

The idea and knowledge of God in theistic psychology is not based on direct experience. If this were the case, it would cease to be a science because one individual's experience of God is not the same as another's, and neither has access to the other. Sensuous consciousness of God is rightly categorized as mystical. Theistic psychology is based on rational consciousness of God. This means that no one can make up what God is or is not, or what God wants or does not want, or how God manages the created universe, or what our fate is in the afterlife.

No one can know these things. They can invent them, but those are mere hypothetical and imaginative portrayals. I for one was never attracted to anyone's idea of God or experience of God because I had no way of verifying their notions. Unless I could understand God from my rational perspective as a trained and practicing scientist, I was unable to get involved, or be interested for very long, in other people's theories and systems.

Rational consciousness of God is based, not on human imagination and intelligence, but on Divine revelation of Himself by God.

This is clearly the only possibility. God created human beings with a mind that can comprehend God's Truth. Truth is rational, hence God's basic character or nature is a Being who is rational. All the laws of nature we have discovered are rational, and the whole fits together rationally. Therefore, to know God rationally is the only way to know God in truth. God is a rational Being. Obviously, God created human beings to possess a rational mind that is capable of knowing and understanding God. From this knowledge we are able to love God if we so choose. This is what God wants, that we love Him more than anything else He has created. Why?

Because by loving God He is able to give us what we were created for, but not otherwise. The purpose God had in creating human beings is that they be born on some physical earth, develop a rational mind, and at death, be resuscitated into an eternal world of conjugial happiness called heaven. This is a noble and loving purpose and we can appreciate it by feeling gratitude.

So it makes rational sense to say that the rational mind God creates in us needs to be given information about God so that we can know God and love Him more than anything else we know. This information comes to us through Divine Speech or Sacred Scripture dictated by God. This is the same as Divine Truth that gives us the facts about God and true reality, rationally understood. Divine Speech must be the source of all information for theistic psychology.

Clearly, if information about reality, about God, and about the universe is made up as someone's theory, we will never know the real reality, the real truth, which only God the Creator possesses. Obviously, the human mind is created to receive communication from God as Divine Speech. If this were not the case science would never know about true reality. It doesn't make sense to separate reality into two parts, one that we can test and another we can only speculate about.

Reality is integrated and cannot be separated. If you separate reality into non-overlapping components you can never understand reality rationally, which it is. God is rational and runs the universe rationally as shown by the rationality of laws we can discover about the physical universe and the rationality of God's revelations.

Theistic psychology is therefore based exclusively on Divine scientific revelations. Nothing is added to it that is from another source. ~Leon James

Today, more than a decade after I wrote the above, it is clear to me that Jung's ideas must also be acknowledged as theistic psychology. I believe that I made a strong case for that in my previous four books and in this current book.

Jung writes:
> I . . . have the feeling that this is a time full of marvels, and, if the auguries do not deceive us, it may very well be that . . . we are on the threshold of something really sensational, which I scarcely know how to describe except with the Gnostic concept of [Sophia], an Alexandrian term particularly suited to the reincarnation of ancient wisdom in the shape of ΨA. ~Carl Jung, The Freud/Jung Letters, p. 439
>
> I have been baptized with impure water for rebirth. A flame from the fire of Hell awaited me above the baptismal basin. ~Carl Jung, Liber Novus, p. 304
>
> It is the mourning of the dead in me, which precedes burial and rebirth. The rain is the fructifying of the earth, it begets the new wheat, the young, germinating God. ~Carl Jung, Liber Novus, p. 243

The scientific framework in the *Swedenborg Reports* includes a series of non-material scientific concepts, as illustrated by the following propositions, each describing a non-material idea:

1. Natural phenomena are effects of spiritual phenomena, these being their cause.
2. God operates the dual universe from Firsts to lasts and from lasts to Firsts, in an uninterrupted series of causation in levels of discrete degrees that correspond to each other.
3. By means of good and truth, God operates physical events from a discrete degree within, thus apart from space. Through good and truth God is omnipresent.

4. Endless earths in the universe are being created to support God's goal for creating human beings, which is to make each one happy and wise to eternity.
5. God creates all things into a discrete series of ends, causes, and effects.
6. All appearances are produced by built-in correspondences between the outward appearance and its inner structure or form.
7. Human beings are born immortal.
8. The entire human race is interconnected by consociation and mutual telepathic influx.
9. There are no industrialized or technological civilizations on other earths, nut there are many planets throughout the galactic universe whose inhabitants are at a level that we would call primitive and pre-literate, but not "savage".
10. Individual growth and development recapitulates ethnic history.
11. God is constantly present with every individual, and manages the sequence of the person's thinking and willing.
12. The mental anatomy of the mind mirrors the physical anatomy of the body. Therefore inferences from one can be made about the other. For instance, the chief motives in our personality dominate our mind like the heart with its circulation dominates the body.

The following charts illustrate how knowledge from the psychological meaning of *Sacred Scriptures* can serve to produce systematized knowledge in theistic psychology. This example discusses the anatomy of the mind and its connection to the afterlife world of mental eternity.

The Charts below first appeared in my book *The Mental World Of Eternity* (2008).

God created the mental world of eternity and the physical world with 12 distinct anatomical levels from highest to lowest. Chart 1 below identifies each level. Levels 1, 2, and 3 are above the human mind. Levels 4, 5, and 6 are the levels of the spiritual mind. Levels 7, 8, and 9 are the levels of the natural mind. Levels 10 and 11 are levels of the spiritual body. Level 12 is the physical body and physical world.

The distinct function, powers, and complexity of operations at each level are indicated in Chart 1.

The 12 levels operate synchronously through the laws of correspondences and symbolism. Chart 2 shows that the 12 distinct levels are present simultaneously.

Level 12 is removed at the "death" of the physical body. Levels 1 to 11 are in the mental world of eternity, which is also called the afterlife world.

The mind of every individual human being contains all the levels.

Chart 3 shows the correspondence between different parts of the body's anatomy in relation to the mind's anatomy and function. This psycho-anatomical relationship is responsible for ordering the afterlife societies in the shape and structure of the body.

Anatomical Chart 1
The Mental World of Eternity
Viewed in Successive Order of Discrete Degrees

Anatomical Layers	Explanation
Layer 1 Spiritual Sun	Mental aura around the visible Divine Human in the created world that can be seen by human beings in layer 4. Source of out flowing mental spheres of good and truth, or of love and wisdom, from which is all willing and all understanding in human minds.
Layer 2 Heaven of Human Internals	From conception to birth. Layer where exist the immortal souls of unborn or still born human embryos. The soul is formed at conception in the mother from the substances that are within the father's semen.

Layer 3 Soul	From birth to eternity. Inherited from the biological father's soul that is carried by correspondence in the semen and its DNA. Created at conception. Forever unconscious to our direct awareness. Also called "God's abode" from which God manages all the layers below. Source of all the individual's uniqueness in qualities and potentials. Can be called an immortal human plant, each created by God with a unique DNA. Contains the archetypes of the collective unconscious.
Layer 4 Spiritual Mind Celestial layer	Also called the "interior spiritual, "the "interior rational," and the "celestial rational." It is the inmost or highest layer of operation for human beings, giving us quasi-omniscience through God's Omni-proprium that is willingly received in the affective organ. In afterlife societies it is called the third or celestial heaven ("highest angels"). It remains unconscious until resuscitation at the death of the physical body (layer 12).
Layer 5 Spiritual Mind Spiritual layer	One degree lower. It also remains unconscious until resuscitation about thirty hours after the death of the physical body. In afterlife societies it is called second or spiritual heaven ("spiritual angels"). Though unconscious to our daily natural mind, it maintains the interior framework of rationality in our natural mind (layer 7).
Layer 6 Spiritual Mind Interior Natural layer	Lowest of the three degrees of the spiritual mind, also called the "spiritual-natural" or "interior natural" level. In afterlife societies it is called the first or natural heaven that is made up of "good spirits". Though unconscious to our daily natural mind, it maintains the interior framework of rationality in our natural mind (layer 7), allowing human beings to construct languages, science, and institutions.
Layer 7 Natural Mind Interior layer Rational	Called the "rational mind." Can contain immaterial ideas principally from the psychological meaning of *Sacred Scripture*, but also from "spiritual conscience". This layer 7 is the locus of reformation and regeneration of the inherited personality. Before regeneration it is in the order of hell (opposite to

	layers 6, 5, 4), when we call "good" whatever pleases us; afterwards, it is in the order of heaven (layers 4, 5, 6) when we call "good" only that which can exist in heaven, as revealed in *Sacred Scripture*. Once this layer 7 is reformed and is undergoing regeneration, the lower natural layers (8, 9) can also be regenerated from their inherited hellish order to a regeneratd heavenly order. Layer 7 becomes inactive after dying-resuscitation in the afterlife.
Layer 8 Natural Mind Exterior layer Materialistic, Sensual	Called the "scientific or materialistic mind" and sometimes the "sensual mind." Contains sense bound or materialistic ideas and interests, like the negative bias in nontheistic science. This is the everyday self ("me") that we know ourselves to be prior to reformation (in layer 7). Contains inherited hellish traits that become habits of life. This layer can become regenerated after layer 7 has been reformed and regenerated. Layer 8 becomes inactive after dying-resuscitation in the afterlife.
Layer 9 Natural Mind Corporeal layer	Called the "corporeal mind." Closest to the physical body. Contains inherited hellish traits. Layer 9 becomes inactive in the afterlife after the dying-resuscitation procedure.
Layer 10 Spiritual Body	Immortal protective covering made of mental substance that contains all the prior layers above in simultaneous order.
Layer 11 Limbus Covering	Inherited from the mother. It is made of mental substance and contains all the prior layers. Remains forever as a natural base for the immortal spiritual body (layer 10) and its contents to which it is connected from birth and subsequent development. Is made of intermediary spiritual-natural substances. Does not disintegrate at death.
	Inherited from the mother and formed in her womb. Temporarily connected by correspondence to the

| Layer 12 Physical Body | spiritual body (layer 10) and the natural mind (layers 7, 8, 9). Disintegrates at death. |

Chart 1 is based on the careful work done by N.C. Burnham, *Discrete Degrees* (1887). The 2001 Internet edition by Ian Thompson is available here: http://www.theisticscience.org/books/burnham/index.htm

Anatomical Chart 2
The Mental World of Eternity
Viewed in Simultaneous Order of Discrete Degrees

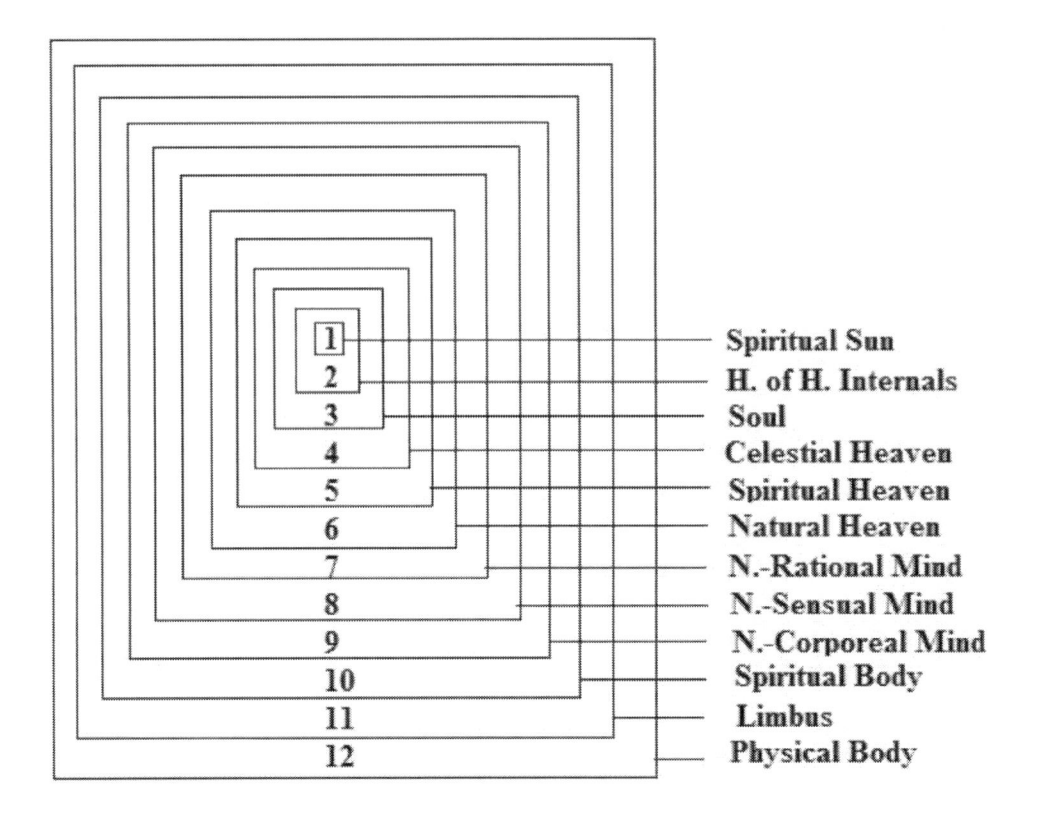

Theistic Psychology - Expanding The Narrative Series—Volume 4
Correspondences, Synchronicity, And Self-Witnessing

```
1  ── Spiritual Sun
2  ── H. of H. Internals
3  ── Soul
4  ── Celestial Heaven
5  ── Spiritual Heaven
6  ── Natural Heaven
7  ── N.-Rational Mind
8  ── N.-Sensual Mind
9  ── N.-Corporeal Mind
10 ── Spiritual Body
11 ── Limbus
12 ── Physical Body
```

The 12 Discrete Layers of a Human Being Viewed in Simultaneous Order

You can see that the highest layer in successive order (1) is the inmost layer in simultaneous order. The inmost of every human being is the Spiritual Sun, and the outermost is the physical body.

Anatomical Chart 3
Body-Mind Correspondences
For Anatomical Layers 4 to 9

PERSONALITY LAYER	CIRCULATORY SYSTEM	RESPIRATORY SYSTEM	NERVOUS AND SKELETAL SYSTEM

148

	A = AFFECTIVE Our Ruling Love	C = COGNITIVE Our Governing Truth	S = SENSORIMOTOR Our External Appearance
Layer 4 CELESTIAL-RATIONAL	HEART, ARTERIES, REPRODUCTIVE ORGANS	LUNGS, BREATHING, LIPS, CHEEKS	HANDS, EYES, RIGHT BRAIN, CEREBELLUM, CHEST, THIGHS

Mentality Themes for Layer 4:

Wife receiving conjugial love from God, while husband receives it from the wife.
Conjunction with God through the Divine Human Omniproprium (Personality).
Love of innocence and protection of children.
Love of fidelity. Altruism.
Perceiving interior truths.
Inspiring in people good thoughts and dreams.
Inspiring in people the love of good.

Layer 5 SPIRITUAL-RATIONAL	A5 STOMACH, LIVER, MASTICATION, ASSIMILATION	C5 ESOPHAGUS, MOUTH, CAVITY, SMELL, TONGUE, TASTE	S5 INTERIOR OF NOSTRILS , EARS, LEFT BRAIN

Mentality Themes for Layer 5:

Discussing and reasoning about theistic psychology topics.
Inspiring people who are seeking to understand theistic psychology and to strengthen conscience.
Helping people in spiritual combat during regeneration efforts.
Rational Theistic Self-analysis (RTS).

Layer 6 SPIRITUAL-NATURAL	A6 NUTRITIONAL EXCHANGE IN CELLS	C6 RESPIRATION, OXYGENATION, AIR SACS	S6 ?

\multicolumn{4}{l}{Mentality Themes for Layer 6: Practicing the human virtues in community life. Inspiring people with being useful. Inspiring people to acquire motor skills. Inspiring in people the rational foundations for aesthetics, art, sports, civics.}
Layer 7 INTERIOR-NATURAL	A7 SPLEEN, PANCREAS, BLOOD, ARTERIES, VEINS, CAPILLARIES	C7 DIAPHRAGM	S7 HANDS, OUTWARD SKIN OR LINING OF ALL INTERNAL ORGANS
\multicolumn{4}{l}{Mentality Themes for Layer 7: Practicing the unity model of marriage. Motivated to master the mental environment. Religious or spiritual views based on what is rationally understandable. Cooperating with God in one's regeneration for eternity. Thinking from scientific dualism and theistic psychology. Valuing sincerity, spiritual responsibility, rationality, diligence, altruism.}
Layer 8 EXTERIOR-NATURAL	A8 GALL BLADDER, KIDNEYS, URETHRA, BLADDER	C8 TEETH	S8 NEURONS, FEET, SKIN, BONES, CARTILAGE, MUSCLES, TENDONS
\multicolumn{4}{l}{Mentality Themes for Layer 8: Practicing the equity model of marriage. Motivated to master the social environment. Thinking from materialism and negative bias in science. Religious or spiritual views based on mystery, authority, and persuasive ideas. Love of legalism, egalitarianism, control. Concerned with parity, duty, honor, recognition, glory. Valuing honesty, social responsibility, patriotism.}

Layer 9 NATURAL-CORPOREAL	A9 INTESTINES	C9 ?	S9 SOLES OF THE FEET, HEEL

Mentality Themes for Layer 9:

Practicing the male dominance model of marriage.
Motivated to master the physical environment.
Desire to punish, to suppress freedoms.
Spirituality based on superstition, magic, psychics.
Xenophobia. Authoritarianism. Dogmatism. Fundamentalism. Literalism.

Illustration And Application
To The Growth Of The Mind

Growth and development take place under two types of influx from God. There is an immediate influx into each layer directly. Simultaneously there is a mediate influx into each layer from the layer above. The mediate influx establishes the vertical community that binds all humanity together through the action of correspondences from a higher layer to a lower layer. In mediate influx each exterior layer is formed by its corresponding interior layer. The immediate influx allows God to manage each layer independently without going through the layers above.

There are two movements in the growth and development of our mind. One is the "ascending" movement, which is upward from layer 9 to layer 7, which constitute the layers of the natural mind. The second movement is the "descending" movement, which is downward from 4 to 6. There is a critical encounter between layer 6 (lower spiritual mind) and layer 7 (upper natural mind). The two movements go on simultaneously as they correspond to each other (e.g., 5A corresponds with 4A, 5C with 4C, and 5S with 4S). Neither ascending nor descending would be possible alone, since our mind would then have no life in it (no sensations, thoughts, feelings).

Growth and development from infancy to old age proceeds progressively and in synchrony between the unconscious descending operations (layers 4, 5, 6) and the conscious ascending operations (layers 9, 8, 7).

During infancy our development is focused on layer 9. This development takes place with the correspondential growth of layer 4.
During childhood our development is focused on layer 8. This development takes place with the correspondential growth of layer 5.

During adolescence our development is focused on layer 7. This development takes place with the correspondential growth of layer 6.

(inversion takes place)

During young adulthood our development is focused on the reformation and regeneration of layer 7 through spiritual combat. This development takes place with the correspondential growth of layer 6.

During adulthood our development is focused on the regeneration of layer 8 to bring it into correspondence with layer 7. This development takes place with the correspondential growth of layer 5.

During old age our development is focused on the regeneration of layer 9 to bring it into correspondence with layer 8. This development takes place with the correspondential growth of layer 4.

Notice the systematic pattern in this development of the layers. You can follow this pattern by looking at the bolded items above. Be sure to understand this pattern fully before you go on with the explanations. You need to learn to reproduce it from memory.

Notice that before the "inversion" the development of the natural layers is by ascending steps from 9 (infancy) to 8 (childhood) to 7 (adolescence). Synchronously with this ascending direction in the natural mind (from 9 to 8 to 7) there is a corresponding descending direction in the spiritual mind (from 4 to 5 to 6).

Notice that after the "inversion" the regeneration of the natural layers is by descending steps from 7 (young adulthood) to 8 (adulthood) to 9 (old age). Synchronously with this descending direction of regeneration in the natural mind (from 7 to 8 to 9) there is a corresponding ascending direction in the spiritual mind (from 6 to 5 to 4).

Both ascending and descending patterns are necessary for mental development, for regeneration, and for opening the layers of our three heavens in eternity (6, 5, 4).

During development in infancy, Layer 4 (unconscious celestial-rational) influences by correspondence the development of layer 9 (conscious natural-corporeal). Then layer 5 (unconscious spiritual-rational) influences the growth of layer 8 (conscious natural-scientific or sensual), and layer 6 (unconscious spiritual-natural) influences the growth of layer 7 (conscious natural-rational). In this way the Divine Psychologist supervises the unconscious development of the spiritual mind (descending sequence), which makes possible the growth of the conscious natural mind (ascending sequence).

In infancy therefore the highest layer of the spiritual mind (celestial layer 4) influences the development of the lowest layer of the natural mind (corporeal layer 9) and the lowest layer of the limbus (layer 11). In turn, the celestial layer of the spiritual mind (layer 4) undergoes unconscious modification by the Divine Psychologist. This involves the storing of mental states of innocence and love that the infant experiences.

Later in adulthood, when the individual is ready to reform and undergo regeneration combats with spiritual truths, these childhood remains of mental states of good (innocence, love, obedience, joy) are used by the Divine Psychologist to motivate the person to continue cooperating with the regeneration process that is going on in the conscious natural mind.

In childhood, the middle layer of the spiritual mind (spiritual layer 5) influences the development of the middle layer of the natural mind (scientific layer 8) and the middle layer of the limbus (layer 11). Remains of good from this period are stored in the spiritual layer of the spiritual mind (layer 5), which undergoes spiritual development as a result of the growth that is taking place in the natural mind's layer 8. This is called the "scientific" mind (or "sensual" mind) because it specializes in operations that stem from sensory input (layer 8S) from the physical body (layer 12) that occurs as the child explores the physical and social environment.

In young adulthood, the lowest layer of the spiritual mind (spiritual layer 6) influences the development of the highest layer of the natural mind (rational layer 7) and the highest layer of the limbus (layer 11). Layer 7 is called the natural-rational mind because it specializes in operations that uphold moral and intellectual reasoning and understanding. The remains of good during this phase are stored in layer 6 of the spiritual mind, which is also called our first heaven.

Now that all the layers of the natural and spiritual mind have been "opened" or operationalized, the individual is ready to undergo reformation and regeneration, which will require all that the person has learned from the external world (science, Sacred Scripture, education, experience) (layers 7, 8, 9), as well as all the remains of spiritual good and truth that God has stored up in the spiritual mind of the individual (layers 4, 5, 6).

The following diagram summarizes the preceding Statements:

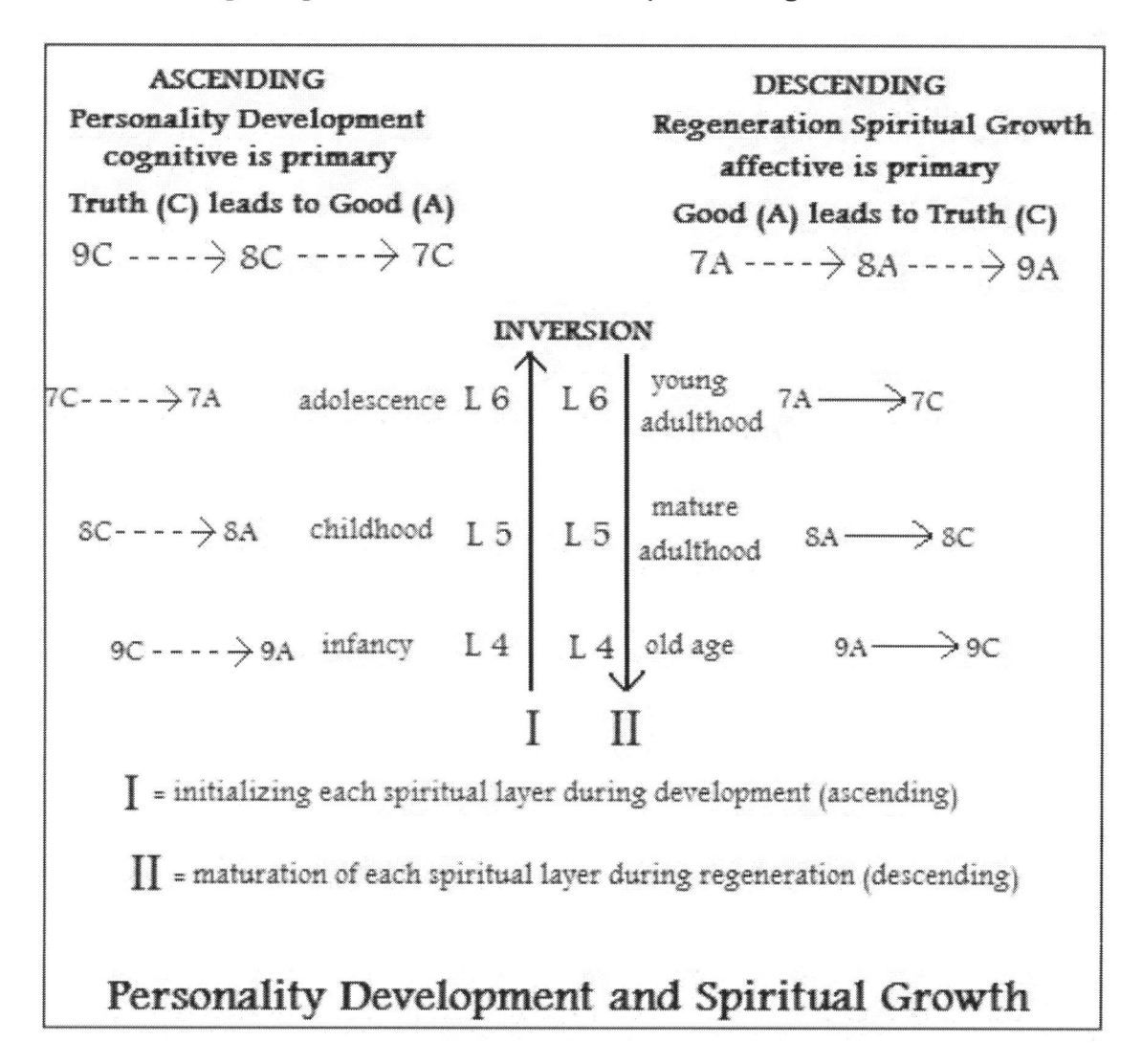

```
ASCENDING                          DESCENDING
Personality Development      Regeneration Spiritual Growth
   cognitive is primary            affective is primary
Truth (C) leads to Good (A)     Good (A) leads to Truth (C)
  9C ----> 8C ----> 7C            7A ----> 8A ----> 9A

                       INVERSION
7C----> 7A  adolescence  L 6  | L 6  young        7A ----> 7C
                              |      adulthood

8C----> 8A  childhood    L 5  | L 5  mature       8A ----> 8C
                              |      adulthood

9C----> 9A  infancy      L 4  | L 4  old age      9A ----> 9C
                              ↓
             I                   II
```

I = initializing each spiritual layer during development (ascending)

II = maturation of each spiritual layer during regeneration (descending)

Personality Development and Spiritual Growth

For additional discussion on layers and mental development see the book on Mental anatomy: http://theisticpsychology.org/books/mental-anatomy.htm or at: https://web.archive.org/web/20161102055709/http://theisticpsychology.org/books/mental-anatomy.htm

Sociology is enlightening to a psychologist.

This is what happens to me. I've been trained and intellectually brought up in psychology. I acquired the idea that psychologists don't read journal articles in sociology and don't go to conferences for sociologists. Later in my career I came across the work of three sociologists that created a paradigm shift in my perspective and methodology in psychology.

One was Erving Goffman's books that describe the micro-details of social interactions in daily encounters. The second sociologist was Harold Garfinkel in his theoretically revolutionary book "*Ethnomethodology*". The third sociologist was Harvey Sacks who wrote a series of key articles that opened up a new methodology and theory on the ethnomethodological analysis of talk in daily exchanges.

I imbibed the theoretical narrative and methodological arguments. The new ethnomethodological approach greatly enriched my understanding of psycholinguistics, the field that I specialized in. I produced in quick succession a dozen articles on conversational analysis. I felt enlightened as a psychologist with a new tool with which to think and explain the phenomena associated with human beings, and especially the mind.

This was in the 1970s. I felt confident that I could write a textbook on the analysis of conversation and how this interacts with personality and mind. I had gathered a lot of pages of detailed notes. I made various discoveries about how semantic structures are aligned in our mind and how these form the pieces with which we think and communicate.

The Writings of Swedenborg are unique in the centuries old literature on science, philosophy, and theology. Everything I knew about psychology and psycholinguistics was enriched by Swedenborg's ethnography of the afterlife. It is not possible to understand human personality without seeing its development from birth, to the afterlife and to eternity.

The Swedenborg Reports, as I often call the Writings, are the only academic source of empirical and observational data on personality development in the afterlife.

And so after studying the *Swedenborg Reports* for more than two decades I took the bold step and announced in my articles and books that a new psychology now exists and it may be called "*theistic psychology*". It is defined as the psychology of personality from birth to the afterlife as derived from the psychological meaning of the verses and phrases in *Sacred Scripture*.

At first I announced that I was describing "*spiritual psychology*". I was searching for a topical entry point into psychology as I was still thinking that the *Swedenborg Reports* could fit into psychology by accepting some of its premises about the afterlife world.

But I soon realized that there was no area of overlap between materialistic psychology and the theistic psychology of Swedenborg. Perhaps subconsciously I was trying to sneak the *Swedenborg Reports* into materialistic psychology! At last I became convinced that not a single idea or concept from theistic psychology can be "imported" into materialistic psychology.

That's because every concept in theistic psychology is non-material and every concept in materialistic psychology is material. There is no overlap or connection point except that of correspondence. Every material idea corresponds to its non-material idea.

****

Volume 4
Section 15

****

15. Post-Materialist Science And Theistic Psychology

So I gave up the idea of importing non-material ideas about personality into materialistic psychology. But I discovered something quite recently that at first made me wonder once more whether or not the two sciences – materialistic and theistic -- can exist together as one science. What gives me this renewed idea is coming across as if by chance a Web page that gave the title as "*Manifesto for a Post-Materialist Science*". That attracted my interest immediately. And sure enough, I loved it.

However once again I had to soon give up the idea of co-existence when it became clear to me that the non-materialist manifesto adds a dual dimension to nature or the natural world. That is, it proposes that the natural world has a dual dimension, namely, one that is material and the other is non-material. Both levels of operation are empirically observable, each with appropriate measuring tools. The non-material dimension of nature is called consciousness and mental operations. The two dimensions interact when mental operations influence physical operations.

I want to quote selections that I want to discuss in relation to theistic psychology.

> *We are a group of internationally known scientists, from a variety of scientific fields (biology, neuroscience, psychology, medicine, psychiatry), who participated in an international summit on post-materialist science, spirituality and society. ...*
>
> *1. The modern scientific worldview is predominantly predicated on assumptions that are closely associated with classical physics. Materialism—the idea that matter is the only reality—is one of these assumptions. A related assumption is reductionism, the notion that complex things can be understood by reducing them to the interactions of their parts, or to simpler or more fundamental things such as tiny material particles.*
>
> *2. During the 19th century, these assumptions narrowed, turned into dogmas, and coalesced into an ideological belief system that came to be known as "scientific materialism." This belief system implies that the mind is nothing but the physical activity of the brain, and that our thoughts cannot*

have any effect upon our brains and bodies, our actions, and the physical world.

3. The ideology of scientific materialism became dominant in academia during the 20th century. So dominant that a majority of scientists started to believe that it was based on established empirical evidence, and represented the only rational view of the world.

5. However, the nearly absolute dominance of materialism in the academic world has seriously constricted the sciences and hampered the development of the scientific study of mind and spirituality. Faith in this ideology, as an exclusive explanatory framework for reality, has compelled scientists to neglect the subjective dimension of human experience. This has led to a severely distorted and impoverished understanding of ourselves and our place in nature.

15. According to the post-materialist paradigm:

a) Mind represents an aspect of reality as primordial as the physical world. Mind is fundamental in the universe, i.e. it cannot be derived from matter and reduced to anything more basic.

b) There is a deep interconnectedness between mind and the physical world.

c) Mind (will/intention) can influence the state of the physical world, and operate in a nonlocal (or extended) fashion, i.e. it is not confined to specific points in space, such as brains and bodies, nor to specific points in time, such as the present. Since the mind may nonlocally influence the physical world, the intentions, emotions, and desires of an experimenter may not be completely isolated from experimental outcomes, even in controlled and blinded experimental designs.

d) Minds are apparently unbounded, and may unite in ways suggesting a unitary, One Mind that includes all individual, single minds.

16. Post-materialist science does not reject the empirical observations and great value of scientific achievements realized up until now. It seeks to expand the human capacity to better understand the wonders of nature, and in the process rediscover the importance of mind and spirit as being part of the core fabric of the universe. Post-materialism is inclusive of matter, which is seen as a basic constituent of the universe.

17. The post-materialist paradigm has far-reaching implications. It fundamentally alters the vision we have of ourselves, giving us back our dignity and power, as humans and as scientists. This paradigm fosters positive values such as compassion, respect, and peace. By emphasizing a deep connection between ourselves and nature at large, the post-materialist paradigm also promotes environmental awareness and the preservation of our biosphere. In addition, it is not new, but only forgotten for four hundred years, that a lived transmaterial understanding may be the cornerstone of health and wellness, as it has been held and preserved in ancient mind-body-spirit practices, religious traditions, and contemplative approaches.

18. The shift from materialist science to post-materialist science may be of vital importance to the evolution of the human civilization. It may be even more pivotal than the transition from geocentrism to heliocentrism.

The Manifesto for a Post-Materialist Science was prepared by Mario Beauregard, PhD (University of Arizona), Gary E. Schwartz, PhD (University of Arizona), and Lisa Miller, PhD (Columbia University), in collaboration with Larry Dossey, MD, Alexander Moreira-Almeida, MD, PhD, Marilyn Schlitz, PhD, Rupert Sheldrake, PhD, and Charles Tart, PhD.
There is a list given of more than 200 scientists who signed or agreed with the manifesto.
Link: http://www.opensciences.org/about/manifesto-for-a-post-materialist-science

----

I recognize two of the names who prepared the wording of the manifesto, namely Rupert Sheldrake and Charles Tart. I should mention that the study and research of "consciousness" became an active field of study in materialistic psychology for the past half-century or more. And of course Jung's work on consciousness began at the turn of the 20th century and went on until 1961, thus a major part of the century.

The post-materialist manifesto argues for the introduction into science of non-material operations in nature. I think this may serve as a stepping-stone to theistic psychology. The contact point might be the non-material properties of mental phenomena. For instance, non-material operations are "nonlocal" and operate from any distance. Mental operations of the will and understanding, such as emotions and thoughts, are non-material and yet thanks to correspondence are able to exert effects on physical objects or properties.

However there is no discussion yet in post-materialist science of God and the afterlife. There is also not yet an awareness of "*discrete degrees*" and "*correspondences*". There is no awareness of the key role of Sacred Scripture as a source of knowledge about mind and personality. There is no awareness of how our personality is influenced by the "*vertical community*" or afterlife societies to which God connects us telepathically.

And there is no acknowledgement of heaven and hell in every human mind and how we avoid the one to achieve the other in the afterlife of eternity. There is no awareness of immortality. There is no understanding that the interaction between non-material and material is by the laws of correspondence and symbolism.

Jung announced one century ago that there is a psychic world that is not derived from the physical world but has its own independent existence and laws of cause and effect. My work on theistic psychology shows that "*mental substance*" is the stuff of which consciousness is made. It is not derived from physical matter. Hence we need to specify what is mental substance and where does it come from.

Descartes (1596-1650) is cited in the history of science for proposing that mind, soul, and consciousness exist in a world separate from the physical body. I think that his idea did not stick in psychology because Descartes did not specify what is the "spirit" substance of which are composed the soul and the mind. He did not know other than it is from God.

Swedenborg (1688-1772) was born in Sweden soon after Descartes left Sweden for Paris, where he passed on from illness. Swedenborg published several scientific treatises on the anatomy of the brain and its functions.

This was prior to age 57 when he suddenly developed dual consciousness. Hence he was not able to give a specific definition of mental substance until after he began his empirical ethnography of the afterlife societies in eternity.

I discuss mental substance throughout this book based on the *Swedenborg Reports*.

November 2017 News article:

> *A scientist claims there is no life after death because the laws of physics make it impossible. After extensive studies, physicist Sean Carroll says for there to be an afterlife, our consciousness would need to be entirely separated from our physical body – which it is not.*
>
> *Consciousness is a series of atoms and electrons which give us our mind, he says. The laws of the universe do not allow these atoms and electrons to continue to operate after our bodies have died. Dr. Carroll, a cosmologist and professor at the California Institute of Technology, explained: 'Claims that some form of consciousness persists after our bodies die and decay into their constituent atoms faces one huge insuperable obstacle: the laws of physics underlying everyday life are completely understood. 'There's no way within those laws to allow for the information stored in our brains to persist after we die,' he wrote in the Scientific American. There's no way information stored in our brains can persist after we die, says Dr Carroll.*
>
> *Dr Carroll says that Quantum Field Theory (QFT) suggests there is one field for each type of particle. So all photons in the universe are on one level, all electrons in the universe are on another level and so on. For life to be able to continue after death, he says tests on the quantum field would have revealed 'spirit particles' and 'spirit forces' – which they have not. 'If it's really nothing but atoms and the known forces, there is clearly no way for the soul to survive death. 'Believing in life after death, to put it mildly, requires physics beyond the standard model,' he said.*

In other words, if we start with the assumption that there is only one world we must conclude that life after death is impossible. This is indeed correct! But if we start with the assumption that there are two independent worlds, then the conclusion is incorrect. Dr. Ian Thompson, a nuclear physicist familiar with quantum theory, has recently proposed a "physics beyond the standard model", which he calls "theistic science". The title of his book is Beginning Science From God

****
Volume 4
Section 16
****

16. Premises And Methodology In Psychology Science

Theistic psychology remains a science as long as it maintains a methodology that allows falsifiability of assertions and theories.

The rendering of non–material ideas through natural language introduces a natural-rational level of thinking that produces a narrative whose details may not be coherent, consistent, or correct. When this happens, the conclusions and implications of the narrative may be shown to be in error, that is, incompatible with the premises of theistic psychology.

Every science consists of a few premises that sound reasonable and acceptable. These premises cannot be proven to be correct but they are assumed to be correct without the necessity of proof. This is why they are called premises. Besides a few premises science has a methodology that allows individual proposals to be replicated or falsified by others. Science proceeds gradually through the contributions of many.

And so both non-theistic and theistic psychology each has premises and methodological explanations. For instance, non-theistic or traditional psychology assumes the negative bias in science. This refers to the materialistic premise that there is only one world, which is the physical world. Therefore mind and consciousness are sourced in the physical brain and body. This premise is asserted without proof, and hence it is that I call it the negative "bias".

In contrast, the premise in theistic psychology is that there are two worlds, one material in time, and the other non-material in the world of mental eternity. I call this the positive "bias" since it is a premise that has not been proven.

Another premise in non-theistic psychology is that natural laws do not require the action or intervention of a Deity or God. In theistic psychology the premise is that there is an intelligent and omnipotent human God who intervenes in every detail of the physical and mental worlds.

Each premise is actually a general statement that collects a number of sub-premises. For instance, in non-theistic psychology the unproven assumption is that natural and biological laws are devoid of human morality and follow their own conditions. But in theistic psychology natural and biological laws are constrained by human moral considerations. Thus, God creates each natural and biological phenomenon for the human purpose of leading individuals to prepare for an afterlife in eternal happiness and justice.

The methodology in non-theistic psychology is tied to measurement. All psychological phenomena must be tied to sensory observations or else they are not admissible into psychological science. For instance, the idea of happiness is grounded in sensory observations such as facial expression, neurological hormones, and self-ratings of subjects. In theistic psychology there is no methodology of sensory measurement or physical observation.

Rather, the idea of happiness is defined by a non-material mental state that is identified with the people of afterlife societies in the *Grand Human* of mental eternity.

All emotions and psychological states in the individual are defined relative to the collective consciousness that belongs to the totality of all afterlife societies in eternity. All psychological states in the *Grand Human* arrangement of societies are defined as positive and healthy, and all psychological states in the *Grand Monster* arrangement of afterlife societies are defined as negative and sick.

****

Volume 4
Section 17

****

17. Methodology In Theistic Psychology

(1) The Method Of Paraphrastic Transformations

Paraphrastic transformations may be considered to be one of the scientific methodologies of theistic psychology.

Example 1:

The following numbered sentences are *paraphrastic transformations* of this sentence:

> *The character of people is made visible in their understanding, which shows itself in their beliefs and lifestyle habits.*

---

(1) People's hidden loves can be seen by their speech and by their choice of words that are chosen by their attitudes and persuasions.

(2) Love in the interior of our mind shows itself as wisdom in the exterior of our mind, and together they produce heaven in our mind. Hence also, self-love in the will shows itself as cunning and spiritual insanity in the understanding, and together they produce hell in our mind.

(3) We become aware of a particular affection in our personality when it conjoins itself with thoughts or images that are experienced as being delightful.

(4) The motive, which lies invisible in the will, conjoins itself with a plan it formulates in the understanding, and this conjunction leads to actions that are delightful to self and useful to others.

(5) People's intentions guide their thinking to justify what they are doing and how they live as being good.

(6) The will of good is within the understanding of truth, and together they produce uses for self and others.

Example 2:

The following numbered sentences are *paraphrastic transformations* of this sentence:

> *One's God-image affects one's relationship with God, hence everything about one's future in eternity.*

(1) What we believe about God influences our relationship with God, which determines everything about our afterlife.

(2) The nature of our faith conditions our relationship with God. If that faith is based on genuine truth from *Sacred Scripture*, it brings closeness and conjunction; but if it is based on falsified truth, it brings distance and separation.

(3) What we know and think about God indicates what relationship we are having with God, and this determines our afterlife of either heaven or hell in eternity.

(4) Closeness and conjunction with God depends on a faith based on genuine truths from God's Word, and conjunction with God produces heaven in our mind, while separation produces hell.

(5) If we desire heavenly love and genuine truth therefrom, which are from God, we are on the path to eternal heaven and to conjunction with God; but if we desire self-love and its falsified truth, which are from self, then we are on the path to eternal hell and to separation from God.

----

(2) The Method Of Correspondences

Another methodology in theistic psychology is the law of correspondences between the mental and physical worlds, as for instance, the details we know of the circulatory and respiratory systems in the physical body gives us detailed information about how affections in our mind produce and interact with our thoughts and beliefs.

The circulatory system in the physical body corresponds to the affective system in the spirit-body, while he respiratory system in the physical body corresponds to the cognitive system in the spirit-body. That they correspond means that the physical body is a perfect model in matter of the spirit-body in substance. All activity in the physiology and biochemistry of the physical body is an embodiment in matter of the psychological operations in the mind to which they correspond.

The method of correspondences allows derivation of psychological principles from the correspondential meaning of the literal verses. The methodology of paraphrastic transformations allows the production of hypotheses and confirmations regarding psychological principles derived from *Sacred Scripture*.

For example, the particular psychological "*lesson of life*" that is sought in the literal story of a "*parable*", is derived from the components of the literal story that are mentioned, such as a "vineyard", which corresponds to our collective beliefs and teachings about God; or, a "lamp" that is mentioned, which corresponds to knowledge from *Sacred Scripture* about psychological states. Similarly when animals are mentioned. The context of the verses reveals the correspondence between a particular species of animals and particular human emotions to which they correspond or represent.

Practicing producing paraphrastic transformations expands our knowledge of psychological dynamics in the human personality. It reveals where are sets and series in psychological states. It reveals how levels operate synchronously through instantaneous operation from "*Firsts to Lasts*", which refers to the flow of creation from God to the world and back to God through the doing of uses by human beings.

(3) The Method Of Substitution

Theistic psychology is a system of thinking about personality and regeneration that involves a narrative of non-material ideas coherently knit together as a synthesis.

The substitution technique involves parallelisms that occur in the verses of *Sacred Scripture* of the *Old Testament*, the *New Testament*, and the *Writings of Swedenborg*. Thee parallelisms are explicitly stated in the literal verses. For example, the following sentences in the *Writings* assert equivalence between sets of expressions or words, as for instance, "*it is the same whether you say that...*" – indicating an equivalent alternate expression. Sometimes it merely says "truth **or** faith", indicating an equivalence in meaning. The following table lists some of these instances and where they can be found in the Writings.

Statements Of Equivalence	Permissible Substitutes	
Divine worship consists of these truths and goods, or that **man** consists of them (AC 10298)	Divine worship	man or person who worships the Divine
truth or faith, since everything of **faith** is **truth**; also it is the same whether you say **good** or **love**, since everything of love is good (HH 232)	truth good	faith love
conjunction of **understanding and will** or conjunction of **truth and good** (HH 370)	understanding and will	truth and good
ruling love or that which he **loves above all things**. (HH 486)	ruling love	what one loves the most
truth or **faith** (NJHD 35)	truth	faith
"**begotten of God**" or "**proceeding from God**;" (TCR 23)	begotten of God	proceeding from God
God is **Good itself** and **Truth itself** or He is **Love itself** and **Wisdom itself** (CAN 8)	God	Good itself and Truth itself
	God	Love itself and

		Wisdom itself
Lord's Divine Human, or the **Divine Love** (AE 146)	Lord's Divine Human	Divine Love
the understanding of truth is described, or **those who are in it** are described (AE 355)	the understanding of truth	those who are in the understanding of truth
the spiritual and natural **mind** or the spiritual and natural **man**. (AE 406)	spiritual and natural mind	spiritual and natural man or person
falsities from the hells, or the **hells** (AE 538)	falsities from the hells	the hells
faith or **conscience** (AC 2325)	faith	conscience
higher and lower ones, or **more internal and more external** (AC 10051)	higher and lower	more internal and more external

In other words, the original verse shown in column 1 is highlighted with its main focus and presented in the middle column. The third column shows the alternate way of expressing that idea by substituting the words that are said to be equivalent in column 1.

Let's take a passage that allows several substitutions according to the table. I have bolded the words in the original, and also in its duplicate paragraph below to indicate the substitutions:

First the original:
The natural **mind**, by its two capacities called rationality and freedom, is in this state that it is capable of ascending through three degrees, or of descending through three degrees. It ascends by reason of **goods** and **truths**, and descends by reason of evils and **falsities**. And when it ascends, the **lower** degrees which tend towards hell are closed, but when it descends, the higher degrees which tend towards heaven are closed. The cause for this is that they are in reaction. These three

degrees, **higher** and **lower**, have neither been opened nor closed in man in earliest infancy, for he is then ignorant of **good** and **truth**, and of **evil** and **falsity**. ~Swedenborg, DLW 274

Now with substitutions:
The natural **man**, by its two capacities called rationality and freedom, is in this state that it is capable of ascending through three degrees, or of descending through three degrees. It ascends by reason of **love** and **faith**, and descends by reason of evils and **the hells**. And when it ascends, the **external** degrees which tend towards hell are closed, but when it descends, the **internal** degrees which tend towards heaven are closed. The cause for this is that they are in reaction. These three degrees, **internal** and **external**, have neither been opened nor closed in man in earliest infancy, for he is then ignorant of **love** and **faith**, and of evil and **the hells**.

It this case, it turns out that the original and the substitutions are so close that the two paragraphs hardly seem different in meaning. Nevertheless, the second paragraph is not merely synonymous with the original but reveals new features that are more interior. To see this requires more detailed study and examination.

Let us take another passage where the substitutions create a more dramatic difference:

Original sentence:
The very essence and life of **faith** is the Lord alone (AC 30)

With substitution:
The very essence and life of **conscience** is the Lord alone

The second sentence containing the substitution is a more interior meaning than the original. We knew that the life of faith is the Lord since faith is truth from the Lord, and what is form the Lord is the Lord. Hence: The very essence and life of faith is the Lord alone. But we did not know that the very essence and life of conscience is the Lord alone. This is a new derived spiritual revelation contained within the first literal revelation. We can now confirm this new perception by finding other passages in the literal that states that the life of conscience is the Lord. As for example:

> The new will with the spiritual regenerate man is conscience (NJHD 1919)
>
> [2] A person does not feel this struggle to be anywhere but in himself, and he feels it as the pangs of conscience. Yet it is the Lord and the devil (that is, hell) who struggle in man; their struggle is to gain control of the person, to see which is to possess him. The devil, or hell, attacks the person and calls forth the evil in him, while the Lord protects him and calls forth the good in him. (TCR 596)
>
> Genuine conscience is given by the Lord through the knowledges of a true faith (SE 3615)
>
> With angelical spirits there are bonds of conscience, which conscience is from the Lord. (SE 3850)
>
> Judgments are based on what is the Lord's when they accord with truths and spring from conscience. (AC 9160)
>
> When conscience dictates, it is in like manner said in the Word that "Jehovah speaks;" because conscience is formed from things revealed, and from knowledges, and from the Word; and when the Word speaks, or dictates, it is the Lord who speaks; hence nothing is more common, even at the present day, when referring to a matter of conscience, or of faith, than to say, "the Lord says." (AC 371)

You can see from these series of passages that a conscience that is genuine is from the Lord and is the Lord: "nothing is more common, even at the present day, when referring to a matter of conscience, or of faith, than to say, "the Lord says."

To recapitulate the three steps of the substitution technique:

First, find parallelisms in the literal verses that are explicitly identified.

Second, make the substitutions and reflect on the new formulation. This new meaning is more interior than the original Letter. It has been enriched by the different series or contexts which are brought together by the substitution.

Third, find new passages that explicitly confirm the new meaning.

(4) The Method Of Discourse Thinking

See below the Section titled "Sudden Memory And The Method Of Discourse Thinking".

(5) The Method Of Self-Witnessing

See below the Section titled "The Mental Technology Of Self-Witnessing"

(6) The Technique Of Graphic Methodology

See List of Diagrams in Volume 9 for entries on "Graphic Methodology".

****
Volume 4
Section 18
****

18. Swedenborg And Jung: Foundation Stones For Theistic Psychology

----
Jung writes:
My dear Bennet, 22 May 1960.

Thank you very much for your kind review of my Aion. There is only one remark I do not quite understand.

Speaking of the hypothesis of archetypes, you say that there is no scientific proof of them yet.

A scientific hypothesis is never proved absolutely in so far as an improvement is always possible. The only proof is its applicability. You yourself attest that the idea of the archetype explains more than any other theory, which proves its applicability. I wonder therefore which better proof you are envisaging.

When you assume the existence of an instinct of migration you can't do better than to apply it f.i. to birds and demonstrate that there are actually birds which migrate.

The archetype points out that there are thought-formations of a parallel or identical nature distributed all over the world (f.i., holy communion in Europe and Teoqualo in ancient Mexico), and furthermore that they can be found in individuals who have never heard of such parallels.

I have given ample evidence of such parallels and therewith have given evidence of the applicability of my viewpoint. Somebody has to prove now that my idea is not applicable and to show which other viewpoint is more applicable. I wonder now, how you would proceed in providing evidence for the existence of archetypes other than their applicability?

What is better proof of a hypothesis than its applicability? Or can you show that the idea of "archetype" is a nonsense in itself?

Please enlighten my darkness.

Yours cordially,

C.G. Jung ~Carl Jung, Letters Vol. II, p. 558-559

Jung dared to enter that great sea of darkness that he discovered in his mind, an empirical experience from which he concluded that the dark sea of the collective unconscious that he found in his own mind is in every human mind. This was one of Jung's most significant discoveries.

How can the same collective unconscious be in every individual mind?

Answering this question requires knowing about the mental world of eternity, which I discuss throughout the book.

Jung's idea is not a material idea and belongs to the mental world of the afterlife where there is no locality, quantity, time, or physical matter. Jung dared to explore the darkness in his mind by wading through its regions, seeing nothing at first, but hearing and feeling only. He discovered living souls of a scary appearance that felt to Jung as being hostile and psychologically dangerous. He also came across benign personalities who were willing to engage Jung repeatedly in conversation and assisted him in his inner explorations. Jung called these human-like beings "*archetypes*".

Jung decided that archetypes were ancient psychological forces that connect to everyone's personality.

Jung writes:
> Archetypes are "real." That is to say, effects can be empirically established whose cause is described hypothetically as archetype, just as in physics effects can be established whose cause is assumed to be the

atom (which is merely a model). Nobody has ever seen an archetype, and nobody has ever seen an atom either. …

… The psyche is something real because it works as can be established empirically. One must therefore assume that the effective archetypal ideas, including our model of the archetype, rest on something actual even though unknowable, just as the model of the atom rests on certain unknowable qualities of matter. … I pursue a scientific psychology which could be called a comparative anatomy of the psyche. I postulate the psyche as something real. ~Carl Jung, Letters Vol. II, p. 53-55

Jung struggled with the question of how to "prove" that consciousness is possible without a "brain". Here is an example of his struggle with scientific methodology that tends to be materialistic and excludes non-material ideas.

Dear Mrs. Eckstein, 16 September 1930

Thank you very much for your long and interesting letter.

It is surely a very interesting problem, the question of the relation between brain and consciousness. Everyday experience tells us that consciousness and brain are in an indispensable connection. Destruction of the latter results in an equal destruction of the former.

… There is no reason why one shouldn't suppose that consciousness could exist detached from a brain. Thus far there is no difficulty for our assumption. But the real difficulty begins when it comes to the actual showdown, namely when you should prove that there is consciousness without a brain. It would amount to the hitherto unproven fact of an evidence that there are ghosts.

I think it is the most difficult thing in the world to produce evidence in that respect entirely satisfactory from a scientific point of view. As a matter of fact, it is the hardest thing I could imagine. I frankly confess I don't know at all how such a proof would look. How can one establish indisputable evidence for the existence of a consciousness without a brain?

I might be satisfied if such a consciousness would be able to write an intelligent book, invent new apparatuses, provide us with new information that couldn't be possibly found in human brains, and if it were evident that there was no high-power medium among the spectators. But such a thing is quite unthinkable.

I therefore consider the possibility of proving an incorporeal consciousness an extremely unlikely one. Trance conditions are certainly very interesting and I know a good deal about them though never enough. But they wouldn't yield any strict evidence, because they are the conditions of a living brain. ~Carl Jung, Letters Vol. 1, p. 76

Jung's dilemma is resolved when we take into account that human beings are born with a physical brain in our temporary physical body on earth and a mental brain in eternity, which is in our immortal spiritual body. When we take into account our dual existence we can see that consciousness is not located in the physical brain but in the brain of our mental or spiritual body. When the physical brain "dies" our mental life and consciousness remains unaffected.

Indeed, it is not possible to prove that consciousness is related or dependent on the physical brain. This is because there is no such dependency except that of correspondence.

And so we can conclude that consciousness activity in the natural mind corresponds to the activity of the physical brain, but does not depend on it.

We each know what consciousness is because this is our normal daily mental state. It is a challenge to define consciousness even though it is so familiar. If we think of it with non-material ideas we can define consciousness as mental substance in the human form. This form is an anatomical embodiment of the individual. It is called the "spiritual body".

We are born in the afterlife of eternity with this immortal spiritual body that is the embodiment of our unique consciousness or mind and personality.

The spiritual body is the human form of mental substance. It has all the external and internal parts and organs of the human body.

The physical body emulates or is a model in physical matter of the spiritual body in mental substance, which is permanent and precedes the physical body in sequence of operation. The physical brain and the mental substance brain correspond in all details of operation and anatomy.

In other words, Jung views his work on archetypes and the psychic world as "empirical", just as much as the physicist's work on the atom is empirical. Both the atom and the archetype are scientific "models" whose validity or usefulness depends on observing or assessing the empirical consequences that follow from the model – in the physical world regarding the atom, and in the psychic world regarding the archetype.

Jung first formulates the existence of the psychic world as separate and independent of the physical world. Empirical observations are therefore possible in the psychic world since it is a world, and this means that there are objects and events to be observed in it. Archetypes are psychic objects that exist throughout the psychic world. Archetypes are real and therefore can be "*established empirically*". Jung writes: "*I pursue a scientific psychology which could be called a comparative anatomy of the psyche*".

Theistic psychology is the empirical study of mental anatomy as given in the psychological meaning of *Sacred Scripture*. Mental anatomy is the anatomy of the mind, or as Jung calls it, "*anatomy of the psyche*". The *Swedenborg Reports* are also proposed as being empirical. They present an empirical ethnography of the mental world of eternity, or what Swedenborg called the "*spiritual world*" of the afterlife.

All of Swedenborg's data about the afterlife world are observational.

He reports what he saw, what he did, what the people said whom he interviewed, what they looked like, what their beliefs were, how they lived, what language they talk, and numerous other lifestyle details.

Jung expressed his admiration for Swedenborg's "visionary" abilities. Unlike Jung who entered the psychic world in relative darkness, Swedenborg entered in full light. Swedenborg explains that God appeared to him at age 57 and told him that his mind was prepared by God since childhood for a super-special and unique mission in the history of science, and indeed, of all the universe.

Swedenborg was given dual consciousness for his mission to write and publish an ethnography of afterlife societies and their connection to the personality and mental health of people who still have their physical bodies on earth.

Dual consciousness means to be conscious and aware simultaneously in the natural mind in eternity that receives sensory input from the physical body on earth, and aware in the spiritual mind that receives sensory input from the spiritual body in the afterlife of eternity. This dual mental state was enjoyed by the generations on earth prior to the historical Fall of consciousness, as I mention in other places when discussing the Fall.

For 27 years Swedenborg carried on his ethnographic interviews and explorations of the afterlife world that is in mental eternity. Meanwhile he was making notes with his physical body on earth to keep track of the observations and interviews that he conducted with the people of the afterlife societies. He then published the notes and conclusions in nearly 30 volumes written in the scientific Neo-Latin that was familiar in the 17th century scientific publications. Swedenborg paid for the publication cost from his pension and then had the publisher send free copies to various bishops and theologians throughput Europe. Most of them ignored what he wrote but some of the clergy in Sweden and Germany sued him in court trying to prove that he was attacking the Church.

However they did not prevail and Swedenborg continued to publish his books until his last work in 1971, and passed on a few months later. Interestingly, some of the clergy who felt threatened had passed on earlier and Swedenborg confronted them in the afterlife trying to show them that they were rejecting the truth. Swedenborg describes in detail several of these afterlife encounters regarding his Writings.

The *Swedenborg Reports* have been translated in more than a dozen languages from the original Latin. They are available on the Web today.

Jung was very fond of the German poet Goethe, and Goethe was very fond of Swedenborg. Jung admired Goethe's skillfulness with which he introduced non-material ideas through dramatic archetypal characters like Faust, and many others. In his autobiography dictated towards the end of his presence on earth (1961), Jung mentions that he was an admirer of Swedenborg, declaring him to be "a great scientist".

Jung writes:

> *I admire Swedenborg as a great scientist and a great mystic at the same time. His life and work has always been of great interest to me and I read about seven fat volumes of his writings when I was a medical student. ~Carl Jung*

.

Carl Jung's legacy of ideas, lectures, interviews, letters, articles, and books have grown a Jungian following today of millions around the world. Jung has had to confront the antipathy and prohibition of twentieth century psychology against non-material ideas such as God, archetype, psychic world, collective unconscious, synchronicity, individuation, and the strong influence of psychic forces on personality and mental health.

One instance of this antipathy to Jung's proposal of the psychic world is exhibited by the brief relationship between Freud and Jung. At first Freud was so impressed by Jung that he saw Jung as a potential successor to himself in the fledgling new psychodynamic theories of neuroses and their psychoanalytic treatment. But then Freud reversed himself and abruptly broke off his relationship with Jung, never to renew communication with him. Later, Jung wrote that the cause was an article that Jung published in which he introduced non-material ideas into psychological theory.

Freud vehemently attacked Jung's idea of the psychic world being a non-material and independent world. Freud's psychology was embodied in the material world of neurology and physiology, while Jung's psychology was embodied in the non-material psychic world. It is not uncommon in science to express professional hostility to colleagues whose proposals include non-material ideas. Freud was not the only one who rejected and ridiculed Jung's concepts.

Unlike the dualism of Descartes, which remained empty, Swedenborg's dualism is highly articulated and forms the basis of his non-material theistic psychology. Like Jung, Swedenborg saw that the mind must be embodied in a non-material world, given that what is mental or spiritual cannot operate or exist in the physical world except by correspondence and symbolism. And since the mind is real, therefore there has to be a mental or spiritual world in which the mind functions and is anatomically embodied.

Swedenborg's proposal of "*spiritual substance*" is in agreement with Jung's proposal of "*psychic substance*", and I should add my own proposal of "*mental substance*". *The three equivalent expressions designate the same non-material entity or substance.*

Swedenborg's account is that God first created the spiritual world of eternity from the stuff of mental or psychic substance that exists eternally in God's human mind and is infinite in variety with no beginning or end. This mental substance is uncreate, and is the 'stuff' that God used to create and fashion the two worlds, the non-material mental world of the afterlife in eternity, and the material physical world of time and locality. In this book I present many details regarding how these two worlds interact synchronously and are unified by correspondences and symbolism.

Throughout his long professional career spanning most of the twentieth century, Jung made repeated attempts to legitimize and introduce non-material ideas in psychology. These include the collective unconscious, archetypes, synchronicity, mandala symbolism in dream analysis, God as partner in our mental health, individuation, mental complexes, the shadow, anima/animus as yin/yang, psychic world, Self, and other important non-material concepts.

I call them non-material ideas and methods because their definition and existence applies to the psychic world of eternity, and not at all to the physical world of time.

God created eternity before creating time. Hence the spiritual world is called the spiritual world of eternity because what is before time, or without time and apart from it, is in eternity. There is nowhere else for anything to be except in eternity or in time.

Psychic entities and psychic influences are dynamic psychological forces that act on the individual's . Jung's *"psychic world"* is synonymous with Swedenborg's *"spiritual world"*, and with my proposal of the *"mental world of eternity"*.

All psychic or spiritual forces exist in the mental world of eternity.

Our mental world belongs to "eternity" because there is no physical matter, space, or time in our mental world, and *what is not in time is in eternity*. The idea of eternity is another key non-material concept in theistic psychology.

Quoting from Wikipedia:
> *Macrocosm and microcosm refers to a vision of cosmos where the part (microcosm) reflects the whole (macrocosm) and vice versa. It is a feature "present in all esoteric schools of thinking. It is closely associated with Hermeticism and underlies practices such as astrology, alchemy, and sacred geometry with its premise of "As Above, So Below". ~ Wikipedia entry, 2017*

From literature we know that the ancient cultures were familiar with the non-material idea that every sub-part in a whole represents the whole in miniature. *Swedenborg explained that the smallest is an image representative of the largest.* This principle was used in earlier times to study the cosmos or universe by studying the human body, as the body was a world in small and all its parts represented some part in the sky of stars and galaxies.

Swedenborg was allowed to have a bird's eye view of the afterlife world of eternity and he saw an immense human body that he called the *Grand Human*.

In order to allow us to study non-material ideas further, I present in the next Section various selections from Jung that clarify how he defined and applied various non-material concepts to psychology and therapy. Following the selections I add my comments to the numbered selections.

****

Volume 4
Section 19

****

Voluptuousness, the lust principle, is Freud; passion for power is Adler; and selfishness-that is myself, perfectly simple. ~Carl Jung, Zarathustra Seminar, p. 1451

He who wants to remain true to love must also overcome sin. ~Carl Jung, Red Book, p. 356

19. Jung On Religion Vs. Psychology

.

.

I think of myself as a Christian since I am entirely based upon Christian concepts. ~Carl Jung, Letter to The Listener, January 21, 1960

Carl Jung writes *in Archetypes Of The Collective Unconscious,* 1934

>**1*
>
>*The hypothesis of a collective unconscious belongs to the class of ideas that people at first find strange but soon come to possess and use as familiar conceptions. This has been the case with the concept of the unconscious in general. After the philosophical idea of the unconscious, in the form presented chiefly by Carus and von Hartmann, had gone down under the overwhelming wave of materialism and empiricism, leaving hardly a ripple behind it, it gradually reappeared in the scientific domain of medical psychology.*
>
>**2*
>
>*For Freud, accordingly, the unconscious is of an exclusively personal nature, although he was aware of its archaic and mythological thought-forms.*
>
>**3*
>
>*myths are first and foremost psychic phenomena that reveal the nature of the soul*
>
>**4*
>
>*Primitive man is not much interested in objective explanations of the obvious, but he has an imperative need-or rather, his unconscious psyche has an irresistible urge-to assimilate all outer sense experiences to inner, psychic events. It is not enough for the primitive to see the sunrise and set; this external observation must at the same time be a psychic happening: the sun in its course must represent the fate of a god or hero who, in the last analysis, dwells nowhere except in the soul of man.*

All the mythologized processes of nature, such as summer and winter, the phases of the moon, the rainy seasons, and so forth, are in no sense allegories of these objective occurrences; rather they are symbolic expressions of the inner, unconscious drama of the psyche which becomes accessible to man's consciousness by way of projection-that is, mirrored in the events of nature.

The projection is so fundamental that it has taken several thousand years of civilization to detach it in some measure from its outer object. In the case of astrology, for instance, this age-old "scientia intuitiva" came to be branded as rank heresy because man had not yet succeeded in making the mental description of character independent of the stars.

*5
*Primitive man impresses us so strongly with his subjectivity
that we should really have guessed long ago that myths refer to something psychic. His knowledge of nature is essentially the language and outer dress of an unconscious psychic process. But the very fact that this process is unconscious gives us the reason.*

*6
An allegory is a paraphrase of a conscious content, whereas a symbol is the best possible expression for an unconscious content whose nature can only be guessed, because it is still unknown.

*7
Why is psychology the youngest of the empirical sciences? Why have we not long since discovered the unconscious and raised up its treasure-house of eternal images? Simply because we had a religious formula for everything psychic-and one that is far more beautiful and comprehensive than immediate experience.

*8
Almost the entire life of the collective unconscious has been channeled into the dogmatic archetypal ideas and flows along like a well-controlled stream in the symbolism of creed and ritual

*9
I am convinced that the growing impoverishment of symbols has a meaning. It is a development that has an inner consistency. Everything that we have not thought about, and that has therefore been deprived of a meaningful connection with our developing consciousness, has got lost. If we now try to cover our nakedness with the gorgeous trappings of the East, as the theosophists do, we would be playing our own history false.

A man does not sink down to beggary only to pose afterwards as an Indian potentate. It seems to me that it would be far better stoutly to avow our spiritual poverty, our symbollessness, instead of feigning a legacy to which we are not the legitimate heirs at all. We are, surely, the rightful heirs of Christian symbolism, but somehow we have squandered this heritage. We have let the house our fathers built fall into decay, and now we try to break into Oriental palaces that our fathers never knew.

*10
Anyone who has lost the historical symbols and cannot be satisfied with substitutes is certainly in a very difficult position today: before him there yawns the void, and he turns away from it in horror. What is worse, the vacuum gets filled with absurd political and social ideas, which one and all are distinguished by their spiritual bleakness. But if he cannot get along with these pedantic dogmatisms, he sees himself forced to be serious for once with his alleged trust in God, though it usually turns out that his fear of things going wrong if he did so is even more persuasive. This fear is far from unjustified, for where God is closest the danger seems greatest. It is dangerous to avow spiritual poverty, for the poor man has desires, and whoever has desires calls down some fatality on himself. A Swiss proverb puts it drastically: "Behind every rich man stands a devil, and behind every poor man two."*

*11
The unconscious is commonly regarded as a sort of encapsulated fragment of our most personal and intimate life-something like what the Bible calls the "heart" and considers the source of all evil thoughts. In the chambers of the heart dwell the wicked blood-spirits, swift anger and*

sensual weakness. This is how the unconscious looks when seen from the conscious side.

But consciousness appears to be essentially an affair of the cerebrum, which sees everything separately and in isolation, and therefore sees the unconscious in this way too, regarding it outright as my unconscious. Hence it is generally believed that anyone who descends into the unconscious gets into a suffocating atmosphere of egocentric subjectivity, and in this blind alley is exposed to the attack of all the ferocious beasts which the caverns of the psychic underworld are supposed to harbor.

*12
True, whoever looks into the mirror of the water will see first of all his own face. Whoever goes to himself risks a confrontation with himself. The mirror does not flatter, it faithfully shows whatever looks into it; namely, the face we never show to the world because we cover it with the persona, the mask of the actor. But the mirror lies behind the mask and shows the true face.

*This confrontation is the first test of courage on the inner
way, a test sufficient to frighten off most people, for the meeting with ourselves belongs to the more unpleasant things that can be avoided so long as we can project everything negative into the environment. But if we are able to see our own shadow and can bear knowing about it, then a small part of the problem has already been solved: we have at least brought up the personal unconscious. The shadow is a living part of the personality and therefore wants to live with it in some form. It cannot be argued out of existence or rationalized into harmlessness.*

*13
*This problem True, whoever looks into the mirror of the water will see
first of all his own face. Whoever goes to himself risks a confrontation with himself. The mirror does not flatter, it faithfully shows whatever looks into it; namely, the face we never show to the world because we cover it with the persona, the mask of the actor. But the mirror lies behind the mask and shows the true face.*

This confrontation is the first test of courage on the inner way, a test sufficient to frighten off most people, for the meeting with ourselves belongs to the more unpleasant things that can be avoided so long as we can project everything negative into the environment. But if we are able to see our own shadow and can bear knowing about it, then a small part of the problem has already been solved: we have at least brought up the personal unconscious. The shadow is a living part of the personality and therefore wants to live with it in some form. It cannot be argued out of existence or rationalized into harmlessness.

*14
Perhaps you will pay attention to the dreams that visit you at such moments, or will reflect on certain inner and outer occurrences that take place just at this time. If you have an attitude of this kind, then the helpful powers slumbering in the deeper strata of man's nature can come awake and intervene, for helplessness and weakness are the eternal experience and the eternal problem of mankind.

To this problem there is also an eternal answer, otherwise it would have been all up with humanity long ago. Then you have done everything that could possibly be done, the only thing that remains is what you could still do if only you knew it. But how much do we know of ourselves? Precious little, to judge by experience. Hence there is still a great deal of room left for the unconscious. Prayer, as we know, calls for a very similar attitude and therefore has much the same effect.

*15
The necessary and needful reaction from the collective unconscious expresses itself in archetypally formed ideas. The meeting with oneself is, at first, the meeting with one's own shadow. The shadow is a tight passage, a narrow door, whose painful constriction no one is spared who goes down to the deep well. But one must learn to know oneself in order to know who one is. For what comes after the door is, surprisingly enough, a boundless expanse full of unprecedented uncertainty, with apparently no inside and no outside, no above and no below, no here and no there, no mine and no thine, no good and no bad. It is the world of water, where all life floats in suspension; where the realm of the sympathetic system, the

soul of everything living, begins; where I am indivisibly this and that; where I experience the other in myself and the other-than-myself experiences me.

No, the collective unconscious is anything but an encapsulated personal system; it is sheer objectivity, as wide as the world and open to all the world. There I am the object of every subject, in complete reversal of my ordinary consciousness, where I am always the subject that has an object. There I am utterly one with the world, so much a part of it that I forget all too easily who I really am. "Lost in oneself" is a good way of describing this state. But this self is the world, if only a consciousness could see it. That is why we must know who we are.

*16
Living begins where I am indivisibly this and that; where I experience the other in myself and the other-than-myself experiences me.

No, the collective unconscious is anything but an encapsulated personal system; it is sheer objectivity, as wide as the world and open to all the world. There I am the object of every subject, in complete reversal of my ordinary consciousness, where I am always the subject that has an object. There I am utterly one with the world, so much a part of it that I forget all too easily who I really am. "Lost in oneself" is a good way of describing this state. But this self is the world, if only a consciousness could see it. That is why we must know who we are.

The unconscious no sooner touches us than we are it-we become unconscious of ourselves.

I will now provide explanations for the Jung selections above:

*1
Jung acknowledges the opposition in empirical psychology to the non-material properties of von Hartman's idea of an "unconscious" and Jung's own idea of a *collective unconscious*. Jung says that the unconscious "reappeared in the scientific domain of medical psychology". That assertion is no doubt accurate for Freud's definition of the unconscious, but it does

not apply to Jung's non-material concept of a *collective* unconscious that is objective and real and thus quite contrastive in kind from the individual unconscious that Freud defined as a subjective mental state that has no independent existence from the physical brain.

*2
Jung points to this contrast by referring to Freud's unconscious as "exclusively personal", thus not collective. As I discuss in the current book, collective consciousness is objective, while individual consciousness is personal and subjective. Jung points out that in Freud's work on the interpretation of dreams (1900), Freud acknowledges and applies "archaic and mythological thought-forms". Again we need to remember that Freud's idea of mythology and religion is material. Freud rejects what Jung accepts as the mental reality of myth and religion as *objective* causative factors in human personality. These objective factors are collective, biological, universal, and transcends what is merely individual. Jung defines the nature of myths as "psychic phenomena that reveal the nature of the soul" (see *3).

*3
"*myths are first and foremost psychic phenomena that reveal the nature of the soul*". Three non-material ideas are woven together in Jung's statement: myths, psychic, soul. Myths are descriptions of archetypes that lie in our personality. Every character in the myth is a representative of the character of the archetype. The character or nature of the archetype cannot be directly observed in our experiencing, hence it is not in our consciousness. But it can be observed through the symbolism of the myth.

This is why Jung says that myths reveal the nature of the soul through mental experience or "psychic phenomena". *Our experience reveals our soul if we interpret the experience as myth*. To do this we need to see the details of our day as details that belong to a myth. Our life is the embodiment of the myth. First comes the myth; and then the embodiment of it in our experiencing.

Swedenborg demonstrates that every verse in the *Old and New Testaments* of the *Bible* is a myth, including every character mentioned and every personal or historical event mentioned. All names, places, numbers, and objects that are mentioned are symbolic representations of archetypes and myths. God's purpose in speaking to us in a dual-meaning mode is to engage our natural thinking and our spiritual thinking simultaneously. Our natural thinking is done through material ideas, while our spiritual thinking uses non-material ideas. God is reaching us through both types of messages, material or historical, and non-material or mental and mythical. I discuss more details of this subject elsewhere in this book.

***4**
Jung acknowledges the psychology of the "primitive man" as the mentality and knowledge from which modern intellectualism departed and is no longer in touch with. Hence is the opposition of science to non-material ideas. Swedenborg relates this mental departure from the pre-modern mind as the "Fall of humankind" that is depicted in the *Old Testament* in the Adam and Eve story of departure or expulsion from Paradise.

It might be of interest to mention here that the earliest generations on earth were celestial creations in the ideal of God. They had an "internal" breathing and did not use sonorous voice powered by the lungs and vocal cords. Instead they had extremely sensitive lips with which they could communicate by moving very slightly in certain ways. It was a visual language that was worth a thousand words for each tiny lip movement.

Further, anatomically they were a whole-brained race. The generations after the Fall were of the split brain race. Having a left and right cerebral hemisphere for our civilization allows us to separate the cognitive and affective systems. The whole-brain celestial race could not think one way and talk another because of the unity of the cognitive and affective systems.

In my earlier books I make the case that the Fall refers to the loss of consciousness in our spiritual mind.

Swedenborg confirms that the earliest generations on this earth was known in ancient history as the Golden Age of civilization. It was followed by successive ages of knowing less and less about the existence of the spiritual mind and world. In the Golden Age there was full knowledge of correspondences, which specify the precise relationship between mental events and properties as causes and their effects in physical events and properties.

Jung studied the laws of physical-mental correspondences in religious symbolism, art, and dreams. Swedenborg studied these laws through *Sacred Scripture*. He discovered that every expression, word, name, or number in the *Old and New Testaments* of the Bible are addressed simultaneously to the conscious natural mind and the unconscious spiritual mind. The literal meaning of verses of *Sacred Scripture* is compatible with the material ideas of our natural mind and consciousness. In contrast, the spiritual or spiritual meaning of the verses is compatible with the non-material ideas of our spiritual mind and consciousness.

Pre-modern civilizations were aware of the non-material ideas that are derivable by implication from the literal meaning. Knowledge and awareness of the science of correspondences sank deeper and deeper into the dark unknown of the collective unconscious. The Fall is therefore a drop or loss of awareness of the reality of non-material ideas and spiritual consciousness.

Jung contrasts therefore the awareness and knowledge of the pre-modern "primitive man" to that of modern civilizations. Elsewhere, Jung relates this loss of consciousness to the etiology of neuroses and the war-prone modern history that we know and lament. Jung made it a theme of his work to bring people back to a greater knowledge of the collective unconscious that actually belongs to the people and is a part of them, even if it is ignored.

Jung considered it especially dangerous for human civilization to continue to ignore the collective unconscious because powerful psychic forces are acting on the mind of individuals, either positively or negatively. He encouraged psychologists and his patients to regain this primitive knowledge that was lost in the Fall, by studying the correspondences that are visible in the symbolism of dreams, religions, and art.

Jung shows that the "processes of nature" such as summer, rain, morning, night, animals, caves, harvest, etc., are "mythologized" and represented symbolically in stories and dreams. He thought it was very important for the mental development of children to expose them to fairy tales and other non-material entities such as spirits, elves, gods, heroes that fight dragons, and animals that can talk. These non-material ideas come out of the collective unconscious and appear in the conscious through these stories and mythical figures. Thus, in Jung's words, the "*unconscious drama of the psyche becomes accessible to man's consciousness*".

Jung laments the fact that astrology, which he calls the "intuitive science" of symbolism and myths, has been treated in science as "heresy", and hence psychology has become ignorant of the objective and causative relationship between personality and the stars. Unfortunately astrology as practiced today has lost its original validity that was based on perception of the collective unconscious forces that influence human minds.

*5
To the modern person, such as we are, the spirituality of primitive cultures that still thrive in a few parts of the globe, appears subjectively intense and personal, based apparently on inner visions that seem far away and less real to us where we are now. Jung says, far away yes, but less real, no. There has been no lessening of the reality of the collective unconscious in our modern days, despite our willful disregard of its reality and its powerful effect on our thinking and feeling every day, and its determinative effect on our mental fate in the everlasting future. This is no small or unimportant matter! The stakes are very high, even as high as they can be. So let us beware!

It wasn't easy, as I imagine, for Jung to have his modern day vision of the psychic world being denied and ignored by modern psychology. Further, it must have been emotionally difficult for Jung to find that he was being misunderstood by critics and followers alike. In a radio interview he made this statement when the subject was brought up: "*Thank God I am not a Jungian. I am Jung*". I'm quoting him from memory so it may not be exact. Still, it is plain to me that the non-material ideas he brought forth into the science of psychology were not going to be understood for quite some time because of the inherent resistance of material ideas to the entry of non-material ideas into consciousness and knowledge. This intellectual difficulty applies not only to critics of Jung's works, but also to followers.

My work in theistic psychology is an attempt to explain and present the non-material ideas found in the psychology of Jung and Swedenborg. *It is easier to understand Jung's non-material ideas once you study the ideas of Swedenborg.* Theistic psychology is the result of integrating Jung's concepts with Swedenborg's ethnographic descriptions of afterlife societies.

As I explain in this book, Jung's archetypes, which is at first a most difficult concept to fully understand, becomes easy to comprehend when it is known that afterlife societies in the psychic world are formed by people who share, what Swedenborg calls, the "ruling love" that governs their personality. Every afterlife society in eternity, which is the psychic world, is mentally governed by an archetype.

Jung discovered archetypes as mental themes that run the minds of all individuals. He discovered them by identifying the meaning of symbols that drive mental activity in imagination and in perceiving the built-in correspondences between nature and the mind. The modern mind of Jung found again the lost knowledge that nature and mind are connected. He was delighted to discover that the people in primitive cultures existing today have persistently shrugged off modernism and materialism. Their conscious natural mind remains open to the flow of non-material ideas that are streaming in from their spiritual mind that contains the collective unconscious.

*6
Jung clarifies the distinction between "allegory" and "symbol". Allegory refers to material ideas, while symbol refers to non-material ideas. When we construct an allegory we make use of the material ideas that are processed through the cerebrum or new brain. The non-material ideas represented by symbols are processed through the cerebellum or old brain. When we produce content in dreams, our cerebrum consciousness is inactive in sleep, while the cerebellum consciousness is active and produces non-material ideas.

The symbol is the vehicle by which a non-material idea in the collective unconscious can enter the individual consciousness in natural mind. The non-material idea thereby becomes comprehensible to the natural mind. A portion of the collective unconscious thus penetrates into natural consciousness. This was the great importance that Jung attached to the symbol, and why he thought children should be exposed to the mythical literature.

The natural mind constructs myths from universal symbols. Modern minds can hear or read the myths, or see the symbolic drawings, and as result they can become receptive to non-material psychology, which they can assimilate it into their personality. This process is healing and restoring. Swedenborg describes it at length calling it *"regeneration"* of personality. It is the process of recovery from the Fall and the restoration of thinking with non-material ideas. A whole new psychology then becomes real to the person, as Jung writes: *"We know from experience that the protective circle, the mandala, is the traditional antidote for chaotic states of mind"*.

*7
Jung laments the sorry fact that psychology in the twentieth century calls itself "empirical" and yet is totally ignorant of the reality and mental importance of the unconscious, which Jung calls a *"treasure-house of eternal images"*. Jung identifies the cause of this ignorance in science to the preemption of "psychic" topics by religion. In other words, religion gives science the excuse for excluding non-material ideas. The argument is that God and the afterlife are religious matters and therefore do not fall in the arena of science. Jung rejects this excuse as invalid.

Jung takes the correct position, in my view, when he argues that God and archetypes are real forces influencing our psychology and personality in our daily lives. Therefore, God and the psychic world of the collective unconscious are part of psychology and science regardless that these topics are also discussed in religion.

Jung is saying here that the religious formulation is artificially and deceptively constructed to appear *"beautiful and comprehensive"*. This makes the religious idea attractive and acceptable. In contrast, the non-material ideas that enter our consciousness when we rely instead on *"immediate experience"* are not as beautiful and seemingly orderly and logical as the religious presentation.

And yet, Jung is saying, that the religious explanation has now real mental power, leaving the individual cheated, under an illusion, and unprotected from the psychic forces. In contrast, the non-material ideas based on experiencing are real and help us progress toward a definitive and individuated restructuring of our personality. In other words, religion becomes effective in healing to the extent that our relationship to God becomes personal rather than collective and ritualistic.

*8

Jung observes that the intellectualism of the West regarding God and the afterlife has been formed by collective worship and by dogmas of religion that are rendered in material ideas. Religion has thereby pre-empted all mental consideration of God, Sacred Scripture, and the afterlife. To Jung this explains why religion in the West has had so much less influence on psychology in comparison to the religions of the East, which were acclaimed by Western intellectuals as passionate and informative regarding spirituality and daily disciplines.

*9

Jung sees in the history of the West a "*growing impoverishment of symbols*" because their interior component of non-material ideas has been gutted and discarded, leaving only a hard inert material shell. Our intellectualism now appears "naked", which means without substance and mental truth. The fascination with the "*gorgeous trappings of the East*" that many Europeans and Americans are feeling has failed to provide the intellectual clothes that would remedy their impoverished ideas of the non-material and the spiritual.

Jung feels that "*our spiritual poverty, our symbollessness*" in the West cannot be remedied or improved by adopting the trappings of the East "*to which we are not the legitimate heirs at all*". Their approach is not for us. We cannot pretend it suits us. As Jung says, "*it is useless to try to break into Oriental palaces that our fathers never knew* ". We cannot retrieve what we have lost by practicing yoga or other Eastern discipline that we do not fundamentally understand. After all, "*We are, surely, the rightful heirs of Christian symbolism*". This remains our mental strength, if we are willing to recapture it.

Two centuries before Jung, we find the same tragic situation being decried by Swedenborg. He argued that the leaders of the Christian religion have imposed a doctrine concerning salvation that is fabricated and mentally devastating. It is the idea that individuals have no motivational power to overcome their inherited selfish personality traits. Hence the method of salvation is faith and not the effort of regeneration that brings personality change from loving self to loving others. As a result of this teaching people accepted their selfish traits and continued to practice them, being confident that are saved because of their faith.

Swedenborg described this a mental death trap. In his state of dual consciousness for 27 years he was able to confirm this conclusion by empirical evidence. He interviewed many people who awakened in the afterlife. Those who described themselves as Christian repeated when asked the dogma salvation by "faith and not by works". Their inherited and acquired personality traits were based in self-love and self-interest. When asked, they were confident in the idea that the Lord will admit them into heaven on account of their faith.

When they were brought near the sphere of heavenly love they realized that they cannot exist in heaven because they would then be deprived of everything they love and by which they feel animated. Personality traits in the afterlife cannot be removed or relearned. This is because the individual is unwilling.

Swedenborg called this type of belief "*blind faith*". To replace it he proposed the idea of "*rational faith*". When I studied his descriptions of rational faith I came to the realization that rational faith is nothing else than theistic psychology.

*10
Before Jung reached adolescence he had already discarded his Christian family religion. He later talks about in his autobiography just before he lost his physical body on earth. He says that he saw through the falsity and hypocrisy of people who were unwilling to live every day in accordance with

the professed belief of loving God and the neighbor. They were horrible to each other, yet they thought they were saved by their blind faith.

But Jung did not reject the personal relationship with God that he had formed in childhood in full innocence that God was real and omnipresent. Clinging to that original powerful experience is what saved him. In two earlier books in this series I document the important fact about Jung that he continued all his life to cling to his personal relationship with God. Jung states in his autobiography that he had made God the central feature of his personal life and, surprisingly, of his therapy. He said that he routinely advised his patients with long-term intractable neuroses to return to the relationship with God they formed in childhood. And he added, those who listened, got better. The others didn't. As Jung writes in a letter:

I share your conviction that genuine religiosity is the best cure for all psyche suffering. The pity of it is that it is exceedingly difficult nowadays to inculcate into people any conception of genuine religiosity. I have found that religious terminology only scares them off still more, for which reason I always have to tread the path of science and experience, quite irrespective of any tradition, in order to get my patients to acknowledge spiritual truths. ... This has forced me to build up a psychology which will open the door again to psychic experience. ~Carl Jung, Letters Vol. I, p. 118

This statement by Jung confirms my proposal that his psychology is theistic. In a previous book on Jung and Swedenborg I theorize that Jung avoided any direct references to Swedenborg because Jung was concerned since the start of his professional career that his new psychology be presented in the mode of science, not spiritism or religious vision. Hence Jung also avoided references to the psychological role of God in the therapy process.

Jung writes:
What is important and meaningful to my life is that I shall live as fully as possible to fulfill the divine will within me. This task gives me so much to do that I have no time or any other. Let me point out that if we

were all to live in that way we would need no armies, no police, no diplomacy, no politics, no banks. We would have a meaningful life and not what we have now—madness. What nature asks of the apple-tree is that it shall bring forth apples, and of the pear-tree that it shall bring forth pears. Nature wants me to be simply man. But a man conscious of what I am, and of what I am doing. God seeks consciousness in man.

This is the truth of the birth and the resurrection of Christ within. As more and more thinking men come to it, this is the spiritual rebirth of the world. Christ, the Logos—that is to say, the mind, the understanding, shining into the darkness. Christ was a new truth about man. Mankind has no existence. I exist, you exist. But mankind is only a word. Be what God means you to be; don't worry about mankind which doesn't exist, you are avoiding looking at what does exist—the self You are like a man who leans over his neighbor's fence and says to him: "Look, there is a weed. And over there is an-I- other one. And why don't you hoe the rows deeper? And I why don't you tie up your vines?" And all the while, his own garden, behind him, is full of weeds.
C.G. Jung Speaks, p. 75

One of Jung's patients who was a long term and seemingly incurable alcoholic, travelled to the United States where he chanced to meet Bill Wilson, the co-Founder of AA. The former patient told him what Jung had advised, to return to his childhood relationship with God. Wilson was deeply affected by this and he went on to form the highly successful Alcoholic Anonymous (AA). The first of the 10 affirmations that members subscribe to when joining, is that as individuals they have no power to heal themselves, but that God alone can do that. I give additional details on how this came about in my book *Jung and Swedenborg on God and Life After Death* (2015).

So the problem of the modern mind is that, having lost the meaning of biological symbols, our natural conscious mind is immersed in material ideas of God that are either accepted or rejected. In either case we are unwilling to open up the spigot of the unconscious. When we attempt it we stand before the "*void and turn away from it with horror*". We then turn to "*spiritual bleakness and pedantic dogmatisms*". This makes our mental state even worse under the powerlessness of its ersatz ideas of salvation and happiness. We become captive of not just one but "*two devils*".

*11
Jung comments on the common belief that the unconscious is "*the source of all evil thoughts*", and where "*dwell the wicked blood-spirits, swift anger and sensual weakness*". This is the horror of the void that terrifies us. It is how "*the unconscious looks when seen from the conscious side*". In other words, it is how we are deceived when we think with material ideas about mental operations in our mind. From the materialistic perspective in our natural mind, entering the unconscious is like entering a "*suffocating atmosphere of egocentric subjectivity*". Jung adds that the mind then enters a "*blind alley*" where we are "*exposed to the attack of all the ferocious beasts which the caverns of the psychic underworld are supposed to harbor*".

I should mention that this negative image of the collective unconscious that Jung refers to was more than fully confirmed by Swedenborg's descriptions of life in the afterlife societies of hell.

*12
Jung warns us ahead of time before we begin our journey to the "inner way". Looking at ourselves to see what is behind our external social persona that Jung calls the "mask". Careful because "*the mirror lies behind the mask and shows the true face.*" This confrontation with oneself "*is the first test of courage on the inner way*". We can come to realize that "*the shadow is a living part of the personality*". It wants to be known and acknowledged. "*It cannot be argued out of existence or rationalized into harmlessness*".

*13
The journey towards self-knowing reveals that we can cooperate with unknown psychic forces in the unconscious. We need their mental energy and direction. We don't have the resources to heal ourselves and to manage our destiny. With this recognition there is a sudden change in our relationship to the unconscious. Now we are "*more inclined to give heed to*

a helpful idea or intuition, or to notice thoughts which had not been allowed to voice themselves before". This is the turning point where non-material ideas from the spiritual mind begin to flow into our natural mind and consciousness. It is the healing of the Fall, and its reversal.

*14
This new condition of humility in our mind gives us new perceptions of non-material ideas and principles. This is the response of the collective unconscious when the individual gives acknowledgement. The collective unconscious becomes supportive and friendly to the individual. Now "*the deeper strata of man's nature can come awake and intervene*". The boogey man is real, but harmless. The unconscious is the self, after all. And more than that, God is there: "*Prayer, as we know, calls for a very similar attitude and therefore has much the same effect*".

God and the unconscious. Man's best friends, whence commeth help. The unconscious is God's tool to help us along the way of individuation and collectivity.

*15
The collective unconscious talks to us "*in archetypally formed ideas*", just as the Word of God talks to us in the ideas of correspondences. We first meet our shadow. Our proprium. Our inflated ego. What we see is ugliness and shame. We feel uncomfortable, compressed, restricted, terrified, full of uncertainty. But wait; there is something beyond the shadow that we can glimpse, beyond the darkness and narrowness of the tunnel of incomprehension. "*Lost in oneself.*"

*16
The healing of our individual consciousness comes with the becoming one with the collective unconscious, which is now to be called collective consciousness. *The goal of individuation is the collectivity*. The two resolve each other by unifying. The collectivity is objective and needs the individuality that is subjective. "*Living begins where I experience the other in myself and the other-than-myself experiences me*". This mutuality is the essence of collective living. Each individual gifts his or her innate potentials to the others, and receives the unique potentials of all others. It is a mental state that is called mutual love. Such is the mental state in heaven.

Volume 4
Section 20

20. Jung Writes On Dogmatism

Thinking which in other respects may be altogether blameless becomes all the more subtly and prejudicially, affected, the more feelings are repressed. An intellectual standpoint, which, perhaps on account of its actual intrinsic value, might justifiably claim general recognition, undergoes a characteristic alteration through the influence of this unconscious personal sensitiveness; it becomes rigidly dogmatic.

The personal self-assertion is transferred to the intellectual standpoint. Truth is no longer left to work her natural effect, but through an identification with the subject she is treated like a sensitive darling whom an evil-minded critic has wronged. The critic is demolished, if possible with personal invective, and no argument is too gross to be used against him. Truth must be trotted out, until finally it begins to dawn upon the public that it is not so much really a question of truth as of her personal procreator.

The dogmatism of the intellectual standpoint, however, occasionally undergoes still further peculiar modifications from the unconscious admixture of unconscious personal feelings; these changes are less a question of feeling, in the stricter sense, than of contamination from other unconscious factors which become blended with the repressed feeling in the unconscious.

Although reason itself offers proof, that every intellectual formula can be no more than a partial truth, and can never lay claim, therefore, to autocratic authority; in practice, the formula obtains so great an ascendancy that, beside it, every other standpoint and possibility recedes into the background. It replaces all the more general, less defined, hence the more modest and truthful, views of life. It even takes the place of that general view of life which we call religion.

Thus the formula becomes a religion, although in essentials it has not the smallest connection with anything religious.

Therewith it also gains the essentially religious character of absoluteness. It becomes, as it were, an intellectual superstition. But now all those psychological tendencies that suffer under its repression become grouped together in the unconscious, and form a counter-position, giving rise to paroxysms of doubt.

As a defense against doubt, the conscious attitude grows fanatical. For fanaticism, after all, is merely overcompensated doubt. Ultimately this development leads to an exaggerated defense of the conscious position, and to the gradual formation of an absolutely antithetic unconscious position; for example, an extreme irrationality develops, in opposition to the conscious rationalism, or it becomes highly archaic and superstitious, in opposition to a conscious standpoint imbued with modern science.

This fatal opposition is the source of those narrow-minded and ridiculous views, familiar to the historians of science, into which many praiseworthy pioneers have ultimately blundered. It not infrequently happens in a man of this type that the side of the unconscious becomes embodied in a woman.
~Carl Jung, Psychological Types, p.442

In the selection just above Jung describes the connection between "*rigid dogmatism*" and "*repressed feelings*" that are acting "*subconsciously*" to influence one's thinking and reasoning. Furthermore, he notes that the dogmatic thinker does not tolerate any modification by others, and goes on a vicious attack when they perceive that someone is not accepting or agreeing with the dogmatic pronouncements just as they are stated.

In addition, there is a complicating factor that can be quite dangerous psychologically, namely, when "*unconscious personal feelings*" become "*contaminated*" by other unconscious factors that piggy backs on top of the repressed feelings. Truth is damaged and falls under the attack of dogmatism. Soon, dogmatic intellectualism becomes a religion of its own even though "*it has not the smallest connection with anything religious*".

A dogmatic belief "*gains the essentially religious character of absoluteness. It becomes, as it were, an intellectual superstition that turns into fanaticism*". An opposition forms between the forces of the unconscious and the thinking of the conscious. "Irrationality" in the unconscious spills over into the conscious, which turns it into superstition and what is contrary to "modern science". Such has also been the fate in the history of science of "*many praiseworthy pioneers who have ultimately blundered*"

In other words, the psychological trait of *dogmatism* involves a distortion in rational thinking that is produced by the person's self-interest. When I was a graduate student in the early 1960s a popular discussion topic was research on how motivational factors influence cognitive operations.

One study that I remember because I replicated the study in our lab at McGill University was the effect of hunger on tachistoscopic perception. Subjects came to lab having been instructed either to eat just before or not to eat for four hours. I flashed random words on a screen for a fraction of a second, and the subject was instructed to say or guess what the word was.

The "hungry" subjects recognized the random words with similar accuracy as the "non-hungry" subjects, but they recognized any food related words faster than the non-hungry group. The conclusion was that the motivation of being hungry lowers the perceptual threshold for hunger related stimuli such as words and pictures.

Research and theory on dogmatism was discussed in the psychology literature following the rise of Nazi intellectualism in the 1930s. Jung was surely familiar with that literature. Jung decried the psychologically dangerous anti-democratic ideology of the 1930s and World War II, which he witnessed all around him in his lifelong home in Berne, Switzerland. The human price paid for the insanity of this dogmatism was the death of one million people per month for five years!

Jung points out the distortion of thinking that is due to another type of dogmatism that has been influencing science in the twentieth century and today. I discuss it in my prior books as the "*negative bias*" in science.

****
Volume 4
Section 21
****

21. The Mental Technology Of Self-Witnessing

The Writings of Emanuel Swedenborg (1688-1771) contain an empirical, objective, and experimental investigation of the afterlife world of mental eternity that is apart from time and apart from space. These Writings are therefore the beginning of a new science that might be called "theistic psychology" that would be a branch of "theistic science", along with other disciplines such as biological theology and spiritual psycho-geography.

The mental world of eternity overlaps with the spiritual world of the afterlife. They are the same. This is because the mind is in the mental world and the same psychic laws apply to both the mind and the mental world. The mind is a non-material collection of organs made of mental substance and arranged in multiple levels of mental operation and activity such as sensation, thinking, consciousness, and motivation.

The mind is an immortal mental body, sometimes called a spiritual body or spirit body. All the anatomy and physiology of the inert physical body on earth correspond to the anatomy and physiology of the living mental body in eternity.

For instance, the physical organ of the heart corresponds and reflects the psychic organ of the will that gives us the ability to be motivated and to struggle to achieve goals by means of feelings, loves, and affections. Similarly, the physical organ of the lungs corresponds and reflects the psychic organ of the understanding that gives the ability to process cognitions, solve problems, and think rationally.

Mental development is therefore nothing else than the growth of the psychic organs of the mind or mental body. A young child has immature affective states and cognitive operations since the organs of the will and understanding are undeveloped. An adult has a fully developed external natural mind, but not yet a fully developed interior rational mind. The development of moral understanding and loves in the natural mind is the outer manifestation of the interior rational mind being opened more and more.

In the afterlife we function with our rational mind, while the natural mind is passive. The rational mind has three levels of activity called natural-rational, spiritual-rational, an celestial-rational. The degree of growth and development of these levels depends on the regeneration of the natural mind and its acquired ability to think with non-material ideas. The more we acquire and practice non-material ideas and principles from theistic psychology, the more we are able to grow the rational mind, all the way to the celestial level of thinking and consciousness. This is the level of life that we will then enjoy in the afterlife of eternity.

The three levels in our rational mind correspond to the three heavens in the *Grand Human* societies. The human mind is therefore an organic construction from mental substance that parallels the mental world exactly, according to the non-material principle that the smallest part of a whole encapsulates in an image the largest or whole. Hence every individual's mind contains all of the *Grand Human* and all of the *Grand Monster* afterlife societies in mental eternity. In other words, "*heaven and hell are within you*".

Swedenborg's observational access to the afterlife societies and his detailed description of them, constitute a unique and rich source of knowledge for theistic psychology. Now the human race has available new knowledge about the mind and its development and operation.

It is clear from the Writings that regeneration is necessary for salvation and heavenly life. Further, we are taught that regeneration is not automatic or spontaneous, but requires our active cooperation. Without this active cooperation there is no regeneration, consequently no salvation. It is therefore crucial to know how we ought to cooperate with God in our regeneration. The research I did on the psychology of self-observation or self-witnessing provides useful behavioral techniques that can help the individual in cooperating in the work of regeneration.

****
Volume 4
Section 22
****

22. Regeneration Self-Witnessing Methodology

People are the only source of objective information on their own private mental world. Personality tests and self-reports are not objective since they rely on interpretation by others. Furthermore, self-reports are summary and generalized descriptions, not particular and unique. Only "*self-witnessing*" can be direct and observational, hence empirical.

Everyone is the sole witness to his or her own private world of thinking and wanting.

Self-witnessing skills are a normal part of human personality and thinking. Our conscious natural mind operates at two levels simultaneously. Through our higher level activity called *natural-rational* we are aware of the operations that are going on in our lower natural called natural-sensory.

Self-witnessing is the activity of verbalizing our ongoing perception of what our mind is doing.

In this Section, I am discussing methods of *systematic* self-witnessing, which is a spiritual daily discipline that people may find useful for their daily regeneration efforts.

A place to begin is to create an inventory or catalog of the major components we see in our own social environment. Our actions and speech in a social environment are called "*situated behaviors*". The word "situated" refers to a place of social encountering. These places serve as tracking devices for where we are and what we are doing there, as for example: the kitchen, the highway, the entrance way to my office, the White House, my wedding, at the veterinary facility, etc.

All human behavior is "situated" because it is carried out in a social setting.

No behavior exists outside or independently of a social setting. For instance, our "food behaviors" are conditioned by family and societal habits, and even when we eat alone in our kitchen at midnight in the dark, we still engage in social behavior because what is in our refrigerator or food closet reflects lifestyle choices, which consists of learned habits and norms of eating.

But in addition to this, our mental behavior is also situated behavior.

The mental setting is independent of all physical settings. I can think of my cats while I'm driving or when I am in the kitchen cooking. I can feel embarrassed when I think about something that I said or did, whether it was a moment ago, or many years ago. My own mental setting creates its own psychological meaning and psychic environment. Each mental setting has its own meaning, feel, and sphere in relation to the mental sphere of others with whom we are in community.

There is therefore an independence of mental behaviors from physical settings, but not from social settings. There is a *horizontal physical society* to which the individual belongs through the physical body on earth. And there is also a *vertical mental society* in whose psychic sphere the individual's mental body is telepathically immersed.

Our individual subjective life of feeling and thinking would be impossible without objective social content that is derived from the immense collective consciousness that is shared by the communities and societies of human beings, past, present, and future.

In our natural mind we think with words that are defined by the dictionary that lists the various common "usages" for each word. We think by means of rules of language and common sense logic that we learn as children from others as well as through our experiencing. We reason by means of rules, values, and justifications that we acquire from our interactions with others.

Therefore private mental behavior is situated socially in a way similar to external public behavior. Therefore the "daily round taxonomy" of human behavior needs to be mapped out equally for private mental behavior as for public external behavior.

The external and internal social environment is quite complex as shown by the list below:

A few components of our *external* social environment:

- my talk with others
- my connections
- my family tree
- my daily routine of activities
- my role, duties, and responsibilities
- my memberships and institutional connections
- my belongings and assets
- my interactions and transactions
- my declarations
- my reputation
- who I hang out with and where
- things I do together with someone
- people who depend on me
- people who love me
- people with whom I've had a fight
- people I'd like currently to meet
- people whom I know who I see or think about only rarely
- people on my invitation list
- things I write down, lists I keep
- the contents of my drawers and pockets
- my nickname
- family sayings
- etc.

A few components of our *internal* social environment

- my talk with myself
- the things I imagine
- my interpretations of what's going on
- my sensations and feelings
- my daydreams
- my prayers and spiritual reflections
- how I assess and evaluate things
- my self concept
- my routine concerns
- things I notice or ignore

- my ambitions
- my fears
- my preferences
- making plans, rehearsing
- things I cannot mention to someone
- what I like to eat
- my mood and energy level
- what I can smell
- my judgments
- my aversions
- my cravings
- my secrets
- my memories
- how I reason with myself
- etc.

Given the complexity of the human environment, the task of cataloguing and itemizing all its numerous components may not be practicable. But we can expect that the external social environment would be normative and therefore similar across individuals within a community. This narrows the variety for cataloguing purposes.

This same normative predictability is present in the internal or private social environment of the individual. There is an urban legend that our private interior environment is individual rather than social. People have the strong illusion that what they think and imagine in their private world of thinking and feeling, is individual and free, in comparison to the external environment of their body, which is public and social.

What I've discovered through this research is that the interior psychological environment is as socially organized and catalogued as the external environment.

What people think, what they imagine, what they fantasize, what they are afraid of, what they are convinced about, and so on, are things they do in common with each other, perhaps unknowingly. Despite it taking place in the private unobservable world of the individual self the activity follows social norms shared with many others in a telepathic community.

In order to reflect this communality and social intersubjectivity I coined a new phrase, "*standardized imaginings,*" to reflect the uniformity with which people function in their "private" mental "alone" operations and activities.

Thinking and emoting was not something idiosyncratic, free, and individual. Our "private" alone world within is fully social and standardized within narrowly prescribed normative limits of determination.

This standardization and uniformity of our mental world was totally unsuspected and I was surprised. It was the first important result I obtained with the self-witnessing research method.

***

Volume 4
Section 23

***

23. Self-witnessing What We Do In Talking

The names I gave to the various groupings and sub-groupings of the "daily round" environment constitute a social psychological theory of what an individual is, and how an individual behaves through the body and in the mind.

The techniques I employed include the recording and analysis of one's external social talk with others, as well as keeping track of one's private internal dialog. The term "self-witnessing" is applied to this approach in general. Self-witnessing offers an effective method for self-objectivity.

I have also used the phrase *"being an audience to yourself"* which refers to the idea that you see yourself as others would see you. This is the definition of objectivity in non-theistic social psychology. If we practice self-witnessing on the daily round we gain an objective view on ourselves. We are less vulnerable to illusions and a fantasy reputation of ourselves.

This objective self-knowledge constitutes an empirical baseline of our habits and traits, as performed through the physical body on earth. Now we can use effective self-modification techniques to manage ourselves better, more rationally, more according to rational choice than family and neighborhood habits and scripts that we happened to acquire in our socialization process. Individuation and healthy psychological development requires that we minimize and separate lifestyle habits of thinking that are received from others and are not individualized to our unique individual needs and styles of expressiveness.

Polls and surveys confirm that the majority of individuals experience on a daily basis a variety of powerful negative emotions, such as rage, hatred, anger, depression, cynicism, and the opposite of compassion and emotional intelligence. Self-witnessing research has uncovered an overwhelming burden of negativity that individuals labor under on a daily basis.

Theistic psychology attributes this human agony of living to the cumulative inheritance of negativity and selfishness that are passed on from generation to generation.

- Why do people prefer behavior styles that are harmful to self and to others in the community?
- Why do people find it hard to remain balanced and rational in their decision-making?
- Why do people make others suffer?
- Why don't people function at a higher moral level?

- Why can't people be happy, contented, productive, and peace loving?

Theistic psychology provides the insight that people are born with an inherited personality that has long lost its connection to the rational mind. In order to regain this higher potential of true humanity, we must change ourselves and acquire a new will and a new understanding. This process of basic personality restructuring is called regeneration.

The self-witnessing methodology is more objective and empirical than personality tests and experiments, which put "subjects" into an artificial situation, and consequently the "data" thus indirectly obtained on people's mental life is hypothetical and interpretive, as they are dependent on tests and on questions regarding what they would do in such and such a situation, as for instance, "On a scale of 1 to 5 how angry would you get if someone…"

These are not only general but also depend on variable recall and other things that influence people in after-the-fact reporting activity. But self-witnessing, self-reporting, and self-monitoring are feasible activities for every ordinary person, and involve "*concurrent reports*" of what one perceives within one's conscious mental world.

One of the most astonishing of theistic psychology ideas is that we are not alone in our private world of the mind. Swedenborg confirms this through thousands of observations in his state of dual consciousness where he was simultaneously conscious in his natural mind through the body on earth, and in his rational mind through the mental body in eternity. In his natural mind he was able to manage the physical body on earth for his busy daily work schedule, while simultaneously in his rational mind he was able to manage the mental body in eternity where he interacted with many people from the afterlife societies that make up the *Grand Human* and the *Grand Monster* of the human collective consciousness.

I made up the expression, "vertical community", to contrast it with what we are familiar with as our social "horizontal" community to which every individual belongs to through a geographic location on earth. In other words, we are born "dual citizens," namely, a horizontal community through the physical body on earth, and a vertical community through our spirit-body in mental eternity.

When our natural mind in eternity is disconnected from sensory input from the physical body, we become fully conscious of our rational mind and through that activity and consciousness we continue life to eternity in one of the numberless afterlife societies and communities.

Swedenborg's observations confirm that the natural and rational mind of all human beings are constantly immersed in a universal telepathic sphere in which every individual contributes and receives thoughts, emotions, and feelings. No individual can survive without being immersed in this collective human sphere.

Further, Swedenborg shows, as in the selection below, that God manages moment-by-moment interconnections and mutual influences between people's mind in such a way as to provide each person with experiences, perceptions, and ideas that contribute to his or her progress in regeneration.

> *It is a great truth that man is governed by the Lord by means of spirits and angels. When evil spirits begin to rule, the angels labor to avert evils and falsities, and hence arises a combat. It is this combat of which the man is rendered sensible by perception, dictate, and conscience. By these, and also by temptations, a man might clearly see that spirits and angels are with him, were he not so deeply immersed in corporeal things as to believe nothing that is said about spirits and angels. Such persons, even if they were to feel these combats hundreds of times, would still say that they are imaginary, and the effect of a disordered mind. I have been permitted to feel such combats, and to have a vivid sense of them, thousands and thousands of times, and this almost constantly for several years, as well as to know who, what, and where they were that caused them, when they came, and when they departed; and I have conversed with them. ~Swedenborg, Heavenly Secrets, AC 227*

24. We Are Never Alone: The Vertical Community

The idea of the vertical community means that we are never alone. We have the illusion that our mental private world is individual and alone, while our physical social world is interactive and public. But now the scientific fact has been uncovered that the mental private world is also a social world in which we are surrounded by many other people. Again Swedenborg writes:

Man [=our natural mind] does not know that in respect to his mind he is in the midst of spirits [=people in the afterlife], for the reason that the spirits with whom he is in company in the spiritual world [of the afterlife], think and speak spiritually [with non-material ideas], while his own spirit [natural mind] thinks and speaks naturally so long as he is in the material body [connected to sensory input from earth]; and the natural man [mind] cannot understand or perceive spiritual thought and speech [non-material ideas], nor the reverse.

This is why spirits cannot be seen [by our natural mind through the physical body]. But when the spirit of man [rational mind] is in company with spirits in their world [after the dying-resuscitation procedure], he is also in spiritual thought and speech with them, because his [rational] mind is interiorly spiritual [rational] but exteriorly natural; therefore by means of his interiors [non-material ideas] he communicates with spirits [afterlife societies], while by means of his exteriors [natural mind] he communicates with men [through the physical body on earth].

> *By such communication man [our natural mind] has a perception of things, and thinks about them analytically. If it were not for such communication [between our rational and natural mind], man [our natural mind] would have no more thought or other thought than a beast [material ideas based on sensory input], and if all connection with spirits [vertical community] were taken away from him, he would instantly die. ~Swedenborg, True Christianity, TCR 475*

Our thoughts and feelings are therefore social events, intersubjective and collective, not private or solitary. The content and quality of our mental experiences are a consequence of the character of the afterlife spirits with whom God connects and reconnects us moment by moment in our thinking and feeling.

There is a simple but powerful relation between our negative thoughts or emotions and the character of the spirits that communicate with our mind. The afterlife spirit societies constitute our vertical community to which we belong and into which we are anatomically and psychically rooted or bonded. Change in our feelings and thoughts is possible only with rearranging the spiritual societies with which we are telepathically communicating.

Every thought or feeling is either from heavenly from the *Grand Human* societies, or hellish from the *Grand Monster* afterlife societies. Swedenborg confirms that rational thoughts and compassionate feelings can only come from heavenly societies, while negative thoughts and emotions can only come from hellish ones. Self-witnessing can be a useful tool for monitoring when in the course of the day we are communicating with heavenly spirits and when with infernal spirits.

****

Volume 4
Section 25

****

25. Self-Witnessing The Threefold Self: Affective, Cognitive, Sensorimotor

Swedenborg writes:

> As is a person's life in general therefore, so is his life in every individual part, indeed in the smallest individual parts of his motives and intentions - that is, of his will - and in the smallest individual parts of his thinking; so that not the least part of an idea can exist in which the same life is not present.
>
> Take someone who is arrogant: arrogance is present in every individual endeavor of his will and in every individual idea of his thought. With someone who is avaricious avarice is in a similar way present, as is hatred with one who hates the neighbour. Or take someone who is stupid: stupidity is present in every individual part of his will and also of his thought, as is insanity with one who is insane. Such being the nature of man, his character is recognized in the next life from one single idea of his thought. ~Swedenborg, AC 1040

In other words our general behavior is created out of particular details, and the same quality characterizes both. Another way of saying this is that our macro-behaviors are made of our micro-behaviors and they both are centrally impelled by the same motivation.

Every act of thinking is motivated just as every act of doing. The same general motive enters into every micro-behavior, or else the behavior would not occur. A particular thought would not occur were it not motivated by some intention, affection, or goal to which the thought is connected.

The expressions "someone who is arrogant" or "someone who is avaricious" or "someone who is stupid" refer to specific mental states that every individual experiences. We have found the enemy, and it is us. We are the ones falling into states of arrogance, avarice, or stupidity. Spiritually considered with a non-material perspective, "arrogance" signifies the "love of self and of cupidities". "Avarice" spiritually signifies "to acknowledge and believe nothing". "Stupid" signifies "the corporeal sensual separated from the rational".

> *Man's interiors are distinguished into degrees, and in each degree the interiors are terminated, and by termination are separated from the degree next below; it is thus from the inmost to the outermost. ~Swedenborg, AC 5145*

Regeneration is to be understood as a psychobiological process of the mind undergoing development and individuation. The mind is of a spiritual or mental substance organ, not of physical matter, because it is constructed out of mental substance from the environment of the mental world of eternity.

The essence of mental substance is God's love and its truth.

Love-substance in the environment of the mental world is absorbed by the affective system of the mental substance body. This psychological absorption process is a gical process and corresponds to the physiology of the physical body when it absorbs, digests, and breaks down chemical foods from earth's environment that enter through the air and through the mouth.

Love-substance is spiritual food for our spirit or mind. It is absorbed and digested in the personality of our rational mind. The digestion of love-substance in the affective system gives us the ability to experience loves and their affections. The absorption and digestion of love-substance supply us with motives, desires, intentions, and enjoyments and pleasures, thus everything central in our life. The instant we cease absorbing love-substance we fall into a swoon without sensations or feelings, and from this, without thoughts and consciousness. Hence it is clear that love in our will is the all and all of our life.

But love cannot embody itself in the experience of an affection without thoughts and meanings in our cognitive system. By absorbing truth-substance from the mental environment of eternity our mind gains the ability to produce coherent thoughts about anything we desire through interest or enjoyment. Now the affections and intentions of the affective system or the will can direct our thoughts to form plans that point that will allow the affections of the will to be embodied in sensorimotor action, which then completes the threefold sequence of love, coherence, and enjoyment. In this way we are alive by the experiencing of love that is completed in the enjoyment of its affections.

Clearly, then, the mind is a rational or non-material organ because it is constructed out of love and its truth, which are from non-material mental substance. Mental substance is from God's mind and it is living, human, immortal, and eternal. The anatomical fibers that constitute the organ of the mind are laid down and coiled in particular directions. *In this mode the mind is able to function as a receptor organ for love and truth substance that flow in from the mental environment of eternity.*

Spiritual growth, individuation, or regeneration consists of two steps in sequence. The first step is to banish and remove the inherited and acquired selfish affections in our external natural mind or social persona. *The second step is to compel ourselves to will what is good from love of what we know is true.* Sacred Scripture instructs us with non-material ideas that are from truth-substance.

This is why Sacred Scripture is called God's Word, since it is the natural correspondence of truth-substance from God's mind and in God's mind.

Since willing and thinking is made of thousands of particular items every hour and day, you can see that we must be able to monitor our willing and thinking sequences all day long to make sure that they agree with the principles of truth that we acquired in our understanding from the study of *Sacred Scripture*, especially in its derived psychological meaning.

It may not be possible to focus on each and every selfish love and enjoyment. There are more of them in our personality than there are seconds in the average person's "lifespan" on earth before the afterlife. But in God's love and grace for the human race, when we reject one ego-love because it is contrary to heavenly life, God removes the rejected ego-love's entire family of affections that are intertwined and cling together.

There is no general way of being regenerated by confessing and by repenting of "all our sins" during prayer, or even by giving charity or doing good to others. These things may be helpful and desirable but they do not accomplish regeneration. The only thing that will accomplish it is to become aware of the particular items in our willing and thinking every day, and judging them in the light of our non-material truths, and desisting from doing and thinking what is contrary to truths because they are sins against God and they prevent our spiritual or rational mind from being opened for full functioning. Our spiritual mind develops to the extent that we are willing to clean out the natural mind from the inherited and acquired ego-loves.

> *A man who examines himself for the purpose of practicing repentance, should explore his thoughts, and the intentions of his will; and there he ought to examine what he would do, if he were at liberty; that is, if he were not afraid of the laws, and the loss of reputation, honor, and gain. A man's evils are in his thoughts and intentions; and the evils which he does with the body are all from thence.*
>
> *Those persons who do not explore the evils of their thoughts and of their will cannot practice repentance; for afterwards they think and will just as they did before; and yet willing evils means doing them. This is meant by self-examination. ~Swedenborg, NJHD 164*

In other words, self-examination is a process of self-monitoring and self-witnessing. This involves monitoring and even note keeping of our mental life in daily tasks and interactions with others. Each exercise involves keeping track in the three "domains" or organs of the mind: affective, cognitive, and sensorimotor.

> *Affective Organ (the will)*
> > What feelings do I have in this situation? Or: What do I feel like doing right now?
> *Cognitive Organ (the understanding)*

What thoughts do I have right now? Or: What are the words and sentences I'm thinking right now?

Sensorimotor Organ (acting, speaking, and sensations):

What sensations am I experiencing right now? Or: What is my body doing and how does it appear to others—my face, my hands, my position, my rhythm, my voice, my breathing, etc.

Keeping cumulative notes in a journal or diary can be useful. Dictating notes with a voice recorder can also be a practical approach. Part of the self-witnessing discipline is to review or analyze the data collected over many samples of one's interactions and behaviors, and to evaluate them as indicators of one's dedication and progress in self-change.

The "small" choices regarding our lifestyle—are we noisy neighbors or aggressive drivers, etc.—carry equal weight or greater weight than the large things of our biography—degrees, income, awards, recognition, important achievements. The little things carry more weight because they are far more numerous given that they are the constituents of the larger things. And the more frequently we perform non-charitable acts, thoughts, or feelings, the more they fix our character habits, and the less we can change.

One area that needs examination is the media entertainment content that we enjoy on TV, movies, comics, novels, and music. The natural mind becomes filled and absorbed when routinely enjoying and tacitly accepting vulgarities, profanities and the lavish portrayal of lusts and violence. Monitoring our exposure and involvement with these things allows us to turn away and to turn back, and so to regain an innocence that teaches us to feel shocked at these rehearsals and dramatic portrayals of selfishness, cruelties, and evils. Similarly, we can examine to what extent we allow ourselves to repeat and enjoy songs with lyrics that are profane and glorify disorderly things.

You can construct a written form on which to keep track of what you are watching and what you were exposed on a daily basis. You can summarize the content of programs, isolating bad behaviors such as abuse against women, corruption of children, bending of ethics, leveling of values, bad driving, and other forms of negativity. You can realize that these disorderly and insane things enter your mind, and if you do not consciously reject them, but instead enjoy them, then your mind is polluted by them.

Mental pollution in your mind increases the telepathic influence on your mind of hellish afterlife societies who revel and relish being immersed in polluted and disorderly thoughts, fantasies, emotions, and enjoyments. The more you make mental pollution into a your regular lifestyle, the more you are enmeshed and anatomically bound to those disorderly afterlife societies.

Eventually they own you and you are part of them, so that in the afterlife you find that society and enter it with a feeling of having arrived at home at last. And there you remain forever, being unable to make yourself leave for another society. Such is the permanent binding power of love in the afterlife of mental eternity.

****
Volume 4
Section 26
****

26. Sudden Memory And The Method Of Discourse Thinking

One of the most significant discoveries I have made in my explorations of theistic psychology is a way of increasing awareness of what we are thinking moment by moment. Thoughts 'fly' by rapidly. The stream of conscious awareness is a rapid that doesn't linger, but is quickly come and gone. I realized in my self-reflection that many secrets are revealed in that stream. If only I could slow it down to the pace of a lazy river!

I then discovered that I can indeed slow it down! I practiced giving a 'blow-by-blow' account of the quickly passing ticker tape that leaves a record of my conscious awareness moment by moment.

I coined a new term for this quickly transitioning conscious awareness: sudden memory.

This was therefore a new addition to the memory sequence known in psychology:
(i) *long term memory* (accessible for days and years);
(ii) *short term memory ("working memory")* (accessible for a few seconds);
(iii) *sudden memory* (instantaneously or suddenly gone)

I was in chase of something that shows itself for an instant on the screen of awareness. If only I could capture it by a snap shot. If only I can slow down the ticker tape of consciousness long enough so I can read its content and record it in memory for later recall and analysis. I got into the constant daily habit of giving a blow-by-blow account of the fast moving ticker tape of consciousness. And lo! One day the Eureka cry was heard in my mind. It said: *discourse thinking*.

Giving a verbal description of the contents of my thinking had the effect of slowing down the ticker tape. Suddenly I became conscious of my thoughts by translating the stream into words and sentences. So I called it *discourse thinking*, or thinking in words.

Our thinking is much faster than the slow vocalizing of speech and writing. So by forcing my thoughts into words the rate of thinking slows down, allowing me an instant of perceiving my sudden memory. I can then put that sequence into short-term memory, and into long-term memory for later analysis and reporting. That has been my lonely secret in my ability to write two or three books a year, all focused on theistic psychology. What I write is a record of my sudden memory. And wonder of wonders, my first draft is my last draft 90 percent of the time. I am not used to editing what I have typed out. This makes sense if indeed what I type is what I perceive on the mental ticker tape of sudden memory.

When the content of sudden memory enters my short term-memory I can examine it with awareness and have a reaction to it. Each time, and though it happens a dozen times a day, I have a reaction of amazement, awe, and joy! Take all the secrets of theistic psychology that I discuss, thousands of them, and each one is surprising, illuminating, humbling, and ecstatically joyful. This may be hard to believe, but it is true, and you can confirm it by practicing the method of discourse thinking as you study the secrets of theistic psychology.

So all this is good news to all of us. It means that our constant mental activity is actually the activity of exploring the immense endless knowledge base or storehouse of humanity's collective consciousness. This mental exploration is the holistic and healthy development of individuation. Jung wrote that as individuation proceeds our ego encompasses more and more of the overall and universal Self of humanity, past, present, and future.

So here we are each of us as unique subjective individuals constantly fishing in the ocean of the collective consciousness. This is our individual consciousness. It is our light of being aware and of understanding the coherence of meaning.

As Jung's work shows, the collective consciousness is ordinarily hidden in the collective unconscious. There is a barrier that is overcome by translation. Symbols in dreams, in religious icons, in stories, in art, in metaphor, and in correspondences in *Sacred Scripture* are the various methods of translating or trans-forming non–material ideas from the collective unconscious into material ideas of individual consciousness in our natural mind.

It is wonderful for all of us to know this great secret. It enhances our self-confidence and our gratitude to God, for giving us this inestimable pearl of value and "greatest of all treasures". We have it in our very grasp in the midst of our mental existence. Nothing can take it away from us. We can peer into reality itself, and we can pick up the treasures that enrich our joy in living.

Think of it: every human being is the center of the universe! All of human knowledge and understanding is already within each one of us. We do not need to seek for truths and wisdom: they are already within each of us. Truth is omnipresent. Knowledge is already present. Learning and discovery are mere appearances.

And oh, what fun and delight it is to access knowledge, understanding, and wisdom. Our individual mind is immersed in the collective consciousness of humanity. You can instantly know and understanding whatever you want to understand. To be born human is to be born with all the knowledge and understanding there is, and all the joys that are within them.

> *It is the rational in fact that coordinates everything in the natural, and in accordance with that coordination fittingly regards the things that are there. Indeed the rational is like a higher faculty of seeing which, when it looks at facts belonging to the natural man, is like someone looking down on to a plain below him.* ~Swedenborg, AC 3283

In other words, with the non-material ideas in our rational mind we can witness what we are doing in our natural mind when thinking and willing in the course of daily activities. Anyone can perform self-witnessing or self-monitoring of thoughts and of the goals or intended outcomes that we desire with our affections.

The stream of thinking and feeling in our natural mind is spontaneous and proceeds automatically as we cope with the moment-by-moment demands of living and doing. We can examine this spontaneous stream by directing our focus on it in a metanoid stance, looking down upon the stream of thinking like on a plain below, or like a river when standing on a bridge and seeing the flotsam go by below.

In this way we inform ourselves of the content and quality of our thinking and willing all day long. Willing something is an internal act. Thinking something is an internal act. We are responsible for all our acts in the sense that acts have consequences that confront us and we have to deal with them. Therefore we are responsible for all our willing acts and all our thinking acts, every one of them, thousands of them by the hour, every day from birth to eternity.

We are nothing but the cumulative collection of those acts. Such as these acts are, such are we, when we arrive in the afterlife, and such we remain forever.

Our consciousness, or life orientation, is such as the content is of our willing and thinking acts hour by hour all day long. This content is made up from the material ideas that operate in our natural mind, and this means that our willing and thinking acts are reduced to the natural and material, having in itself no rational, non-material, or spiritual dimension and content.

And so our consciousness is constricted and restricted to what we can see with material ideas. The natural self-centered ego personality sits in darkness as to what actually takes place in the mind and in life. If our natural mind believes in God and the afterlife we call it a "blind faith" because there is no knowledge, perception, and vision of the mental world of eternity, which requires non-material ideas to be seen and understood rationally.

With the non-material ideas that are handed down to us from our rational mind, if we accept them and do not battle with them, we can see and perceive as in an image or symbol the "other side" of our actual reality, the side of eternity into which we are born and in which we live forever with our immortal mental substance body.

> *The man who has the interiors of his mind open can see the evils and falsities that are with him, for these are below the spiritual mind. On the other hand, the man with whom the interiors have not been opened is unable to see his evils and falsities, because he is not above them but in them. ~Swedenborg, HH 532*
>
> *In the spiritual world, into which every man comes after death, the question that is asked is not, What was your faith, or what was your*

doctrine? but, What was the nature of your life? Was it of this or that quality? Thus the inquiry is concerning the nature and quality of the life; for it is known that such as one's life is, such is his faith and also his doctrine, because the life fashions doctrine and faith for itself.
~Swedenborg, DP 101

To the extent that we function in our daily tasks from the interior activity of altruism and decency, to that extent our physical and mental disciplines will have become spiritual. *By "spiritual" is meant that which relates the individual to the afterlife of mental eternity.* To do something that is motivated by altruism is to want to avoid hurting others or inconveniencing them.

This feeling of wanting to avoid hurting others is present when we are regenerating and thus striving to live in accordance with God's principles of spiritual charity and mutual love.

The focus therefore needs to be on how the inside world of altruism in our willing, can direct the relatively "outside" world of thinking and of action. As we perform our routine acts outwardly through the physical body on earth, we need to monitor what is happening simultaneously in our thinking (cognitive system) and willing (affective motivational system). As for instance:

- What are we enjoying or hating about what's going on?
- What are we thinking that we do not show?
- What is delightful to us?
- What are we hoping will happen next?
- What are we prepared to do or say?

Swedenborg observed that it's common for people to arrive into the afterlife not being aware of who they actually are, or what affections and ideas are active in their subconscious mind.

For instance, when both married pairs have passed through the dying-resuscitation procedure, they meet in the afterlife and spend time together in deeper explorations of their relationship, whether it is to last forever or whether it ends now. Swedenborg reports that husbands in general do not at first recognize their wives in the afterlife, while wives instantly recognize their husbands. This is because husbands are less aware of what fills their own subconscious motives, while the wife has an inner perception of her husband's subconscious mind.

But it's otherwise with husbands who prepare themselves appropriately for conjugial love by undergoing the process of regeneration, which is a process by which they strive by daily self-witnessing discipline to uncover their subconscious resistance to conjugial love and to altruism, and following that, to strive to remove the resistance.

What are the activities going on in our subconscious mind, which is a "hidden" portion in our natural mind? The subconscious is the source of our inherited ego-loves, our selfishness, and our evils of character that are damaging to self and community. Swedenborg explains:

> *There are innumerable things in every evil. In man's sight every evil appears as one single thing. This is the case with hatred and revenge, theft and fraud, adultery and whoredom, arrogance and high-mindedness, and with every other evil; and it is not known that in every evil there are innumerable things, exceeding in number the fibers and vessels in a man's body.*
>
> *Hence it follows that all these in their order must be restored and changed by the Lord in order that the man may be reformed; and this cannot be effected unless by the Divine Providence of the Lord, step by step from the earliest period of man's life to the last. ~Swedenborg, DP 296*

Since there are innumerable things in every one of our evil affections, it is clear that we must cooperate with God who can remove them from us to the extent of our cooperation and willingness.

The very least we can do is to keep track of the major evils in the main categories of living by becoming conscious of them through the daily practice of self-witnessing.

You can see that a type of general confession and self-examination carried out once or twice a year or month, is not going to be effective in knowing and removing our particular evils, which are so numerous. Self-witnessing our willing and thinking activity hour by hour every day is necessary in order for us to become aware of our specific evils. And when we shun a specific evil, God is able to remove the clumps of evils that are attached to that particular evil.

For example, there are innumerable evils attached to being overweight from overeating and under-exercising. We must take charge of it in our willing and thinking, day by day, so as to shun the harmful delights that cause us to overeat and under-exercise. To the extent that we struggle under this yoke, trying to subdue and control ourselves, to that extent God can remove the many evils that are attached to this general one.

The same goes for all our daily habits and routines that are from evil affections, such as our emotions of
- anger,
- impatience,
- swearing and cussing,
- adulterous thoughts,
- enjoyments of vulgar entertainment,
- our bending the rules of honesty and fairness to our favor,
- our neglect of duties and promises,
- and many such things.

These are the things in which are hidden from our consciousness the innumerable evils that anatomically consist of mental substance fibers that are tying us to some hellish afterlife societies. The organic fibers, roots, and connections are broken by God to the extent that we do our share and cooperate in the general evils of which we can become conscious through the practice of self-witnessing as a daily spiritual discipline.

All these forms of lusts must be changed one by one; and the man himself, who with respect to his spirit appears as a human monster or devil, must be changed to become like a beautiful angel. ~Swedenborg, DP 296

Regeneration is a gradual and piecemeal process that alters our appearance from the ugliness and monstrosity of ego-loves to the beauty and wisdom of the angels in heavenly afterlife societies.

Detesting one evil doesn't make us detest another, especially when the other is hidden in our subconscious because we do not witness it and identify it. Swedenborg explains:

A wicked man [selfish states of mind] from himself continually leads himself more and more deeply into his evils [ego-loves or selfish lusts]. It is said, from himself, because all evil is from man [natural mind], for man turns good [altruism] that originates from the Lord into evil, as was said above.

The real reason why the wicked man immerses himself more deeply in evil is that as he wills and commits evil he advances into infernal [afterlife] societies more and more interiorly and also more and more deeply.

Hence also the delight of evil increases, and so occupies his thoughts that at last he feels nothing more pleasant. He who has advanced more interiorly and deeply into infernal societies becomes as if he were bound with chains.

So long as he lives in the world [still connected to the physical body on earth], however, he does not feel his chains, for they are as if made from soft wool or from fine threads of silk, and he loves them as they give him pleasure; but after death, instead of being soft they become hard, and instead of being pleasant they become galling. ~Swedenborg, DP 296

Who is the "wicked man" spoken of here? It is we, every individual, before being reformed and regenerated. In that state we tend to lead ourselves more and more deeply into our evil affections, loving them more and more, feeling them delightful and pleasant like nothing else, by which we are tied more and more to the many hellish afterlife societies.

At first we think about our evil affections, turning them over in our mind as we consider whether we should satisfy them or not. If we give in and do them, we advance more deeply into associations with the "infernals" in the afterlife society to which we are connected and from which we have the desire to do them and experience their pleasure and delight. Then, if we continue to will them despite our conscience, we "*plunge ourselves to a depth from which we can be led out only by actual repentance*" (DP 296).

> *Evils in the external man cannot be removed by the Lord except through man's instrumentality.* ~Swedenborg, DP 114

Since the historical Fall of Consciousness everyone is born with a natural mind that inherits the cumulative evils that come down from parents and ancestors (AC 4317). These evils are in the will or affective system of the natural mind and are the source of falsities in our cognitive system, the two always going together. The carrier of this hereditary evil is the "very inward form" of the will, which is the source of all our motives, interests, and delights.

We inherit the love of self in the will so that we love others less than ourselves, and only when they "honor" us or agree with us. We hate all others and would take away all their possessions if we could, and treat them cruelly if they do not agree to serve us.

When we become conscious in the afterlife it becomes manifest that we love self alone, and others only to the extent that they honor us or agree with us. Otherwise we hate them and desire to cheat them, to dominate them, to abuse them, or to destroy them. These hatreds are hidden from our conscious awareness while we are still tied to the physical body. And yet everyone is able to become aware of them by self-witnessing their thoughts and feelings.

Knowing that we are all this way may motivate us to monitor our willing and thinking all day long, so that we may become aware of our actual evils in operation. We must witness ourselves in order to discover when and where we wish for something bad to happen to someone, or when we feel envious of someone's good fortune, and how we use our imagination to delight ourselves with denigrating others and ignoring their expectations, needs, or requests to us.

In the process of regeneration we cooperate as-of self with God by choosing to reject a particular evil that delights us or fulfills our needs. This is what makes recovery from evil possible: *our choosing to reject it*.

Whatever we do in freedom is done from love and therefore it is a higher rational love that makes us reject lower evil loves. As a result, in the afterlife, we arrive with a mind filled with non-material rational loves, within which we can live as a heaven because God's good and truth flows in from within these non-material rational loves.

By self-witnessing our willing and thinking every day we are indicating to God that we are willing to cooperate in the process of our regeneration. We acknowledge that God is managing the timing and content of what comes to our awareness and insight into our sins or evils. God wants us to witness the evil affections and delights that are in our personality and with which we are so familiar but only semi-conscious. God brings them to our conscious awareness to the extent that we are willing to desist from them because they are sins against God and against the heaven in which we want to exist. And further, God keeps out of our awareness those evils that we are not ready to give up willingly.

It's very important to have a scientific or medical perspective on regeneration, for this knowledge helps us to cooperate more with the Lord. The slow down is not on the Lord's side. He would go more rapidly. But we are holding Him back like a toddler at a street crossing—you end up picking up the child and carrying it across. But the Lord cannot pick us up and carry us to heaven, or else He would, do not doubt that! So He has revealed to us in a scientific way what the process entails and how we are to cooperate for maximum pace. For instance, He has revealed that He cannot remove sins clinging to us by our love, so He wants us to voluntarily desist from them and to detest them. Then He can remove them.

Volume 4
Section 27

27. Our Evils Cannot Be Removed

No one can shun that of which he is ignorant. (...) Evils cannot be removed unless they appear. ~Swedenborg, DP 278

Regeneration involves the process of freely rejecting our evils even though they delight us tremendously. It is not possible to reject our evils generally and collectively, as just discussed. It is only possible to reject particular evils one by one. Therefore if we don't make lists, how are we going to keep track of the evils so that we may reject them?

This is a practical issue. If we run a department store without an inventory, can we succeed? We must identify something before we can sell it or reject it. *Therefore it is often useful to make lists and inventories of our evils and falsities just as we make lists of things to do on a busy day.*

Sacred Scripture instructs us that God cannot remove our evils in secret or unconsciously. Removal of evil loves in our personality along with their pleasures, enjoyments, and delights requires a conscious and voluntary act of "giving up" and rejecting the love and its delights. Swedenborg adds:

> *This does not mean that man is to do evils in order that they may appear, but that he is to examine himself, not his actions only, but also his thoughts, and what he would do if he were not afraid of the laws and disgrace; especially what evils he holds in his spirit to be allowable and does not regard as sins; for these he still commits.* ~Swedenborg, DP 278

It is critical for us to understand that evils remain in our personality even when they are silent, passive, or inactive. Hence God manages to create social situations every day and hour in which the silent evil suddenly erupts and goes into action. We then have an opportunity to witness the evil tendency, to identify it, to see how it is contrary to God and heaven, and thereupon to choose to reject it and condemn it even with its delights and enjoyments. This is effective because God can then remove that evil since it is a free voluntary choice by the regenerating person.

The cooperative process in regeneration is between God and the individual. First, we ought to "examine ourselves." It is specified that the self-examination must have a threefold focus:

- our feelings or motives in the will (affective system)
- our thoughts and beliefs (cognitive system)
- our public acts and speech (sensorimotor system)

In other words, God commands us to examine our minute-by-minute willing, thinking, and acting or speaking.

What are these particular types of evils? These the evils that we "do not regard as sins." For example, we may have long standing habits of thinking about others in a derogatory way. We never bring this out to the surface and would not want others to know about it. We see it as merely an inward habit that we take care not to allow them overt consequences. Just a kind of quirk—we might think. But this is fooling ourselves. Swedenborg explains:

> *In order that man may examine himself an understanding has been given him, and this separate from the will, that he may know, understand and acknowledge what is good and what is evil; and also that he may see the quality of his will, or what it is he loves and desires.*
>
> *In order that he may see this his understanding has been furnished with higher and lower thought, or interior and exterior thought, to enable him to see from higher or interior thought what his will is doing in the lower or exterior thought. This he sees as a man sees his face in a mirror; and when he sees it and knows what sin is, he is able, if he implores the help of the Lord, not to will it, but to shun it and afterwards to act against it; if not wholeheartedly, still he can exercise constraint upon it by combat, and at length turn away from it and hate it. ~Swedenborg, DP 278*

In other words, the higher thought can witness the lower thought "as a man sees his face in a mirror." Our personality in the natural mind is born filled with inherited evils. Each evil works in clumps with other evils and each clump is rooted anatomically in one of the hellish afterlife societies to which our parents and ancestors are rooted. These roots are inherited. They are the source of the delights and pleasures of evils and ego-loves. These are the pleasures and enjoyments that we must be willing to give up, even if at first only with regret and chagrin.

> *When he sees it and knows what sin is, he is able, if he implores the help of the Lord, not to will it, but to shun it and afterwards to act against it; if not wholeheartedly, still he can exercise constraint upon it by combat, and at length turn away from it and hate it.*
>
> *Now, and not before, he first perceives and also feels that evil is evil and that good is good. This then is what is involved in examining oneself, seeing one's evils and recognizing them, confessing them and afterwards desisting from them. ~Swedenborg, DP 278*

****
Volume 4
Section 28
****

28. Metanoid Self-Witnessing Or Being An Audience To Yourself

A man's mind is his spirit ~Swedenborg, DP 296

To focus on the thousands of acts of willing and thinking every day, means to monitor and keep track of them. Note that normal social life does not require this kind of self-knowing. Society requires that we know things outside of ourselves, like the history of our country, or the multiplication table, or how to read instructions and write messages. But there is no social, legal, or professional requirement that we monitor our feelings, motives, thoughts, and interior dialog with ourselves.

Once in awhile, if we get called on the witness stand in court, we might have to report on some of our willing and thinking activities. We are asked, Why did you do this? Or, What did you decide then? Or, Were you in love with her at that time? Etc. It is required by law that we answer honestly, but knowing the answer is not a requirement. In that case we reply, "I don't remember," and the court accepts it. But the court does hold us responsible for knowing things outside of ourselves, such as, Did you see him or not? and, Were you ever contacted by this person, etc.

And yet, for our eternal fate in the afterlife of eternity, this external knowledge is not at all crucial, and will only last us as long as we are connected to the physical body, while the usefulness of the interior knowledge will last us to eternity. Clearly, the interior knowledge is immeasurably more important than the external knowledge, and yet, prior to our reformation, everyone favors the external knowledge, and pursues it, hardly paying attention to the far more crucial interior knowledge, which is knowledge about the character of our willing and the content of our thinking all day long.

> *The knowledge of a thing must come first in order that there may be a perception of it. ~Swedenborg, AC 5649*

As I discussed earlier, self-witnessing can access our "sudden memory", which refers to the stream of thought and feeling that is our actual mental life in the natural mind. This stream of thought is the outward form of our affections, namely their embodiment. The quality of our affections is the result of the particular afterlife societies with which we are in telepathic contact as the sequence of thoughts proceeds. God continuously manages the details of all such contacts as a way of activating dormant affections and silencing those that are active.

When we practice daily self-witnessing we are able to "tune in" to the stream of thought while carrying out routine tasks. This is not like meditation or deep reflection, which are activities that occur when we stop our tasks and sit doing nothing, thus disengaged from the surrounding pace of events.

The stream of thinking accompanies every act and is a characteristic of human life. Every person is able to tune in and listen to that mental stream and to become aware of it. What is amazing is that the instant one tries to reflect on what was snatched from the stream, it is mostly gone. One cannot remember what it was. It's quite unsettling.

How do we get hold of what we snatch from the stream of sudden memory long enough so we can describe it in words and examine it in greater detail?

You may be familiar with this experience when, upon awakening, you are still affectively filled by the sphere of your vivid dream, but the instant you try to reflect on what it is so you can put it in words, it remains unavailable to the conscious mind, staying just out of its reach—like the "tip-of-the-tongue" phenomenon when you're trying to think of a name or word you know but can't quite think of it.

Modern psychology teaches that there are two types of memory: short term and long term. The first lasts for several seconds—like the phone number we look up and then dial. If we wait more than a few seconds to dial it, we have to look it up again. We move things from short term to long term memory by repetition and rehearsal with the motive to recall it later.

So you can memorize things in this way and place them permanently in your long-term memory where you can recall it when you want to. Sudden memory seems to work for a second or two and then it's gone. This is why I named it "sudden" memory—suddenly come and suddenly gone. This is the reality of our stream of consciousness under normal conditions. But self-witnessing skills allow you to snatch things from sudden memory and put them into short term, then long-term memory where the record of the thoughts can be verbalized, analyzed, and evaluated.

As mentioned above, I discovered that trying to make myself think in words and sentences slows down the stream of consciousness so that it's easier to become aware of what it is.

This is somewhat like giving a "blow-by-blow" account of what one is thinking and feeling to an imaginary audience or recorder. It seems to slow down the stream for a while, enough so that one's short term memory retains more of it and one is able to get a fix on what the topic is and its direction.

In short term memory we can be aware and evaluate, and put anything we want into long term memory by mentally rehearsing or making a verbal record of it. In this way the mental discipline of self-witnessing pays off because it gives conscious access to one's normal everyday affections and thoughts.

Daily self-witnessing practice enables us to exert rational and moral control over our interior dialog, daydreams, and emotional reactions to things moment by moment all day long. It reveals attitudes and interests. One can exert control by consciously choosing to stop or interrupt a particular line of thinking and feeling.

I use the expression "*self-regulatory sentences*" for instructions we can give ourselves to control the stream of thinking, as for example, "Stop it. Why are you wasting time thinking these useless things?" Or: "That's not a nice thing to think." Or: "How low can I get to be so fascinated by that sort of thing?" Etc.

This gives people greater conscious control over their mental life allowing them to clean out the mental pollution that reigns in it from heredity and culture. It is not possible for humans to do anything without the accompanying thinking stream. By controlling this process, we control a portion of our natural mind.

This process is inhibited and destroyed when we do not remove the mental pollution by our own daily efforts, as-of-self, but looking to God for determination. It is God who performs the regeneration process, which can be done only to the extent that we cooperate as-of self by means of daily conscious effort. God's removing act is within our as-of self effort. Without this effort there is no removing.

We need to learn to erect walls and filters as guards in our mind to prevent polluted ideas and pleasures from entering our personality and lodging there. Our culture of entertainment as social cynicism specializes in manufacturing large quantities of polluted ideas, pictures, and situations. They are called polluted because they cannot be taken into a heavenly sphere.

Without such vigilance exercised every hour of our waking time our mind gets inundated by mental pollutants, psychic poisons, psychological viruses, and all sorts of unpleasant, sleazy, scortatory, and idiotic suggestions, images, and situations. The mind is weighted down by them, even sinking to the animal life.

Have you listened in on yourself lately? We cannot trust the reputation or opinion we have of ourselves, for this is unreliable, biased, and self-serving. The check mark we place on self-rating scales are inflated or deflated in accordance with our vanities: How good am I? How often do I get mad? Am I ever unkind or gross? What kind of mistakes do I make? How happy are the people around me with my conduct? Etc. To answer such questions objectively and accurately we must witness our life.

To react to what we observe is to make an evaluation of our willing and thinking. This evaluation is from a rational level, looking down, while the stream of thinking we are observing is from a lower natural level. An analogy might be standing on a bridge and looking down on the flow of a semi-transparent river and inspecting its contents—stones, fish, plants, debris. These things represent the content of our mind—knowledges, truths, and falsifications of truths. The flow of the river is the sequencing of the thoughts, their reasoning and coherence.

Swedenborg writes about self-witnessing his eye movements while walking in an unfamiliar city in the spiritual world:

> That Cruel Spirits And Adulterers Love Nothing More Than Filth And Excrements. (((((I have spoken) previously of this [fact] that to such spirits, filth and excrements are very pleasant, so that they prefer the pleasantness of beholding such things to all other pleasantnesses, and not only filth and excrements, but also foul, loathsome, and horrid intestines of animals, to that degree, that when they act through man they snatch away all his interior sense, as also [his] sight, to such things, because they, are delighted therewith.
>
> This also was shown me by manifest experience; when I walked in the street, they carried away my eyes to all such things; wherever there was filth, excrement and intestines, thither they directed my eyes, although I was ignorant where were such

things in the street, because not observed by me. Still they saw these, whilst I was wholly unobservant, and thither directed my eyes, either to [my] side, or about [my] feet, or near and farther from thence; and the did not turn my eyes to anything else. ~Swedenborg, SE 2843

I find it quite instructive to monitor my eyes as I walk on the street or as I read a magazine or watch TV. The eyes respond to our interest, to our affections, to what we find delightful. As our eyes roam they settle on this or that object, body part, or detail. The eyes are quick. You have to catch yourself and become conscious of where they settle for how long, and where they keep coming back to.

These eye movements will reveal interests and delights that we do not wish to publicize because they are filthy and scortatory, as the passage above describes. As Swedenborg walked in the street, the spirits with him "*carried away my eyes to all such things; wherever there was filth, excrement and intestines, thither they directed my eyes, although I was ignorant where were such things in the street, because not observed by me.*"

Monitoring our eyes will reveal to us what filthy things are of interest to us from heredity. These filthy interests are not our own affections, they are the affections of the filthy spirits. But we are tied to those spirits by heredity and the filth remains with us *unless consciously removed*. It is called "filthy" because they cannot enter into a heavenly sphere of life. If we are unwilling to give up filthy things we cannot enter into a heavenly afterlife society.

> *Since spirits* [telepathic connection with afterlife societies] *take possession in that way of all that forms a person's thought and will, and angels take possession of what is even more interior, so that he is joined very closely to them, the person cannot avoid the perception and sensation that he himself is the one who thinks and wills.* ~Swedenborg, AC 6193

Our inherited connections with evils spirits cause our minds to be filled with blasphemous thoughts and curiosities.

Swedenborg writes:

Anyone who is governed by bodily and worldly love, and not at the same time by spiritual or by celestial love, does not have any but evil spirits with him, even when external holiness exists with him. Good spirits cannot in any way be present with such a person, for they perceive in an instant the kind of love which governs a person. There is a sphere emanating from the interior parts of him which the spirits perceive as plainly as man by his sense of smell perceives offensive and foul odors floating around him in the air. ~Swedenborg, AC 4311

****

Volume 4
Section 29

****

29. Macro-Behaviors Are Regenerated By Means Of Micro-Behaviors

All acts that we perform occur in a sequence and in a social setting. For example, we awake at dawn, drive to the park for a run, drive back, fix and eat breakfast, and clean up the kitchen. This is a morning routine that takes up a small portion of every day. Note that in order to describe it we use expressions that refer to "macro-behaviors", or behavior units that are fairly general, like "driving to the beach" or "cleaning up the kitchen." You can see that each detail mentioned, has sub-components that are not mentioned.

For instance, my wife and I spend about one hour at the beach park walking every morning, which is a unit of behavior composed of multiple sub-routines. One for instance, has to do with saying good morning to the other walkers and runners. This has many details to be described since it varies with each stranger that we say good morning to. We could write a book on the many details about how we transact this complex social event that takes one and a half seconds-- saying "Good morning."

An hour-long walk is an event that is packed with details of sub-events. For example, admiring the sunrise—which varies every morning, listening to the waves—which varies with the specific place or the weather, watching the frigate birds high in the sky looking for favorable air currents, and numerous other things, like the dogs, the fisherman who gives the dogs treats, each dog responding to it in its own way, and the things my wife picks up, whether it's a broken piece of glass, or a wounded bird that she then needs to drive to the oceanic institute where they take care of them.

When we get to describe even more specific behavioral details, we enter the "micro-behavior" world. Most people do not describe things at this level for it would be too boring and even meaningless, thus interfering with normal communication. For example:

I could describe what I do with my cell phone, which I don't want to leave in the car at the beach park parking lot, fearing another break in as we had twice before over the years. When I enter the car I place the tiny little phone on the tray, then when I arrive at the beach, I pick it up and put in my right back pocket. I have my wallet in my left back pocket. I have my keys in my left side pocket. I avoid putting the cell phone with the keys for it makes a noise as I walk. Etc. Etc.

Who could stand endlessly discussing such details on our daily round of routines? So we don't. And even each of these sub-details has sub-sub-details, like how I put the phone in my back pocket as I exit the car. My back pocket seals with a Velcro strip so I have to manage to open the flap held tight by the Velcro, as I hold the cell phone in the hand. This takes some practice to do effectively. Etc. Etc.

And then there are finer details to each of these little movements, as when I have a cut that is still healing on my finger and try to avoid opening the wound by putting pressure on it at a certain angle. In each of these micro-behavior details there is a threefold stepwise execution. First, I have a motive, like protecting my cut finger from being injured as I open the Velcro flap. Second, I have a thought, like monitoring the angle of pressure on the cut on my finger and judging at which point I should no longer put pressure. Third, I have a sensorimotor execution of the hand rotation, the right amount of force exerted, and precise finger movements.

The spiritual importance of micro-descriptions of behavior is that every micro-behavior, no matter how small in the overall sequence, is an outcome of a specific motive. And all motives are compatible either with a heavenly afterlife society or with a hellish one.

No micro-behavior can occur without a motive. From the Writings we know that all the heavens form a one, and all the hells form a one. Therefore all our motives and affections form a one. This is why the Writings speak of our ruling love. The ruling love rules all the other loves that are under its subordination. If there is selfishness or stupidity in our mind at any particular time, then every sub-routine and microbehavior we perform has this selfishness or stupidity in it. The motive driving our macrobehavior enters into every microbehavior of which it is constituted. And the motive always belongs to the will, supported by the thought. You can see then that willing and thinking is performed in numerous sequence of micro-behaviors built into macro-behaviors.

Self-modification of macro-behaviors is achieved in two steps. First, there must be a general motive or goal, such as going to the beach at dawn. All the sub-behaviors and their micro-behaviors depend on this one macro-behavior motive. The morning one of us decides to sleep in, all the micro-behaviors at the beach do not occur. In regeneration, the motivation to modify macro-behaviors must therefore come first. For example, I may decide that it is my citizen's duty to pick up sharp pieces of glasses I see as I walk, so as to prevent injury to those who walk barefoot. In the past I did not do this. Now I'm motivated to be a better beach citizen and to stop acting with indifference towards the danger. This begins my regeneration effort with regard to this one area. It starts with a macro-motivation.

Now I need to struggle to regenerate all the micro-behaviors. For example, I see something a few feet away that might be a piece of glass. I should go over there and examine it, but I don't want to break my aerobic pace, so I keep walking. I feel bothered. Now I can continue to walk or I can turn back. I'm in a struggle. And so on. You can see that the micro-behaviors confront the actual issues involved in carrying out the macro-behavior. Motives are set within motives in a complex hierarchy and we cannot regenerate the macro-behavior unless we tackle and modify the lower issues attendant to the micro-behaviors.

When the Internet was still in its early years I posted an article in which I state that clicking on a link is an important spiritual decision. Later I found out that one of the blogs that picks "crazy" articles on the Web each week selected mine. My article explained that the micro-behavior of clicking or not clicking is at once a social decision, a moral decision, and a spiritual decision. Clicking on the Web is like deciding to enter an unknown house or to travel to an unfamiliar country. Most of the time you don't know what you're getting into, whether it is safe or risky, acceptable or shocking, pleasant or boring.

Clicking on a Web page is a spiritual act because it is motivated by an interest, attraction, curiosity, and anticipation. These are operations of our will in the affective system of our personality. If we are undergoing regeneration we need witness precisely what that interest or motive is, whether it is compatible with heaven or with hell. Hence is the spiritual importance of clicking or not clicking.

Metanoid self-witnessing is a mental literacy skill that allows us to monitor and evaluate the moment-by-moment stream of willing and thinking that constitutes an hour or a minute of our daily round of behaviors at the macro and micro levels of operation.

The Writings speak of this metanoid or dual focus in connection with self-examination, repentance, and regeneration (e.g., DP 114).

Swedenborg writes:

[A person] can from wisdom above view the love that is below, and in this way can view his thoughts, intentions, affections, and therefore the evils and falsities as well as the goods and truths of his life and doctrine; and without a knowledge and acknowledgment of these in himself he cannot be reformed. ~Swedenborg, DP 16

Without self-examination, recognition, acknowledgment, confession and rejection of sins, thus without repentance, there is no forgiveness of them, thus no salvation, but eternal condemnation. ~Swedenborg, DP 114

Evils In The External, Man Cannot Be Removed By The Lord Except Through Man's Instrumentality.

It is only religion which renews and regenerates a person. Religion is allotted the highest place in the human mind, and sees below it the social matters which concern the world. Religion too climbs up through these as the pure sap rises in a tree to its top, and from that lofty position it has a view of natural matters, just as someone on a tower or a mountain has a view of the plains beneath. ~Swedenborg, TCR 601

The will inclines from birth towards evils, even to those which are enormous; hence, unless it were restrained by means of the understanding, a man would rush into acts of wickedness, indeed, from his inherent savage nature, he would destroy and slaughter, for the sake of himself, all who do not favor and indulge him. ~Swedenborg, ISB 14

Constant self-witnessing is a method that allows us to cooperate with God for our regeneration. When you begin self-witnessing one striking aspect of it is to become conscious of the macro and micro-integration of our willing and thinking.

For example, I think about taking in the car for servicing. This is a macro-topic in my day's schedule, to be integrated with many other macro-topics like sending email to someone, grooming the cat, shopping for groceries, reading the Writings, preparing dinner, and so on. Every macro-topic is kept in place by priorities of motives or affections in the will. But every macro-topic is constructed of an integrated series of micro-topics, each of these being maintained by a hierarchy of goals, sub-motives, affections, and preferences in the will.

For example, vacuuming the pool is made of sub-tasks (1) getting the pole from its place behind the plants without injuring the plants; (2) taking off the brush attached to it and affixing the hose nuzzle extension on wheels; (3) curling or snaking the long hose into the water to fill it with water and empty it of air; and at least a dozen other sub-tasks. Each sub-task has a series or hierarchy of affections that determine the style, rate, and effectiveness of my willing, thinking, and performing the movements of hands, head, and body. Each sub-task offers plenty of opportunity for inherited and acquired evils to break out and take over, producing errors, ineffectiveness, damage, injuries, anger, egocentric affectational styles, neglect, laziness, carelessness, and many others.

Self-witnessing reveals the astounding complexity of the ordinary behaviors that we perform mentally and physically every day and hour. Every micro-act or detail is managed by God through heavenly and hellish afterlife societies in our vertical community. God connects us and disconnects us moment by moment as we perform our willing that is prompted by affections, and our thinking that is prompted by knowledge and beliefs, and our sensory and motor activities that are prompted by our mental activities.

But self-witnessing in itself is not a spiritual or religious activity. *What makes it spiritual is the motive we have in doing it.* A spiritual motive for self-witnessing makes it into a spiritual or religious discipline. God enjoins us to examine our willing and thinking so that we may evaluate each mental act in the light of what we have learned from *Sacred Scripture*. This is the spiritual motive for self-witnessing.

****

Volume 4
Section 30

Theistic Psychology - Expanding The Narrative Series—Volume 4
Correspondences, Synchronicity, And Self-Witnessing

****

30. Examples From The Daily Round Archives

The Ten Commandments [are] the starting-point of reformation.
~Swedenborg, TCR 582

The following examples are from anonymous entries in the collection of self-witnessing reports of the Daily Round Archives.

Category 3A Logging Activities (Time, Duration, Place, Participants, Occasion, Nature of Activity)

(i) 4:12 P.M. "(ii) 3 min. (iii) in our parking stall (iv) me and my daughters; (v) unloading the groceries from the car; (vi) carrying groceries upstairs, checking the mailbox, putting grocery bag on the kitchen floor, telling the kids to hurry up"

(i) 4:15 P.M. "(ii) 13 min.; (iii) at home; (iv) me and my daughters; (v) putting away the groceries: (vi) taking groceries out of the bags and telling children to put them away and start doing their home-work, use the bathroom, then Sit down in the parlor"

(i) 4:28 P.M. "(ii) 2 min; (iii) at home: (iv) me; (v) in my bedroom; (vi) changing my clothes, combing my hair, and putting NY clothes away"

(i) 4:30 P.M. "(ii) 32 min; (iii) at home in the parlor: (iv) me and my daughters; (v) helping children to do their homework; (vi) lying down on the couch, talking to the children, listening to the stereo"

(i) 5:02 P.M. "(ii) 1 hour, 7 min; (iii) at home, in the parlor; (iv) me and my daughters; (v) lying on the couch; (vi) sleeping"

(i) 6:09 P.M. "(ii) 2 min,: (iii) at home on the couch; (iv) me and my daughters; (v) lying down on the couch: (vi) children wake me up and tell me to start cooking dinner--they're hungry, TV is on, and I start to sit up"

(i) 6:11 P.M. "(ii) 3 min,; (iii) at home, on the couch; (iv) me and my daughters; (v) discussing what to eat for dinner; (vi) .sitting down and smoking a cigarette"

Category 3E1.4 Situated Sensations and Feelings, Microdescriptions of Sensory Observations, Retinal Sensations

I am leaving the theater after watching a matinee feature: as I walk out of the theater, my eyes suddenly squint at the glare of the sun; the muscles around my eye tighten. My pupils experience and sharp but momentary pain; as I become accustom to the glare of the sun. The muscles around my eye begin to relax, I open my eyes to its normal position; the pain in my pupils gradually diminish towards the back of my head$_1$ there is a slight throbbing in my eyes but it quickly diminishes; my vision is now normal and comfortable.

Category 3E1.7 Situated Sensations and Feelings, Microdescriptions of Sensory Observations, Smells and Odors

I preheat the oven before roasting the duck; as I prepare the duck there is a faint odor in the kitchen; I sniff at the duck, then at my hands; the smell doesn^{1}t seem to be the duck or my hands; I start sniffing at the pot of vegetables on the stove; its not the vegetables; I take many short sniffs and several long ones; smells like something burning; I hear some sizzling and smoke coming out of the oven; my entire body is now tense; I rush to open the oven; smoke is coming out of it but there is not-thing in there that would burn; I grab a potholder and quickly open the broiler, beneath the oven; there it is the drippings from the steak we had two days ago sizzling on the rack; I begin to relax; I remove the rack and place it in the sink; my body begins to relax; the smell of steak slowly leaves the air; I continue to prepare the duck.

Category 3B4 Situated Interior Dialogue, Reviewing-Making Plans and Lists

I'm driving home and thinking to myself what should I do first when I get home? First, I'll wash the clothes then clean the house while the clothes are in the washer and dryer; then I'll start to prepare dinner, no I better not, I think I'll take a bath after I'm through cleaning house: then I'll take the clothes out of the dryer fold them before starting dinner, that way I won't have to interrupt my cooking to pick up the clothes and fold them; after dinner I'll rest for about half an before I start studying; I wonder if I should call Rita and ask her if she would like to go to the library me tonight, no, I better not, otherwise we might end up in the bar having a few drinks and I won't get a chance to study; let's see first wash clothes, then shower, then cook dinner, relax for a little while, then study--sounds good, I think to myself, yeah, that's what I'll do tonight.

Category 3B6 Situated Interior Dialogue, Rehearsals and Practicings

I'm talking to Helen on the phone and she mentions Eddie called her and they talked for half an hour, I'm wondering if I should tell her that he called me the other night. no, I don't think I should, she might take it the wrong way. I'm wondering if I should say 'oh yeah, he called last night to see how every thing was going with me, he didn't say much, we only talked for about ten minutes or perhaps I should tell her that he had forgotten her number and that's why he called. No, maybe I should say, 'oh, that's nice, how is he doing?' and not mention to that he called me. Hmm, Nah, I don't think I should say anything at all about his call. Perhaps if he had wanted her to know that he called he would have told her himself... but he didn't... wonder why? On, well, forget it, it's not important anyway. I know, I'll just say that he called just to say hello and that he was doing fine...yeah, that's it, that's what I'll say.

Category 5A8.1 Regular Lists And Belongings, Inventories Of Ownership, Documents And Mementos, Official-Legal-Medical

My official legal documents include: birth certificate of self and children, marriage certificate, divorce decree, social-security card for self and kids, legal ownership paper for my car, car insurance document, check book, HMSA medical card, drivers license, school tuition agreement papers for children's school, BEOC award letter and tuition waiver, medical statements, bank statements, transcript from U.H. and Leeward Community College, school receipts for children, telephone bill receipts, rent receipts, student identification card, rental agreement paper, student fee slip, high school diploma, an associates degree in art and, science from Leeward Community College.

Personal-Biographical: I am looking in my bedroom for my personal things as I do not leave them lying around the house, here is a list of things that I've found on my book shelf which is 5' x 5':

> 1. A Bank of Hawaii statement in a blue envelope ,on my bookshelf, it is there because I forgot to balance my check book for last month.
>
> 2. A karate trophy for most outstanding dated 1968 on the book shelf. It is as a bookend.
>
> 3. There are forty-one albums and two tapes: Sinatra (9), Herb Ellis (2), Al Green (1), Charlie Byrd (3), Don Ho (2), Matt Monroe (1), Dionne Warwick (4), Jerry Vale (1), The Beatles (1), Sergio Mendes (3), Simon and Garfunkel (1), Best of '66 (1). Doris Day (1). Peter and Gordon (1), New Vaudeville Band (1), This is Broadway (1), Follow the Sun

Around the World (i), Johnny Rivers (1). Liz Damon and the orient Express (1), Barbra Streisand (1), Gladys Knight & the pips (1), Carol King (1), Olivia Newton-John (1), Nat King Cole (1), and a Vikki Carr and The Strauss Family tapes on the shelf.

4. There are thirty-three hardback books and one-hundred and twelve paperback books on the shelf ranging in subject matter from politics to sex.

5. There are fifteen manila folders containing notes, handouts, and exams from previous courses.

   1. There are four folders, all black, which contain old notes from previous courses.
   2. One faded, old Frisbee that my daughter found outside while playing.
   3. There are two bottles of cutex, one is a base coat the other is called frosted pink, a bottle of cutex remover (half empty), a bottle of baby powder, one snoopy bank, white, that my ex-husband gave me- there's no money in it, one old, metal fan that was a wedding gift, one large old yellow candle that a friend gave me, and four blank cassette cartridges all on the shelf.
   4. On my dresser I find one bottle of apricot oil that I bought at a make up party, a ceramic dinosaur, that my daughter gave me last year for Christmas, a wedding pic of my brother and his wife, in a clear plastic cover, in a folding silver frame there's a picture of My mother and out dog, two pictures of my daughters when they were one and two years old, and picture of myself at Christmas time, 1967, a yellow scratch pad that has "fix car on Saturday" written on it, and & pencil holder with two pens in it on my dresser.

      10. In my closet there is a box containing eight albums, two blue ones, three red ones, and three

white ones. The white ones contain wedding pictures, high school photos of friends and family; the red and blue albums contain pictures of my children; there's a small white box containing all the negatives from all the photos.

11. There is one portable sewing machine in a green case, one old Singer sewing machine in a brown wooden cabinet, one green and yellow beach chair, one sewing table for the portable sewing machine, two shoe boxes containing a black pair of shoes and a white one, one pair of sandals next to them, beige in color, on the floor, and two sets of Scrabble, one tape deck, two file boxes, gray in color, and four evening purses-beige, black white, and off-white all on the shelf in the closet.

12. In a small, old shoe box on the shelf I find a brand new black shoe lace, small gold colored safety pins, a deck of Hanafuda cards, and an old combination lock that I once used for my locker in high school, I probably put them there so that I could find them easily but in fact I had completely forgotten about them.

Category 5B1.3 Routine Concerns: Selected Inventories, Privacy, From the Ears of Particular Others

I am standing outside of class and it is raining. My. girlfriend and I are talking about the course. She says that she has a hard time understanding the professor. I agree with her and mention that he is boring and doesn't seem to know how to communicate well with students, considering that that is what he teaches. Just then he walks in front of us and enters the room. I feel uneasy, I ask my friend if she thinks he overheard what I just said. She just shrugs. I think he did, but maybe he thought that she said it and not I. I don't know, I hope not."

Category 5B1.4.1 Routine Concerns, Selected Inventories, Privacy, From the Knowledge of Particular Others, Involving Your Activities

> I am at home, opening my telephone bill for this month. John is sitting down beside me. I look at the bill and wonder if he is going to pay for his long distance call. He knows I don't have the money to pay for the whole bill by myself. I'm hoping that he asks to see the bill. No, he doesn't ask. I don't want to mention it to him, he might think that I'm assuming he won't pay for it. I'll just leave it on the dresser and hope that he is nosey enough to look at it himself and mention that he's going to pay for his half. I hope.

Category 5B1.4.2 Routine Concerns, Selected Inventories, Privacy, From the Knowledge of Particular Others, Involving Your Ideas

> I am talking to my sister and she mentions that she doesn't want to have any more children because her husband is presently unemployed. She asks if I know of any sure method of birth control without having sterilization and taking the pill. I tell her that she should consult her physician and discuss the matter with her husband. I did not wish to pursue the matter as I know that it would only add to her confusion and a heated argument and hurt feelings might ensue. If she were not older than I, I would have told her that she should take the pill, which she is strongly against, The subject is then dropped and I ask her how she's doing in her present job.

Category 5C1.4 Noticing Observations, Visual Sightings, People in Public Places

> Today, at Ala Moana shopping center, I saw Professor Z. He was wearing a printed red and white aloha shirt, white flared trousers, and white buck shoes.

Category 5C2.1.3 Noticing Observations, Relationship Events, Noticeables About People You Know (physical appearance, mood, etc.), Unmentionables Within the Relationship

Today I noticed Professor B wearing two different colored, different size rubber slippers. One was green and the other was brown. His pants are too short and his aloha shirt looks wrinkled, as if he didn't iron it. This is the umpteenth time I've seen him dress in such a manner.

Category 5D5 Description Of Transactions, Exchanging Information

While sitting outside of the classroom, I see a friend of mine approaching. She sits with me and we start to talk of school. She asks if I was accepted into the dental hygiene program. I say no I wasn't. I ask if she was, she says no. We then start to discuss the requirements for the program and how a person is selected into the program. She tells me that perhaps we should apply to the nursing program instead and proceeds to inform me of there requirements.

Category 5D6 Description Of Transactions, Making Arrangements

Faye called me tonight and invites me to have a drink with her at the bar tonight. I agree. She tells me if it would be alright if we meet in about one hour at Latin Villa. I say that that would be fine. I then call my neighbor and ask her if it would be possible for her to watch the kids for me tonight. She agrees.

Category 5D7 Description Of Transactions, Working Out a Problem

...them both to the cashier. Once its paid for, I take the package and leave the store, I go downstairs and buy a drink for myself, feeling proud that for once I bought a gift ahead of time instead of waiting till the last minute. After finishing my soda, I go to my car and leave.

Category 5K3 Non-Joint Activities, Mentioning a person to Someone

While talking to Carol on the telephone, we both mention a total of seven people; She mentioned four people, three from the store and her roommate. I mentioned John's name, Tom's and my sister's brother-in-law.

Category 5K4 Non Joint Activities, Avoiding a Person

> After dropping off the kids at school, I came home to do some studying. Just as I park my car, I see my neighbor arriving home. I hurry out of my car and pretend not to see him. Just as I'm about to walk upstairs, he shouts "Hi Nan, how you doing? I smile at him and say alright but keep on walking...can't stop now or I'll be stuck for hours talking to him! He looks at me and I feel that he would like me to say something so that he can start rapping. I keep on walking, Making sure that I don't look back again.

God is unceasingly present, and continually striving and acting in man.
~Swedenborg, TCR 74

****

Volume 4
Section 31

****

31. Swedenborg On Self-witnessing And Regeneration

Swedenborg writes:

Spiritual freedom is from the love of eternal life. Into this love and its delight no one comes but the man who thinks that evils are sins, and consequently does not will them, and at the same time looks to the Lord. As soon as a man does so, he is in this freedom; for no one has the power not to will evils because they are sins and so to refrain from doing them, unless from a more interior or higher freedom which is from a more interior or higher love.

At first this freedom does not appear to be freedom, and yet it is; and later it does so appear, when the man acts from freedom itself according to reason itself, in thinking, willing, speaking and doing what is good and true. This freedom increases as natural freedom decreases and becomes subservient; and it conjoins itself with rational freedom which it purifies.

[7] Everyone may come into this freedom provided he is willing to think that there is an eternal life, and that the temporary delight and bliss of a life in time are but as a fleeting shadow compared with the never-ending delight and bliss of a life in eternity. This a man can think if he wishes, because he has rationality and liberty, and because the Lord, from whom these two faculties are derived, continually gives him the ability to do so. (DP 73)

From infancy to childhood, and sometimes on into early youth, a person is absorbing forms of goodness and truth received from parents and teachers, for during those years he learns about those forms of goodness and truth and believes them with simplicity - his state of innocence enabling this to happen.

It inserts those forms of goodness and truth into his memory; yet it lodges them only on the edge of it since the innocence of infancy and childhood is not an internal innocence which has an influence on the rational, only an external one which has an influence solely on the exterior natural.

When however the person grows older, when he starts to think for himself and not, as previously, simply in the way his parents or teachers do, he brings back to mind and so to speak chews over what he has learned and believed before, and then he either endorses it, has doubts about it, or refuses to accept it.

If he endorses it, this is an indication that he is governed by good, but if he refuses to accept it, that is an indication that he is governed by evil. If however he has doubts about what he has learned and believed before, it is an indication that he will move subsequently either into an affirmative attitude of mind or else into a negative one. (AC 5135)

It is the same with all things that belong to man's very life, as with those which relate to his understanding, and those which relate to his will. These also follow in order from interior to exterior things. Exterior things are memory-knowledges with their pleasant feelings; and outermost things are those of the senses, which communicate with the world by the sight, the hearing, the taste, the smell, and the touch. (AC 9216)

The interior can perceive what takes place in the exterior, or what is the same, that the higher can see what is in the lower; but not the reverse. Moreover they who have conscience can do this and are accustomed to do it, for when anything contrary to the truth of conscience flows into the thought, or into the endeavor of the will, they not only perceive it, but also find fault with it; and it even grieves them to be of such a character. (AC 1914)

[2] What the interior man is, scarcely anyone knows, and it must therefore be briefly stated. The interior man is intermediate between the internal and the external man. By the interior man the internal man communicates with the external; without this medium, no communication at all is possible. The celestial is distinct from the natural, and still more from the corporeal, and unless there is a medium by which there is communication, the celestial cannot operate at all into the natural, and still less into the corporeal.

It is the interior man which is called the rational man; and this man, because it is intermediate, communicates with the internal man, where there is good itself and truth itself; and it also communicates with the exterior man, where there are evil and falsity.

By means of the communication with the internal man, a man can think of celestial and spiritual things, or can look upward, which beasts cannot do. By means of the communication with the exterior man, a man can think of worldly and corporeal things, or can look downward; in this differing little from the beasts, which have in like manner an idea of earthly things. In a word, the interior or middle man is the rational man himself, who is spiritual or celestial when he looks upward, but animal when he looks downward.

[3] It is well known that a man can know that he speaks in one way while thinking in another, and that he does one thing while willing another; and that there exist simulation and deceit; also that there is reason, or the rational; and that this is something interior, because it can dissent; and also that with one who is to be regenerated there is something interior which combats with that which is exterior. This that is interior, and that thinks and wills differently from the exterior, and that combats, is the interior man. In this interior man there is conscience with the spiritual man, and perception with the celestial. This interior man, conjoined with the Divine internal man that was in the Lord, is what is here called "Abram the Hebrew." (AC 1702)

Summarizing the points in the above Swedenborg selection on regeneration and self-witnessing:

1. Regeneration involves inner freedom and the voluntary choices we make from love. Everything else is partially or wholly coerced and not in freedom.

2. At the start of our regeneration we have the experience that freedom is to choose what an ego-love desires or wants. And to feel un-free or coerced when we try to resist giving in to the ego-love that is selfish, and to choose instead being considerate of others or altruistic love.

3. There is natural freedom in the natural mind and rational freedom in the rational mind. As we progress in our regeneration natural freedom diminishes and rational freedom increases. Eventually all natural freedom gives way to "coercion" or obedience to the rational mind. The natural mind and the rational mind are then acting in synchrony and correspondence. That is when they reach their full potential of function and health.

4. Our rational mind has the ability to compel our natural mind to think and act in accordance with the order of the rational mind. For instance, our rational conscience gives us regrets, pain, and fear when we think, speak, or act contrary to the order of our rational mind, as when we speak and intend from the desire to satisfy an ego-

love. Ego-loves are contrary to the rational order of mutual love and altruism.

5. Additionally, our rational mind appeals to the rational common sense that we follow in our natural mind.

6. For instance, it points out that resisting ego-loves may be challenging our motivation but it is well worth it when we figure (a) that rational pleasure is far greater and satisfying than natural pleasure; and (b) that natural pleasure lasts a few decades at the most while we are connected to the physical body on earth. But the rational pleasure lasts forever in the afterlife of mental eternity.

7. As regeneration proceeds there is a growing influence of non-material ideas from our rational mind on the material ideas in our natural mind. This influence is possible because of psychological states of innocence in childhood that are called "remains". God causes these states of innocence to remain in our personality structure even though they sink into the sub-conscious while we grow up into adulthood. In adulthood when we choose to undergo regeneration the non-material ideas of our rational mind hook up with these unconscious remains in our natural mind synchronizes with them.

8. When we reach adulthood, God prompts us by an inner motive to "chew over" the beliefs and lifestyle practices that we have adopted. We can then have three reactions:
(a) we can endorse the materialistic beliefs and lifestyles, and confirm them as right;
(b) we can have doubts about our materialistic beliefs and experience conflict from the goodness and truths of our remains or conscience;
(c) we can reject the materialistic lifestyle and with the help of remains we can undergo regeneration.

9. To the extent that we reject our materialistic beliefs because they conflict with non-material ideas in our remains, to that extent we are being effective and successful in our regeneration. It is a sign that we are progressing in our individuation whose ultimate goal is to approach the collective consciousness of humanity that is

omnipresent in the mental world of eternity into which we are born. All our human potentials are sourced and rooted in the collective consciousness.

10. The anatomical structure of our mental body consists of two levels of mental activity and consciousness called natural and rational. The natural mind with its material ideas is exterior and therefore lower in complexity of function and ability. The rational mind with its non-material ideas is interior and therefore higher in complexity of function and consciousness.

11. The higher rational mind is aware of the ongoing activity in the lower natural mind. What is lower cannot see what is higher, but what is higher can see what is lower. For instance, when we think of something very selfish and harmful we suddenly feel a warning pang from our conscience, and this indicates that we were monitoring at the level of our conscience what we were thinking at the level of our material mind. Sub-conscious and unconscious self-monitoring is therefore a feature of the human mind.

12. Regeneration involves this one-way tunnel vision because we need the magnified vision of non-material ideas in our higher rational mind to influence and manage the blind material ideas of the lower natural mind. The goodness of love and the truth of rationality are the non-material ideas in the rational mind that are to synchronize with the material ideas of our natural mind, such as treating people with appropriate consideration and respect.

13. Our rational mind operates at two levels. The lower level of the rational mind synchronizes with the natural mind. As well, the lower level rational mind synchronizes with the higher level rational mind. In other words, the lower rational thinking is intermediate between the lower natural thinking with material ideas and the higher rational thinking with non-material ideas.

14. Hence it is clear that the lower rational thinking can be either with material ideas or with non-material ideas. When the lower rational mind thinks with material ideas it is communicating with the natural

mind, but when the lower natural mind thinks with non-material ideas it is synchronizing with the higher rational mind.

15. Good and truth are the source of all non-material ideas and can be understood only with the higher rational mind. However they can be communicated or synchronized with material ideas through the intermediary of the lower rational mind.

16. When we are regenerating, the non-material ideas of goodness and truth are in spiritual combat with the selfishness and insanity of material ideas and ego-loves that are embedded in our inherited personality. The non-material ideas are in the interior rational mind while the material ideas are in the external natural mind. The interior must battle with the exterior and compel it to align itself in synchrony.

Volume 4
Section 32

32. The Daily Round Archives Classification Scheme (DRA)

I reproduce below a copy of the "daily round archives" that I constructed several years ago in my research on self-witnessing. I wanted a listing of the categories of activities, places, and settings that form our daily life of activities in our various roles. I realized that such a classification system couldn't be a true catalog of everything that makes up an individual's daily life. But I figured that if it's detailed enough it could serve as a significant map of the "daily round" of regular activities. This would then be a valuable instrument for keeping track of ourselves in multiple behavior areas and psychological states in our efforts of regeneration.

I. MAJOR CLASSIFICATION LEVEL

Zone 1: Biographic Record (White)

Zone 2: Tribe (Yellow)

Zone 3: Role (Green)

Zone 4: Psychohistory (Blue)

Zone 5: Territoriality (Brown)

Zone 6: Appearance (Black)

[Note: For explanations about the color code see End Note 4.]

II. SUBCLASSIFICATION LEVEL

Zone 1: Biographic Record

1a My Vita

Zone 2: Tribe

2a My Talk

2b Connections

2c Family Tree

Zone 3: Role

3a Logging Activities

3b Situated Interior Dialogue

3c Situated Standardized Imaginings

3d Situated Psychologizings

3e Situated Sensations And Feelings

3f Situated Feeling Arguments

3g Situated Fantasy-Daydream Episodes

3h The Elevated Register

3i Responsibilities and Duties

3j Social Memberships

Zone 4: Psychohistory

    4a Situated Attributions

    4b Situated Evaluations And Assessments

    4c Situated Judgments

    4d Interviewing The Self

Zone 5: Territoriality

    5a Regular Lists And Belongings

    5b Routine Concerns: Selected Inventories

    5c Noticing Observations

    5d Description Of Transactions

    5e Transactional Strategies: Episodes When

    5f Declarations

    5g Slogans

    5h Epithets

    5i Hangouts And Group Activities

    5j Reporting Joint Activities

    5k Non-Joint Activities

Zone 6: Appearance

    6a Interviewing Others

MICRO CLASSIFICATION LEVEL

   Zone 1: Biographic Record

      1A. My Vita

         1A1 Current Status in Community

         1A2 Background

         1A3 Topic focus

         1A4 Personal

            1A4.1 Favorites

            1A4.3 Fears

            1A4.2 Ambitions

   Zone 2: Tribe

      2A My Talk

         2A1 Analysis of Argument Logic

            2A1.1 Schema of Argument Structure

            2A1.2 Description of Operational Talking Procedures

            2A1.3 Schema of Behavioral Strategies in Talk

         2A2 Analysis of Relationship

            2A2.1 Case History

            2A2.2 Relationship Dynamics

            2A2.3 Tabulation of Pair Types

2A2.4 Tabulation of Role Types

2A3 Analysis of Sequence

2A3.1 Schema for Move Embeddings

2A3.2 Tabulation of Adjacency Relations

2A4 Analysis of Setting

2A4. 1 Discourse Analysis

2A4. 2 Tabulation of Derivative Relations

2A4. 3 Tabulation of Implicit Meanings

2A4. 4 Tabulation of the Rhythm of Exchange

2A4. 5 Transactional Engineering through Talk

2A5 Analysis of Topic

2A5. 1 Breakdown of Topics Exchanged

2A5. 2 Topical Annotations

2A5. 3 Topical Chart of Transcript

2A5. 4 Topicalization Dynamics

2A6 Transcript Annotations

2A6.1 Explanations

2A6.2 Stage Directions

2B Connections

2B1 People I Live With

2B2 People Who Are My Immediate Family

2B3 People Who Are My Extended Family

2B4 People Who Are Acquaintances of the Family

2B5 People I Know From Work

2B6 People I Regularly Socialize With

2B7 People Who Have Provided Me with Professional Services

2B8 People Who's change in Financial Status Would Affect My Financial Status

2B9 People Who Are Non-Intimates and Non-Family whose Ill Health or Death Would Affect Me

2B10 People Whom I Might Ask for a Recommendation

2B11 People Who Influenced My Intellectual and Personal Maturity

2B12 People I Don't Know Personally But Whose Ideas Affect Me

2B13 People Who Have or Could Ask 'Me for a Reference

2B14 People I see Regularly for Service or Supplies

2B15 People I'd Like Currently to Meet

2B16 People I Know Whose Words I Quote or Stories I Tell

2B17 People Whom I Believe to be Admired by My Parents

2B18 People Whom I Know Who I See or Think About Only Rarely

2C Family Tree

Zone 3

3a Logging Activities

3A1 Time

3A2 Duration

3A3 Place

3A4 Participants

3A5 Occasion

3A6 Nature of Activity

3b Situated Interior Dialogue

3B1 Overlays of Comments to Self

3B2 Value Expressions

3B3 Preparing Schedules

3B4 Reviewing-Making Plans and Lists

3B5 Emotionalizing Episodes

3B6 Rehearsals and Practicings

3B7 Annotations, Memorizings, Editings

3B8 Unmentionables Within the Relationship

3c Situated Standardized Imaginings

3d Situated Psychologizings

3e Situated Sensations And Feelings

    3E1 Microdescriptions of Sensory Observations

        3E1 .1 Aches and Pains

        3E1 .2 Stretchings and Exercise

        3E1 .3 Blushing

        3E1.4 Retinal Sensations ~ etc.

        3E1.5 Appetite and Cooking

        3E1.6 Energy Level

        3E1.7 Smells and Odors

3f Situated Feeling Arguments

    3F1 Figuring Out a Conflict

    3F2 Making Resolutions

3g Situated Fantasy-Daydream Episodes

    3G1 Elaboration of Dramatized Scenarios

    3G2 Construction of Catharsis Stories

    3G3 Re-contacting Nostalgic Memories

    3G4 Working out Alternative Realities

3h The Elevated Register

    3H1 Praying-Invocations

    3H2 Altered States of Consciousness

3H3 Meditations-Reading of Scriptures

3H4 Poetic Expressions

3i Responsibilities and Duties

3j Social Memberships

Zone 4: Psychohistory

4a Situated Attributions

4b Situated Assessments/Evaluations

4c Situated Judgments

4d Interviewing Self

4D1 Who Am I

4D2 What Am I

4D3 How Am I

4D4 What Do I Look to You

Zone 5: Territoriality

5a Regular Lists And Belongings

5AI Invitations

5A2 Announcements

5A3 Subscriptions

5A3.1 Periodicals

5A3.2 Membership Dues

5A3.3 Contributions

5A4 Bills

5A5 Closets

5A6 Drawers

5A7 Objects

5A8 Documents and Mementos

    5A8.1 Official-Legal-Medical

    5A8.2 Personal/Biographical

        5A8.2. 1 Prizes

        5A8.2.2 Letters

        5A8.2.3 Gifts

        5A8.2.4 Albums

        5A8.2.5 Souvenirs

5A9 Personal Effects: Selected Inventories

    5A9.I Purse/Wallet

    5A9.2 Car Glove Compartment

    5A9.3 Your Own Drawer for Stuff

    5A9.4 Clothes Closet

5b Routine Concerns: Selected Inventories

    5B1 Privacy

        5B1.1 From the EYES of Particular Others

        5B1.2 From the NOSE of Particular Others

5B1.3 From the EARS of Particular Others

5B1.4 From the Knowledge of Particular Others

    5B1.4.1 Involving Your Activities

        5B1.4.1.1 Places

        5B1.4.1.2 People

        5B1.4.1.3 Purchases

        5B1.4.1.4 Bills

    5B1.4.2 Involving Your Ideas

        5B1.4.2.1 Memories

        5B1.4.2.2 Attitudes

        5B1.4.2.3 Opinions

5B2 Information: Record Keeping

    5B2.1 Schedules

    5B2.2 Shopping Lists

    5B2.3 Date and Address Books

    5B2.4 Check/Bank Books

    5B2.5 Biographical

        5B2.5.1 Diary

        5B2.5.2 Notes

        5B2.5.3 Resolutions

5c Noticing Observations

5C1 Visual Sightings

    5C.1.1 Physical State-Appearance of Things and Places

    5C1.2 Change in Normalcy Signs

    5C1.3 Weather

    5C1.4 People in Public Places

5C2 Relationship Events

    5C2.I Noticeables About People You Know

        5C2.1.1 Physical Appearance

        5C2.1.2 Mood

        5C2.1.3 Unmentionables Within the Relationship

        5C2.I.4 Disoccasioned Mentionables

5C3 Auditory Pickings-up

    5C3.1 Overheard Snatches of Talk

    5C3.2 Sounds, Noises

5d Description Of Transactions

5D1 Gossiping

5D2 Catching Up on News

5D3 Having an Argument

5D4 Joking

5D5 Exchanging Information

5D6 Making Arrangements

5D7 Working Out a Problem

5D8 Sharing Secrets/Confess ions

5D9 Routine Reviews/News of the Day

5e Transactional Strategies: Episodes When I:

5EI Lied

5E2 Avoided

5E3 Persisted

5E4 Pursued

5E5 Insisted On

5f Declarations

5F1 Problems

5F2 Concerns

5F3 Secrets

5F4 Disoccasioned Topics

5F5 Superstitions

5g Slogans

5GI About Appearance

5G2 About Health

5G3 About Diet

5G4 Folk Wisdom

5h Epithets

    5H1 Pet Peeves (self and others)

    5H2 Family Sayings

    5H3 Nicknames (self and others

    5H4 Personal (self and others)

    5H5 Regularized References To:

        5H5.l Time

        5H5.2 Place

        5H5.3 Events

5i Hangouts And Group Activities

    5I1 Places

    5I2 Circumstances of Crowding With

    5I3 Activities with Others

    5I4 Rights and Privileges

    5I5 Reputations

5j Reporting Joint Activities

    5J1 Doing Something With Dates, Appointments

    5J2 Telephone Calls

    5J3 Writing/Receiving Notes, Letters, Memos, Ads, etc.

    5J4 Paying Bills

5k Non-Joint Activities

5K1 Doing a Task for Another Person

5K2 Buying a Gift for Another Person

5K3 Mentioning a Person to Someone

5K4 Avoiding a Person

5K5 Going to See/Looking for a Person

5K6 Having a Mental Exchange with Someone

Zone 6: Appearance

6a Interviewing Others

6A1 Who Am

6A2 What Am

6A3 How Am I

6A4 What Do I Look Like To You

****
Volume 4
Section 33
****

33. Summary And Overview

The proposal in this book represents my attempt to integrate and synthesize the basic concepts in Jung's psychology and the ethnographic facts about the afterlife that are found in the *Swedenborg Reports*. The result of integrating Jung and Swedenborg offers a new synthesis for psychology that may be called *"theistic psychology"*. It is psychology "from God" and treats of God's direct and active management of the mental operations of every individual, from birth to endless immortality.

This must come as huge news to most people, as indeed it was for me when the idea first presented itself to my mind. By "huge news" I mean unexpected, surprising, and totally changing everything in our idea of ourselves as an individual. The idea of privacy and independence of our mental world is shattered forever.

We are never alone! Not only God is present, but also whole societies of people that are living in the afterlife of eternity. Such is the amazing telepathic co-presence of all human beings with each other, past and present, and the future to join the mental collectivity of all humanity.

Theistic psychology is called "theistic" because it is derived exclusively from the psychological meaning of God's Word in *Sacred Scripture*. Theistic psychology differs from religion, which is derived from the *literal* meaning of *Sacred Scripture* and its historical details. The literal meaning of *Sacred Scripture* in all religions is historical and culture-specific, and hence non-transferable cross-culturally, but the psychological meaning is universal and culture free, and hence scientific and applicable to all humanity.

It is not yet known that the *Sacred Scripture* of all religions and cultures contains a universal non-religious but theistic psychological meaning. I have discovered this by examining small samples of the *Sacred Scripture* of several of the major historical religions that are translated into English and available on the Web. I have concluded that by using correspondences and symbolization we can derive the same theistic psychology from the *Sacred Scripture* of all of them.

This uniformity and compatibility of all *Sacred Scripture* is due to the fact that God speaks to the sensuous mind of human beings, which is cultural and religious, and at the same time to their rational mind, which is psychological, biological, and universal. There is only one God. It is clear that God raises up different religions in different cultures and times. The connection between them is the culture free psychological meaning that applies regardless of cultural and historical context.

I will number the summary propositions for easier review and reference.

***

1

I begin from the beginning. God has created two worlds, one being the physical or material world that is in time and fixed space, and the other being the non-material world that is in eternity, which means "not in time or fixed place". The physical world in time is made of inert matter and energy, while the non-material world of eternity is made of living mental substance that provides immortal life.

What is physical or material is non-living and inert, while what is spiritual or non-material is living and human.

The two worlds are connected by the laws of correspondences and symbolization. This will be further explained below. It should be noted that the non-material world is also called the spiritual world, and this is also called the mental world since all things that are spiritual, such as love, wisdom, goodness, truth, heaven, hell, are mental operations in the human mind.

The spiritual world of eternity is the same as the mental world of eternity, which is the same as the afterlife world of eternity.

2

Human beings are born in the spiritual world of eternity with an immortal spiritual body. This spiritual body is made of living mental substance that abounds in the atmosphere of the spiritual or mental world of eternity. Simultaneously with the spiritual body, God creates a material biomedical physical body on earth that is made of inert chemicals but *is created to react by correspondence to our spiritual body in eternity*.

Our mind is located in this immortal spiritual body from birth onward. We are born into the spiritual world of eternity and never leave it. We are born immortal. You are there now!

3

The spiritual body contains the organs of our mind, which is our unique personality and individual consciousness. The exterior anatomy of the spiritual body is called the "*natural mind*". The interior organs make up the "*spiritual mind*". With our natural mind we mostly think with material ideas that are appropriate to earth conditions. With our spiritual mind we think with non-material ideas that are appropriate to afterlife conditions in the mental world of eternity.

4

The external natural mind in our spiritual body grows and develops through the sensory input from the physical body on earth. The interior spiritual mind in our spiritual body develops through the non-material ideas that correspond to the material ideas of the natural mind. In this way the two minds and worlds remain connected and synchronous.

Our natural mind in our spiritual body in eternity mostly operates with material ideas that we abstract from the sensory organs of the physical body on earth. This creates the powerful illusion that we are alone in our mind and that we are the physical body. That illusion ceases when sensory input switches to the spiritual body in the afterlife. We then lose all contact with the physical world.

Our natural mind now remains inactive but continues to form the basis of content through correspondence with the spiritual mind. This is why the afterlife world and the dream world are comprehensible through content familiar to us in the natural mind.

Our spiritual mind operates with non-material ideas that we construct from the sensory organs of the spiritual body. The natural mind tends to reject non-material ideas and doesn't know anything about the spiritual mind. However the inmost portion of the natural mind is called the spiritual-natural mind. We can re-arrange our rational mind to be in agreement with the spiritual-natural level of thinking and feeling. This occurs gradually with regeneration.

5
When the physical body "dies", the spiritual body in eternity is cut off from sensory input from earth. The natural mind in the spiritual body now becomes relatively inactive because it no longer has sensory input from the physical body. The sensory organs of the spiritual body now provide the input. This allows us to see and interact with all the people in the afterlife. Everyone in the afterlife spontaneously begins to use a universal human language that is inborn shared by all human beings.

This gives us an opportunity to encounter with people who have been in the afterlife for countless millennia, and as well, with people whose natural mind was developed from a physical body on other planets throughout the universe. By focusing their attention on the natural mind they can still talk about the conditions on earth at that time. Swedenborg talked to some who had contact with earth conditions prior to the historic Fall of Consciousness. They did not have the illusion as we do of thinking that we are in the body on earth. They had dual consciousness and received sensory input from both worlds. This is the state in which Swedenborg was for 27 years during which he wrote the 27 volumes of the *Swedenborg Reports* (1743-1771).

6

The mental world in which you are thinking right now as you are reading this is the same mental world in which all human beings are thinking, past, present, and future. When we lose contact with our physical body on earth, we start our activities in the afterlife with the use of our immortal spiritual body. Now we are able to see and explore the afterlife world of eternity where are located the countless afterlife societies where people live with each other in telepathic collective consciousness.

7

The operations of our spiritual mind influence the operations of our natural mind. The two operations are always active together or synchronously. However, the natural mind is not conscious of this influence or connection.

In "this life" we are unconscious of our spiritual mind but conscious of our natural mind. In the "afterlife" it is the reverse: we become more and more conscious in our spiritual mind, but less and less conscious in our natural mind.

In "this life" through the physical body on earth we are immersed in individual consciousness and we are not aware of the telepathic collective consciousness of afterlife societies.

What we now call the collective unconscious becomes in the afterlife the collective conscious.

8

In this life, the collective unconscious acts upon and influences the conscious natural mind. Jung and Swedenborg studied how this influence takes place. Jung discovered that the unconscious mind is collective to all humanity and hence called it the "collective unconscious".

9

Swedenborg discovered that the natural mind and the spiritual mind communicate by means of symbolization or correspondences in meaning between natural material ideas and spiritual non-material ideas. He proved that the verses of *Sacred Scripture* contain an literal meaning intended for the natural mind, and a hidden psychological meaning intended for the rational mind that is in correspondence with the spiritual mind. God speaks simultaneously to both minds, and the two different messages are correspondences of each other.

The rational mind is the inmost part of the natural mind. It has the ability to think with non-material ideas. The sensual mind, which is the lower part of the natural mind, is not capable of thinking with or understanding non-material ideas.

God addresses the literal meaning of any verse in *Sacred Scripture* to the sensual part of the natural mind. It consists of historical events and the lives of various people with whom God is interacting. The literal sense also spells out God's commandments of how human beings are to behave with each other and how they are to worship God. This historical and behavioral focus serves to create particular religions that exist in historical perspective.

10

The hidden psychological meaning of a verse is God speaking to the rational mind with non-material ideas. The message of this non-material meaning may be called *theistic psychology* since it is the content that God provides for the instruction of our rational mind. These are non-material ideas concerning our thoughts, feelings, and personality traits that God is regenerating. The psychology of regeneration is given to us by God through the psychological meaning of *Sacred Scripture*.

11 Jung's discovery of psychobiological archetypes in the collective unconscious parallels Swedenborg's discovery of afterlife societies in the spiritual world. Jung's *psychic world* is the same as Swedenborg's *spiritual world*. Both agree that the psychic or spiritual world is non-material, organic, living, human, and in eternity without time and space.

I would add here my idea that the psychic or spiritual world is the same as the mental world that is familiar to all of us from daily consciousness. The word "psychic" and "spiritual" both refer to "mental".

Hence we have three expressions that are equivalent:
- the psychic world of eternity
- the spiritual world of eternity

- the afterlife world of eternity
- the mental world of eternity.

There is only one eternity.

The mental world of eternity is constructed out of non-material mental substance. The physical world of time and place is constructed out of material chemicals and energy.

Mental substance is the stuff from which everything is created. It is God's omnipresent and infinite mind that contains uncreate and eternal mental substance that appears in infinite variety as love, goodness, wisdom, truth, intelligence, consciousness, feelings, sensations, desires, intentions, and so on. The human mind exists in these mental operations. We receive these varieties of human substance through the sphere of the mental world.

Human minds populate the mental world of eternity, which is the field of creative activity for God who may be described as the Divine Human, the original human, the infinite human, or the omnipresent human.

Human life or activity is the continuous reception of God's mental substance, which every individual receives in a unique way. We each receive this Divine Human inflow according to our unique personality, and God gives us the freedom of choice in how we choose to react and make use of the inflow, even to invert the inflow of good and truth into their opposites of adulterated good and falsified truth.

Whichever we do we experience the built-in psychological consequences, whether wholesome and happy, or depraved and suffering. These consequences continue to eternity.

12

Each mental society in the afterlife is composed of individuals who share a similar mental character, so that they can form a *collective intersubjectivity* with each other, which is also called telepathic.

The collective character of every afterlife society in mental eternity is distinguished by its particular *chief archetype* or "ruling love" in the individual's personality. Jung described the nature and character of many archetypes that he discovered through the study of the world's religious and artistic symbolisms, including that of children's stories and dreams.

Jung showed that the dreams of human beings use the same archetypal symbolism as he discovered in religious, artistic, and children's imagination.

Swedenborg discovered that this symbolized meaning in dreams is the same as the correspondences in *Sacred Scripture* that link material ideas in the literal sense of the verses to non-material ideas in the implied or psychological sense.

13

Swedenborg discovered that there are numberless afterlife societies throughout the spiritual world of eternity, which he explored for 27 years continuously in his dual consciousness. Each afterlife society lives in collective intersubjectivity or consciousness that is produced by instant telepathic sharing of thoughts and feelings between all members.

They also experience a collective cardiac and pulmonary rhythm allowing them to breathe in unison and have a synchronized heart beat.

14

Through my study of Swedenborg and Jung I discovered that Swedenborg's "*spiritual world of eternity*" and Jung's "*psychic world of the collective unconscious*" are names for the same world. I proposed a third name for it, calling it the "*mental world of eternity*".

My proposal is that the mental world familiar to each of us and in which we all think and feel right now, is actually the world of eternity. Since the mental world is not in physical space and time it is called the mental world of eternity.

15

An astonishing discovery is made when we see the identity between "mental", "spiritual", "psychic", "afterlife", and "eternity".

It is the discovery that we are born into eternity and never leave. Hence we are immortal.

This means that we are not born on earth and we are not on earth.

Instead we have a physical biomedical body or avatar on earth that is functionally connected to our non-material spiritual body in the mental world of eternity.

16

Human beings have a split consciousness. Our cognitive consciousness operates in correspondence to the cerebrum or new brain in the spiritual body. Our affective consciousness operates in correspondence to the cerebellum or old brain in the spiritual body. The physical body replicates the anatomical locus of these two brain functions.

Consciousness is an organic mental state or operation, and therefore in order to be activated it must have an embodied mind or spiritual body that is constructed with the constituents of mental substance. The natural mind and the spiritual mind together form an anatomical structure that is called our "spiritual body", or if you prefer, our "mental body" born into mental eternity.

The mind is our spiritual body. The spiritual body is the embodiment of the mind.

The spiritual body is nothing but the non-material anatomical embodiment of our mind and its mental operations such as thoughts, feelings, and . Because it is constructed of mental substance, our mind is born immortal. Mental substance is eternal, living, human, non-material, and mental or psychic.

17

When we are born we possess two minds in the immortal spiritual body, the exterior natural mind for the development of individual consciousness, and the interior spiritual mind for the development of collective consciousness. The biomedical body on earth is our physical body, while the spiritual body in the mental world of eternity is our mind.

Our spiritual body or mind is living, but our physical body is inert.

18

Putting together the ideas of Jung and Swedenborg, I conclude that human beings are born with an immortal spiritual body in the mental world of eternity, which is also called the afterlife world or the psychic world. The spiritual body is made of eternal mental substance that fills the psychic world.

Our spiritual body in eternity where we are now has the same external and internal anatomy as the biomedical physical body on earth. The two correspond to each other in external appearance and in internal organic structure, and biochemical and genetic functioning.

But the body on earth is made of physical matter and is not capable of mental operations such as sensations, thoughts, or feelings. The physical body's brain operates electrochemical patterns of energy. The information in the brain patterns of the physical body on earth corresponds to the thoughts in our spiritual body in mental eternity. This functional connection begins at birth and ends at the physical body's so-called "death", a term that is used by people who do not yet know that human beings are not born on earth and can never be on earth. The physical body on earth is temporary and when it no longer functions we say that it "died".

Since the physical body is a material construction it has no capacity for mental operations such as sensations, thoughts, feelings, or consciousness. All mental activity occurs in our living spiritual body in mental eternity, and none of it on earth in physical space and time.

19

Without a functioning physical body on earth the natural mind of our spiritual body in eternity is cut off from all sensory input from the physical world. When this happens, we suddenly become conscious in our spiritual mind. All sensory input is now into our spiritual body from the afterlife world of eternity.

With sensory input now coming from the mental world of eternity we discover that this is the afterlife world where everyone who lost their physical body from the beginning of history can be found there, and with whom we can interact and have relationships.

20

In the afterlife there are numberless societies that form themselves into social units of distinctive collective consciousness. Each archetype or specific mental character of a society influences our spiritual mind, which passes on this influence to the natural mind. There is therefore a unified or collective consciousness throughout humanity.

The collective consciousness of the archetype is unconscious to the natural mind. But as Jung and Swedenborg have shown it is possible to become conscious of archetypes through symbolization and correspondences.

God gives *Sacred Scripture* in order to instruct human beings about the archetypes in the afterlife, and to instruct us on how to lead a life that can produce a personality with an intact or healthy archetype structure.

21

In *Sacred Scripture* God addresses simultaneously both our spiritual mind and our natural mind. People familiar with *Sacred Scripture* know that God speaks in two different ways. The majority of verses present the history of events in which God selects a prophet, speaks to him, and commands him to write down what God said and what the prophet witnessed around him.

The identity of the participants to various miracles is also given. As well, God reveals the commandments that everyone must obey under threat of damnation in eternity. This may be called the historical portion of *Sacred Scripture*. It is also the literal meaning of the verses. This is addressed to our natural mind in which we think with material ideas that apply to the physical conditions on earth.

22

Our spiritual mind reacts to the correspondences of the literal verses that are read in our natural mind through the sensory input of the physical body reading the physical book. But instead of hearing the historical and natural descriptions as we do in our natural mind, we now hear the mental correspondences to these events, places, names, numbers, and so forth. Each of the details that are mentioned in the literal sense of the verse has its own mental correspondence, or as Jung would say, its archetypal significance.

In other words, God speaks to our spiritual mind in the language of symbology and correspondences. Each physical detail in the literal verses reveals something about our psychology in relation to God.

For instance when the natural mind reads that *"God made it to rain"*, the spiritual mind transforms it to *"God gives instruction and knowledge"*. Or when the natural mind reads that someone "shot a bow", the spiritual mind thinks of fighting a temptation. Or when the natural mind reads that there is a "famine in the land", the spiritual mind thinks that there is a want of non-material ideas due to the individual's rejection of God's commandments and living contrary to them.

23

Swedenborg demonstrates that all the Books of the *Old and New Testaments* use the same double communication, one natural on the outside literal portion, and the other spiritual on the interior psychological meaning. What is most remarkable is that the same translation process of correspondences applies to all 66 Books of the Bible despite the historical fact that they were written independently by dozens of writers who were not familiar with each other over the course of two thousand years.

And also remarkable to me is that when I took a few samples of text of *Sacred Scripture* in other major religions I confirmed that the correspondences are similar. In other words, in the implied psychological sense God talks the same way to all humanity of all religions and times. The spiritual mind of all human beings is not divided, as is the natural mind that is immersed in different historical religions.

24

God is instructing our rational mind in its own operations, its psychology and mental anatomy. This is essential knowledge for our regeneration and individuation, and for our mental growth and development from birth to eternity. This body of psychological knowledge about the necessary regeneration of our personality may be called *theistic psychology*, or the psychology from God.

Jung and Swedenborg are prolific contributors to theistic psychology, though they did not use this phrase. The study and knowledge of theistic psychology involves studying the psychological meaning of God's Word and of talking with God. In this process of conscious mental co-presence or intersubjectivity, God enlightens our natural mind so that we can perceive and understand non-material truths and ideas. Theistic psychology teaches non-material facts and principles that are contained in the psychological meaning of the *Word of God*.

25

In the afterlife we live in the mental world of eternity, which Swedenborg called the "spiritual world" and Jung called the "psychic world". This is the world into which our mind is born with our immortal spiritual body that operates our natural and spiritual mind. This living spiritual body is functionally connected to the inert physical body on earth, which is a copy or model in material form of the spiritual body, which is not material but mental and substantial. Mental stuff is a real substance out of which our mind's anatomy is made. Physical matter is temporary and not living, but mental substance is eternal and living.

We can activate and move the inert physical body on earth through our thoughts and feelings in the spiritual body, which is in mental eternity. When the physical body on earth stops functioning, our spiritual body is liberated from being restricted to earth conditions. For the first time we can then see the afterlife societies in mental eternity.

26

Human life is the organic unfolding of the individual's immortal biography such as God sets it at birth. It is the individual's soul that contains that unique biography. The soul gradually unfolds itself, liberating its unique packet of human potentials.

God's mental substance is organic, human, eternal, and infinite. *All creation was made out of this mental substance*. First, God formed the mental world of eternity into the shape and structure of the human body. All locations in the afterlife world can be marked as to their relative location through the anatomy of the body. Swedenborg discovered afterlife societies in "the province of the right eye", or in "the stomach", or in "the region below the buttocks", and so on.

What is most remarkable is his discovery that the chief archetype characterizing a particular society is described by the physiological functions of the organ in which they are located in the afterlife world. For example, the people who were located in the "region of the stomach" were able to induce anxiety in anyone who was brought into telepathic communication with them. Or, the couples that were located in the "womb" area of the afterlife world were most solicitous in their care for infants who lose their physical body shortly after birth. The spiritual bodies of these children need to be taken care of and properly instructed so that the person can grow into an adult mind.

The relative arrangement of afterlife societies in the shape of the human body creates the *Grand Human*, for mutual love societies, and the *Grand Monster*, for self-love societies.

Theistic Psychology - Expanding The Narrative Series—Volume 4
Correspondences, Synchronicity, And Self-Witnessing

List Of Sections For All 12 Volumes

Section Contents Of Volumes: 1 to 12
This List is reproduced at the end of each Volume

Volume 1
Individuation And Collective Consciousness: Discovering Our Immortal Self In A Telepathic Universe

Preface To The Series

1. Jung And Swedenborg: The New Frontier Of Psychology
2. The Historic Fall Of Consciousness
3. The Mental World And The Afterlife World
4. Knowing The Psychic Forces In Our Personality
5. Sacred Scripture And Personality
6. What Makes Sacred Scripture Sacred?
7. The Collective Unconscious And Collective Consciousness
8. Jung's Explanations Of Ego, Self, Spirit, Consciousness, And Unconscious
9. Individuation And Collective Consciousness
10. Consciousness And Sacred Scripture
11. Our Mind Is A Body
12. Collective Consciousness And The Telepathic Universe
13. The Chain Of Uses: From First To Last
14. You Are Immortal, Omnipresent, and Omniscient
15. Instantaneous Creation, Freedom, And Responsibility
16. God And The Anatomy of Infinity
17. God And The Spiritual World Of Eternity
18. Born Into The Afterlife Of Mental Eternity
19. Anatomy Of Our Immortal Spiritual Body
20. Our Temporary Physical Body On Earth
21. What About My Pets?
22. What News From Earth
23. What News From Heaven
24. More On Swedenborg
25. More On Jung
26. Encountering God
27. Gravity And Love
28. Archetypes Of Love
30. Meaning Is The Embodiment Of Experiencing.
31. Archetypes As Emotional Meaning
32. Where Do Our Thoughts Come From?

293

Theistic Psychology - Expanding The Narrative Series—Volume 4
Correspondences, Synchronicity, And Self-Witnessing

33. Jung And Swedenborg's Relationship To God
34. Jung On God And On Theologians
35. Opposition To Swedenborg's Works
36. The Last Judgment
37. Jung's Psychology With Non-material Ideas

List Of Sections For All Volumes
God, Immortality And Theistic Psychology Series
Other Books by Leon James
About the Author
End Of Volume 1

Volume 2
Personality And Afterlife Lifestyles: Getting Ready For Eternity

Preface To The Series

1. Positive And Negative Archetypes
2. Astrology, Personality, And The Grand Human
3. We Are Linked To Each Other
4. The Historical Fall That Killed Dual Consciousness
5. The Telepathic Universe
6. The Vertical Community
7. Tragic Consequences Of Ego-Loves
8. We Are Always On Stage, We Are Never Alone
9. Human Beings Are Immortal Mental Beings
10. Swedenborg's Dual Consciousness
11. Recapitulating The Narrative Of Theistic Psychology
12. Existential Illusions
13. Psycho-Geography Of Archetypes
14. Dual Consciousness
15. Ants And Termites
16. The Joy Of Individuation
17. The Grand Human And Earths In the Universe
18. Individual Consciousness Needs The Collective Unconscious
19. The Yin/Yang of Individual And Collective Consciousness
20. Killing Off Death
21. Consciousness, Sweet Love, And The Afterlife
22. Individuation Is The Lifting Of Restrictions To Omnipresence
23. The Embodiment Of Archetypes In Afterlife Societies
24. Our Personality Chooses Heaven or Hell
25. To Be Human Is To Be Omnipresent And Omniscient
26. Regeneration And Individuation

27. Jung On The Process Of Individuation
28. What's Wrong With Self-love?
29. Selfish Traits And Infernal Fire
30. Trouble Archetypes
31. What Are The Evils That Need To Be Regenerated?
32. Biological Definition Of Good And Evil
33. Collective Consciousness And The Telepathic Universe
34. Individuation And Collective Consciousness
35. Consciousness As Mental Substance
36. De-Individuation And Mental Hell
37. Our Spiritual Body In Eternity Needs A Physical body On Earth
38. The 12 Anatomical Layers of a Human Being
39. Born With Two Bodies
40. Why The Illusion of Selfhood Is Necessary
41. The Illusion of Selfhood And De-Individuation

List Of Sections for All Volumes
God, Immortality And Theistic Psychology Series
Other Books by Leon James
About the Author
End of Volume 2

Volume 3
Sacred Scripture, Dreams, And Archetypes The Secret Connection

Preface To The Series

1. The Secret Connection And The Secret Knowledge
2. Thinking With Material And Non-Material Ideas
3. Extraverted And Introverted Modes of Thinking
4. Three Levels Of Thinking And Loving
5. How God Manages Our Mind
6. Learning The Mental Skill Of Spiritualizing Everything
7. Spatial And Non-Spatial World
8. God Viewed With Non-Material Ideas
9. Anatomy Of Mind: Natural, Rational, Spiritual
10. Becoming An Individual In A Collective Universe
11. Practicing Thinking With Non-Material Ideas
12. Practice Exercises For Thinking With Non-Material Ideas
13. The Artist And The Collective Unconscious
14. Symbolizing In Dreaming
15. Dreaming Consciousness And Our Dreaming Body
16. Theistic Psycholinguistics

17. Idioms Shape Our Thinking Through Built-In Correspondences
   Physical-Mental Correspondences In Our Daily Speaking and Thinking
18. Bible Animals Teach Us What Inclinations Are In Our Personality
   Correspondences Between Human Personality And Animal Archetypes
19. Taxonomy Of Spiritual Neologisms
20. Correspondences In Sacred Scripture
   (1) What are "correspondences"
   (2) Why we need a physical body on earth
   (3) How the natural mind and spiritual mind interact
   (4) How correspondences influence our thinking
   (5) Preparation for regeneration
21. The Conscious And The Unconscious
22. And God Spoke, And There Was Light
23. God Is Within You
24. Psychology of Regeneration In Sacred Scripture
25. Theistic Psychology Vs. Biblical Counseling and Therapy
26. Rational Theistic Self-Analysis (RTS)
27. The Seven Steps Of Psychological Regeneration
28. Synthesizing Jung And Swedenborg
29. Our Dreams Are Produced By Afterlife Societies
30. The Two Levels In Our Natural Mind
31. The Bridge of As-of Self

List Of Sections For All Volumes
Other Books by Leon James
About the Author
End Of Volume 3

Volume 4
Correspondences, Synchronicity, And The Spiritual Discipline Of Self-Witnessing

Preface To The Series

1. Selecting Our Afterlife Society
2. Lifestyles In The Afterlife of Mental Eternity
   There Are Three Heavens
   Collective Societies
   There Are Three Heavens
   Clothes In Heaven
   What Personality We Need For Heaven
   Palaces, Streets, And Government In Heaven
   Children In The Afterlife
   Marriage In The Afterlife]

Selfish Traits And Infernal Fire
Afterlife Hell Societies
3. Free Full Text Access To Swedenborg's Writings
4. Jung's Psychology Of The Collective Unconscious
5. The Collective Unconscious
6. Jung On The Thoughts In Our Mind
7. The Archetypes of Afterlife Societies
8. Dual Consciousness And The Unity Of Opposites
9. Explanation Of Key Concepts Used In Theistic Psychology
    Afterlife, Dying, Death
    Archetypes And The Soul
    Born Into Mental Eternity: Spiritual Body, Physical Body
    Collective Conscious And The Collective Unconscious
    Consciousness
    Family Spirits
    Heaven And Hell
    Individuation
    Infinity, God
    Mental Substance: Love And Truth
    Mental Anatomy
    Personality, Symbolism, And Talking With God
    Psychology
    Regeneration Of Personality
    Theistic Animism
    Theistic Psychology
    Uses: Selfish And Altruistic
10. Conclusions From What Precedes
11. Synchronicity And Correspondences
12. Archetypes In Sacred Scripture
13. Durkheim's Description of Collective Consciousness
14. Natural Psychology And Theistic Psychology
    Anatomical Chart 1 The Mental World of Eternity Viewed in Successive Order of Discrete Degrees
    Anatomical Chart 2 The Mental World of Eternity Viewed in Simultaneous Order of Discrete Degrees
    Anatomical Chart 3 Body-Mind Correspondences For Anatomical Layers 4 to 9
    Illustration And Application To The Growth Of The Mind
15. Post-Materialist Science And Theistic Psychology
16. Premises And Methodology In Psychology Science
17. Methodology In Theistic Psychology
    (1) The Method Of Paraphrastic Transformations
    (2) The Method Of Correspondences
    (3) The Method Of Substitution
    (4) The Method Of Discourse Thinking
    (5) The Method Of Self-Witnessing

    (6) The Technique Of Graphic Methodology
18. Swedenborg And Jung: Foundation Stones For Theistic Psychology
19. Jung On Religion Vs. Psychology
20. Jung Writes On Dogmatism
21. The Mental Technology Of Self-Witnessing
22. Regeneration Self-Witnessing Methodology
23. Self-witnessing What We Do In Talking
24. We Are Never Alone: The Vertical Community
25. Self-Witnessing The Threefold Self: Affective, Cognitive, Sensorimotor
26. Sudden Memory And The Method Of Discourse Thinking
27. Our Evils Cannot Be Removed
28. Metanoid Self-Witnessing Or Being An Audience To Yourself
29. Macro-Behaviors Are Regenerated By Means Of Micro-Behaviors
30. Examples From The Daily Round Archives
31. Swedenborg On Self-witnessing And Regeneration
32. The Daily Round Archives Classification Scheme (DRA)
33. Summary And Overview

List Of Sections For All Volumes
Other Books by Leon James
About the Author
End Of Volume 4

Volume 5
Regeneration And The Vertical Community: How God Manages Our Psychological States

Preface To The Series

1. Sacred Scripture And Theistic Psychology
2. Archetypes And Mental Anatomy
3. Physiological Correspondences Between Mind and Body
4. Citizens Of Two Worlds
5. Our Natural Mind And Our Rational Mind
6. Regeneration And The Split-Brain Race
7. Character Reformation And Regeneration
8. Non-Material Permanence And Material Impermanence
9. Mental Substance And Our Immortal Mental Substance Body
10. The Seven Days of Creation; The Seven Phases of Regeneration
11. Our Worst Enemy: Ego-Loves
12. The Loves Of Insanity
13. Selfish Love Versus Altruistic Love
14. The Kingdom Of God Is Within

15. Jung on God, The Fall, And Atheism
16. Jung: I Must Become A Christ
17. Personality Regeneration
18. Christ's Archetypical Life
19. Individuation and Regeneration
20. The Christian Message
21. The Fallen Ego
22. The Day of Judgment
23. Jung's God-Image
24. The Kingdom Of God Is Within You
25. Integrating the Thinking Of Jung and Swedenborg
26. Self-love And Its Spiritual Anatomy   138
27. Individuality, Consciousness, And Relationship
28. Individuation: Living The Symbolic Life
29. Male Mind, Female Mind
30. The Two Psychological Phases In The Afterlife
31. Theistic Psychology, Sacred Scripture, And Correspondences
32. Why God Allows Evils
33. The Individual And The collective
34. Non-Theistic Psychology vs. Anti-Theistic Psychology
35. Reconciling Naturalistic And Theistic Psychology
36. The Premises Of Theistic Psychology
37. The Difference Between Logical And Rational
38. Jung On God-Man And Psychology
39. Jung On Archetypes
40. Vertical Community: The Presence Of Others
41. The Politics Of Atheism In Science
42. Jung On Judaism And Freud
43. Dual Consciousness And The Fall
44. What Is Mental Eternity? Are We There Now?
45. Psychology Without A Soul
46. Individuation And Remains
47. Jung: God Is Reality Itself
48. On The Psychological Function Of Error
49. Past, Present, And Future
50. Instantaneous Creation
51. Basic Propositions In Theistic Psychology
52. Immortality: There Is No Exit From Living
53. The Vertical Community
54. Spiritual Significance Of Social Networking
55. Ego To Ego
56. Anatomical Levels Of Our Mind
    Chart 3: Body-Mind Relationships In the Mental Body
57. More On The Incarnation Event
58. Technology And De-Individuation

Theistic Psychology - Expanding The Narrative Series—Volume 4
Correspondences, Synchronicity, And Self-Witnessing

59. Archetypes And The Soul

List Of Sections For All Volumes
Other Books by Leon James
About the Author
End Of Volume 5

Volume 6
Natural and Spiritual Marriage: Moving Into Eternity Together

Preface To The Series

1. The Mental Anatomy Of Marriage
2. Jung On Male And Female Psychology
3. Swedenborg On Love and Sexuality In Marriage
4. Formation Of Man And Woman As Reciprocal Units
5. The Oneminded Pair
6. Husband-Centered, Equity-Centered, And Wife-Centered Interactions
7. Spiritual Marriage Within And Between Partners
8. Swedenborg On General Principles In Marriage
9. Natural and Spiritual Conjunction In Marriage
10. Ego-Loves And Ego-Insanities: Male Mind, Female Mind
11. Anatomical Diagrams Of Marriage
12. Married Love And Sex In Afterlife Societies
13. The Origins Of Male Virility
14. The Happiness Of Conjugial Couples
15. The Collective Self Of Eternally Married Partners
16. Conversational Analysis In Marriage
17. Studying How Married Partners Talk
18. Practicing Writing Couples Dialog
    Husband-Centered Interactions
    Equity-Centered Interactions
    Wife-Centered Interactions
19. Writing Dialog For A Series Of Scenes
    First Sample Dialog: Husband-Centered
    Second Sample Dialog: Husband-Centered
    Third Sample Dialog: Equity-Centered
    Fourth Sample Dialog: Wife-Centered
    Fifth Sample Dialog: Wife-Centered
    Sixth Sample Dialog: Wife-Centered
    Exercise 1
    Exercise 2
20. Disjunctive And Conjunctive Replies Of Husbands

1) Negation, Denial, Refusal
2) Disloyalty, Secrecy, Lies
3) Abusiveness, Swearing, Yelling
4) After Disturbing His Wife, Not Making Up Sufficiently
21. Checklist Exercise For Couples

List Of Sections For All Volumes
God, Immortality And Theistic Psychology Series
Other Books by Leon James
About the Author
End Of Volume 6

Volume 7
Sayings And Aphorisms In Theistic Psychology Emanuel Swedenborg, Carl Jung, And Leon James

1. Sayings of Emmanuel Swedenborg -- Entries 1 to 77
2. Sayings Of Carl Jung -- Entries 1 to 215
    Accepting Death
    Death as a Goal
    Life After Death
    God Alone is Real
    Why I Am Not A Catholic
    The Nature Of God
    I Don't Need To Believe In God, I know
    A Personal God
    Religious Experience
    What Happens After Death
    One Needs Death
    Descent Into Hell
    Preparation For Death
    Death is Part of Life
    Death is the Bridge
    Devil and Neurosis
    Immortality and the Soul
    Christianity and Atheism
    Battling The Demons: The Life Of The Shadow
3. Sayings Of Leon James: Parts A to D
Preface
    Part A: Love, God, Regeneration, Afterlife -- Entries 1 to 216
    Part B: Truth, Sacred Scripture, Science -- Entries (1) to (166)
    Part C: Aphorisms On Love and Marriage -- Entries (1) to (99)
    Preface

Theistic Psychology - Expanding The Narrative Series—Volume 4
Correspondences, Synchronicity, And Self-Witnessing

Part D: Experiencing Poetry Insights -- Entries 1 to 1337
Preface

List Of Sections For All Volumes
Other Books by Leon James
About the Author
End of Volume 7

Volume 8
Topics And References in Theistic Psychology

1. Afterlife Societies, Their Lifestyles, And Personalities
2. List of All Sections For 18 Volumes Of Principles Of Theistic Psychology
3. Subject Index For 18 Volumes Of Principles Of Theistic Psychology
4. List Of Intellectual Discoveries
    Pre-Swedenborgian Ideas (for the period 1960-1980)
    Post-Swedenborgian Ideas (for the period 1981-2018 and onward)
5. List Of Documents Sent To The Swedenborg Library Reserve Shelf, Bryn Athyn
6. List Of Publications
7. Annotated Directory Of Articles And Books By Leon James

List Of Sections For All Volumes
God, Immortality And Theistic Psychology Series
Other Books by Leon James
About the Author
End Of Volume 8

Volume 9
Schematic Diagrams And Charts In Theistic Psychology

1. Reformation, Enlightenment, Regeneration
2. Freud, Jung, Swedenborg: Overlap in Word Usage
3. Overlap Of Mental Levels with Sacred Scripture
4. Sensorimotor, Cognitive, and Affective Operations
5. Integrating Technological, Mental, and Social Systems
6. Levels Of Mind and Mental Operations
7. The Circuit of Behaviors in Daily Activities
8. Social, Technological and Psychological Systems
9. Natural and Spiritual Understanding of Sacred Scripture
10. Factual, Intelligent, and Wise: Three Levels of Human Operation

11. Affective, Cognitive, and Sensorimotor Interaction in Behavior
12. Daily Emotional Spin Cycle in Feelings, Thoughts, and Actions
13. Affective and Cognitive Inversion in Man and Woman
14. The 12 Layers of Mental Anatomy in Successive and Simultaneous Order
15. Natural and Spiritual Perspective in Man and Woman
16. Correspondence Between Physical and Mental Body
17. Schematic Representation of a Human Being
18. Male and Female Mental Anatomy
19. Two Stages of Unity Between Man and Woman
20. Mental Genetics for Masculine and Feminine
21. Anatomy of the Mental Body
22. Materialism, Humanism, Theism: Stages of Development
23. The 12 Anatomical Layers of a Human Being
24. Mental Anatomy of Conjunction in Marriage
25. Personality Development With Stages of Growth
26. Three Phases in Marriage: Dominance, Equity, Unity
27. Maturation and Regeneration of Our Natural Mind
28. Consciousness Prior and After Regeneration
29. The Natural Mind in Successive and Simultaneous Order
30. How Mental Anatomy Integrates with Technology
31. Relationship Between Successive and Simultaneous
32. Dominance, Equity, Unity: Male and Female Conjunction
33. Spirituality, Regeneration, and Divine Speech
34. Affection, Thought, Speech: End, Cause, Effect
35. Graphic Methodology: Patterns of Anatomic Correspondences
36. Elevation of Consciousness Through Reception of Divine Speech
37. Graphic Methodology: Three Levels of Meaning in Sacred Scripture
38. Three Levels of Consciousness Before and After Regeneration
39. Natural and Spiritual Marriage Prior and After Regeneration
40. Spiritual Sun: Source of Spiritual Heat and Light in Mind
41. Mental Anatomy and Phases of Regeneration
42. Three Levels of Good and Truth in Mental Anatomy
43. Theistic Psychology, Sacred Scripture, Religion, Literacy
44. The Four Options on the Daily Emotional Spin cycle
45. Correspondence Between General, Specific, Particular
46. Spiritual Psychobiology of Marriage: Two Phases of Conjunction
47. Two Phases of Marriage Union: External, Internal
48. Mental Anatomy: Descending and Ascending Consciousness
49. Celestial and Spiritual Race: Sensuous and Rational Consciousness
50. Old Will, New Will: Mystical vs. Rational Consciousness
51. Ritual Faith, Mystic Faith, Rational Faith
52. Theistic Psychology vs. Religion
53. Vertical Community: Celestial, Spiritual, Natural
54. God, Levels of Mind, and the Descending Flow of Life
55. Child Development, Mental Anatomy, and Influx

56. Graphic Methodology: Ennead For 36 Mental Zones
57. Spiritual Geography Map with Jacob's 12 Children
58. Sensuous and Rational Consciousness in Mental Development
59. Mental Levels and Anatomical Zones in Human Development
60. Historical Ages and Collective Consciousness
61. Stages in Human Development and the Circuit of Consciousness
62. Ethnosemantic Hexagram And Degrees Of The Mind
63. Degrees Of Consciousness And Intellectual Content
64. Descending And Ascending Paths For Undergoing Regeneration
65. Descending And Ascending Paths For The Regenerate
66. World Of Spirits = The Mind
67. Theistic Psychology And Religion
68. Conjugial Influx In The Wife
69. Conjugial Influx In The Wife And Husband
70. Love And Wisdom In The External And Internal Mind
71. Divine Celestial And Divine Human
72. Anatomy Of Man And woman
73. Conjunctive Vs. Disjunctive And Personal Vs. Formal
74. Map Of The Daily Emotional Spin Cycle
75. Relationship Between Sacred Scripture, Religion, And Theistic Psychology
76. Evolutionary Steps In The Development Of Religion
77. Map Of Mental Eternity In The Afterlife
78. Anatomical Levels Of Consciousness, Heaven, And Hell
79. Daily Emotional Spin Cycle: Feeling, Thinking, Doing
80. Three Levels Of Information: Knowledge, Intelligence, Wisdom
81. Model Of Ecological Constructionism
82. The Negative Spin Cycle In Daily Emotions
83. The Positive Spin Cycle In Daily Emotions
84. The Four Options And The Two Bridges
85. The Red Bridge
86. The Blue Bridge
87. Social Biological Technology In Second Life Social Practices
88. Urgent, Persistent, Intermittent Information Needs
89. Affective, Cognitive, Sensorimotor Systems
90. Causes And Solutions To Aggressive Driving
91. Affective Load, Information Needs, Affective Engagement
92. Burnham: Anatomy Of External And Internal Mind
93. Burnham: Anatomy Of Mind In Three Degrees
94. Information Literacy: Identification, Modeling, And Loyalty
95. 12 Steps In The Daily Emotional Spin Cycle
96. Socialization And Taxonomy In Communication
97. Microdescriptions In Social Communication
98. Graphic Methodology: Nine Zones Of Externalization And Internalization
99. Graphic Methodology: Externalization And Internalization
100. Interior Dialog And External Transactions

Theistic Psychology - Expanding The Narrative Series—Volume 4
Correspondences, Synchronicity, And Self-Witnessing

101. Graphic Methodology: Biography, Personality, Behavior
102. Graphic Methodology: Biography, Personality, Behavior
103. Graphic Methodology: Sociolinguistics And Psycholinguistics
103. Graphic Methodology: Self, Life, Issues
104. Social Categories
105. Social Role, Schedule, Location
106. Social Role, Survival, Intellectual Climate
107. Sounds, Normalcy, Entertainment, Talk
108. Group Dynamics: Influence Through The Presence Of Others
109. Personality, Attitudes, Interpersonal Relations
110. Zimbardo: Psychology And Life
111. Interior Dialog, Standardized Imaginings, Relationship Management
112. Influence On Behavior Through Presence Of Others
113. Community Management With Enhancing Forces
114. Collective, Automatic, And Integrated Self 127
115. Graphic Methodology: The 12 Masters Of Social Psychology
116. Analysis Of Talk On The Daily Round
117. Bilingual Transfer Effects
118. Model Of Bilingual Description
118. Model Of Bilingual Transfer Effects
119. Model Of Compound And Coordinate Bilingualism
120. Model Of Bilingualism, Ethnocentrism, And Orientation
121. Factors: Socio-cultural, Instructional, and Learner
122. Approaches And Methods In Research
123. First And second Language Acquisition
124. Daily Round Self-witnessing
125. Graphic Methodology: Source, Cause, Effect
126. Graphic Methodology: Highest, Intermediate, Lowest
127. Graphic Methodology Quiz On Personality Development
128. Graphic Methodology Quiz 1 On Money Thoughts
129. Graphic Methodology Quiz 2 On Money Thoughts
130. Graphic Methodology On Food Behavior Change
131. Graphic Methodology On Dynamic Concepts Of Personality
132. Graphic Methodology Quiz On Negative Emotions
133. Graphic Methodology On Nine Masters Of Social Psychology
134. Graphic Methodology On Performance And Behavior
135. Graphic Methodology On Behavior Change
136. Graphic Methodology On Pragmatics And Administration
137. Graphic Methodology On Socio-Psychological Futures
138. Graphic Methodology On Intention And Utterance In Language Use
140. Striving, Planning, And Mapping Issues On The Daily Round
141. Graphic Methodology: Language Teachers and Communicative Competence
142. Graphic Methodology: Group Dynamics And Goal Achievement
142b. Graphic Methodology: Culture, Socialization, And Self
143. Venn Diagram: Overlap In Loves And Reasonings In A Dyad

144. A Three-Factor Theory Of Social competence
145. Symbolic Representation Of Social Competence Theory
146. Localizing Daily Round Events in Time And Space
147. Schematic Of Daily Round Map
148. Sociomap Of Buying Pants
149. Sociomap Of Buying A Car
150. Topical Emphases In Three Books On Language Teaching
151. Sociodynamics And Social Behaviorism
152. Social Occasions In Bird Aviary
153. Zones Of Social Co-Presence
154. Schema Of Leon James Home Page With Student Reports
155. The WIB Home Page Schema
156. Ethnosemantic Trigrams
157. The Color Hexagram In Ethnosemantic Structures
158. Sets Of Ethnosemantic Trigram Structures
159. Ethnosemantic Trigram Structures For Correspondences
160. The Cube Of Understanding In Ethnosemantic Structures
161. Quadrangular, Triangular, And Line Arrangement In Ethnosemantic Structures
161. Quadrangular Solution For Watergate In Ethnosemantic Structures (part 1)
161. Quadrangular Solution For Watergate In Ethnosemantic Structures (part 2)
162. WIB Student Schema For World Ideas Bank
163. Leon James And Students Home Page Schema (part 1)
164. Leon James And Students Home Page Schema (part 2)
164. Leon James And Students Home Page Schema (part 3)
165. Graphic Methodology: Sociological Research Colloquium
166. Personality Map
167. Evils, Falsities, Goods, Truths, And Striving
168. Heavenly And Hellish Dynamics In Personality
169. Religion, Redemption, Truth, And The Word
170. Religion, Death, Atheism, And The Torah
171. Ego: Functions, Evolution, Bodies (part 1)
172. Ego: Functions, Evolution, Bodies (part 2)
173. Male And Female Anatomy Of Love And Wisdom
174. Regeneration And The Divine Human
175. Road Rage Quick Test
176. Driving Informatics
177. The 72 Coordinates And Movements In Ethnosemantics (part 1)
178. The 72 Coordinates And Movements In Ethnosemantics (part 2)
179. The 72 Coordinates And Movements In Ethnosemantics (part 3)
180. The 72 Coordinates And Movements In Ethnosemantics (part 4)
181. The 72 Coordinates And Movements In Ethnosemantics (part 5)
182. The 72 Coordinates And Movements In Ethnosemantics (part 6)
183. The 72 Coordinates And Movements In Ethnosemantics (part 7)
184. The 72 Coordinates And Movements In Ethnosemantics (part 8)
184. Table of Correspondences Between Physical Space and Mental Space

185. Synergy And Correspondence Between Physical And Mental Body
186. Schematic Representation Of A Human Being
187. Schematic Representation Of Male And Female Mental Anatomy
188. Two Stages Of Unity In Marriage
189. Mental Anatomy Of Man and Woman
190. Anatomy Of The Mental Body
191. Discrete Layers Of The Mental Body
192. Consciousness Themes Prior And During Regeneration
193. The 12 Layers Of Human Mental Anatomy
194. The 12 Anatomical Layers of Creation, Existence, and Reality
195. Maturation and Regeneration of Consciousness

List Of Sections For All Volumes
God, Immortality And Theistic Psychology Series
Other Books by Leon James
About the Author
End Of Volume 9

Volume 10
Articles In Theistic Psychology Part 1 of 3

Foreword

Article 1: Ten Rational Conclusions From The Proposition That God Exists
    (1) God is a Person, at once Divine and Human
    (2) God's Omnipotence Must Control Every Event
    (3) God is Perfect in Love and Rationality
    (4) There are Two Worlds, Material in Time And Non-Material in Eternity
    (5) Humans are Born Dual Citizens, In Time and in Eternity
    (6) The Eternity of the Afterlife is Our Mental World Now
    (7) We Are Born With Heaven and Hell in Our Mind
    (8) Heaven is a State of Marriage Between Soul Mates
    (9) Divine Speech as Sacred Scripture Produces Consciousness and Enlightenment
    (10) Salvation, Regeneration, Wisdom Are Attained By Spiritual Discipline

Article 2: Theological and Psychological Aspects of Mental Health: The Marriage of Good and Truth
    Introduction
    Psycho-Spiritual Aspects of Mental Health
    Levels of Transcendence: The Breadth and Height of the Self
    Applications: Modern Psychological Concepts and Mental Health Symptoms Mapped unto Swedenborg's Nomenclature

Symbolism In Dreams And Myths
Conclusion
Endnotes

Article 3: Swedenborg's Dual Consciousness
- Abstract
- Introduction on Swedenborg
- The Issue of Consciousness in Dualism
- The Dual Universe And The Dual Mind
- Spiritual Consciousness And Love Substance
- Resuscitation Of Consciousness In The Dying Process
- Consciousness Raising Applications To Daily Life
- References

Article 4: The Coming Swedenborgian Revolution In The Social Sciences And Humanities
- Introduction
- Scientific Revolutions Are Normal
- Where The Revolutions Will Occur
- The Negative Bias Versus The Positive Bias In Science
- Swedenborg's Triune Model Of The Universe

Article 5: Overcoming Objections to Swedenborg's Writings Through the Development of Scientific Dualism
- Introduction
- Scientific Revelations
- Spiritual Revelations
- How Swedenborg Has Been Portrayed
- Evaluating Swedenborg
- Resistance To Swedenborg
- Is Swedenborg's Dualism Scientific?
- The Six Minimal Premises Of Dualist Science
- Extracting Dualist Concepts From Swedenborg's Writings
- It Is Not Known Revealed
- Scientific Puzzles For Dualist Science
- The Two Main Branches of Dualist Science
- Conclusion
- References

Article 6: Carl Jung and Alcoholics Anonymous: Is a Theistic Psychopathology Feasible?

Article 7: Two Perspectives on Swedenborg's Writings: Secular and Religious
- The Essentials Of The Religious Perspective
- The Issue Of Collateral Readings

Theistic Psychology - Expanding The Narrative Series—Volume 4
Correspondences, Synchronicity, And Self-Witnessing

    Scientific Revolutions Change Things
    Gurdjieff And Spiritual Growth Groups
    The Affirmative Principle in Science

List Of Sections For All Volumes
God, Immortality And Theistic Psychology Series
Other Books by Leon James
About the Author
End Of Volume 10

Volume 11
Articles In Theistic Psychology Part 2 of 3

Foreword

Article 8: The Reciprocal Relation Between Science and Revelation
    The Controversy
    Pre-modern Versus Modern Minds
    The Significance For Science Of The Second Advent
    Traditional vs. New Christian Mentality
    Science Education And Understanding the Writings
    Scientific Paradigm Shift To Dualism
    The Writings As the Word: Secular and Religious View
    Is Science Limited?
    Scientific Revelations
    New Church Ministers As Scientists
    The Writings Contain Scientific Revelations
    Swedenborg's Dualist Science
    The Mental Spiritual Connection
    Dualist Science And the Writings
    Four Ways Of Intellectualizing About God
    When Prophecy Fails Science
    Footnotes

Article 9: New Church Education With Dualist Concepts
    Introduction
    Integrating Secular And Religious Concepts
    Principles For An Integrated Model Of Instruction
    Constructing Integrated Concepts 43
    Quotations From New Church Academy Educators

Article 10: Freud, Jung, and Swedenborg
    Introduction

Table 1a: Keywords for Freud, Jung, and Swedenborg
Table 1b: Intense Topic Focus
Figure 1: Contrasts and Overlap in Topic Focus for Freud, Jung, and Swedenborg
Table 2 Comparing Freud, Jung, and Swedenborg on Various Characteristics
Freud and the Individual Unconscious
Freud's Atheism and Materialism
Stages of Evolution of An Individual
Kant, Emerson, And William James
Religious Psychology
Descartes And Leibniz In The Afterlife
End Notes

Article 11: The Scientific Meaning of Christmas
　　　The Incarnation Event: God Enters the World Of History And Science
　　　Completion of the Creation Of The Human Race

Article 12: Anti-Semitism and Holocaust Theology
　　　1. Tenets Of Holocaust Theology
　　　2. The Victims In The Afterlife
　　　3. The Spiritual Meaning Of Anti-Semitism
　　　4. The Old Testament's View Of The Chosen People
　　　5. All Old Testament Details Represent The Lord
　　　6. The Meaning Of "Jews" In The New Church Mind
　　　7. Anti-Semitism Is An Evil Love Of The Unregenerate Mind

Article 13: A Brief History of God and Humanity
　　　God And Levels of Creation
　　　Feelings Determine The Quality Of Our Afterlife
　　　The Incarnation Event
　　　Regeneration And Theistic Psychology
　　　Why Is There Hell

Article 14: The New Evolution Of Rational Spirituality Of God
　　　The Mental World Is The World of Eternity
　　　Our Life in Eternity
　　　Why We Need Sacred Scripture
　　　The Hidden Correspondential Sense Of Sacred Scripture
　　　Why We Need Theistic Psychology
　　　The New Evolution In Rational Consciousness Of God

Article 15: The Spiritual Content of Yoga
　　　The Correspondences In Yoga Sayings
　　　Correspondential Meaning of Asanas (Postures)
　　　The Correspondential Meaning of Mudras

Theistic Psychology - Expanding The Narrative Series—Volume 4
Correspondences, Synchronicity, And Self-Witnessing

    The Correspondential Meaning of Breath and Breathing
    Breathing Explained In Swedenborg's Writings
    Correspondences To Body Positions
    Correspondences In Hindi Sacred Scripture
    Quotes from the Bhagavad Gita and Their Spiritual Meaning
    The Correspondential Meaning of the Upanishads

List Of Sections For All Volumes
God, Immortality And Theistic Psychology Series
Other Books by Leon James
About the Author
End Of Volume 11

Volume 12
Articles In Theistic Psychology Part 3 of 3

Foreword

Article 16: Born Into Mental Eternity
    Abstract
    I Experience, Therefore I am
    The Dual Universe And Our Dual Citizenship
    Immortality And The Afterlife In Mental Eternity
    Implications For Human Consciousness
    The Theory Of Heaven And Hell
    References

Article 17: The New Focus on Theistic Psychotherapy
    Introduction
    Recent Developments
    Conclusion
    References

Article 18: The Affect of Symbols: Creating the Graphic Differential Through Synesthesia and Metaphor
    Abstract
    Introduction
    The Pan-cultural Semantic Differential
    Cross-Cultural Generality Of Visual-Verbal Synesthetic Tendencies
    The Cross-cultural Graphic Differential
    Method
    The Participating International Sites
    Results

Discussion
References
Figure 1: The Pictographic Opposites in the Graphic Differential
Table 1: The Fifty Stimulus Concepts

Article 19: Spiritual Psychobiology
- Abstract
- Introduction
- The Three Levels Of Behavior
- Swedenborg's Laws Of The Other World
- Behavioristic Criteria For A Scientific Theory
    1. Organicity
    2. Objective Reality
    3. Operational Definitions
    4. Empiricism
    5. Usefulness
- The Organic Basis Of All Phenomena
- The Method Of Psychobiological Correspondence
- Applications Of Swedenborg's System
- Behavioral Consequences Of Swedenborg's System

Article 20: Carl Jung's Psychology of Dreams and His View on Freud
- Introduction
- Freud And Jung On Dreams
- Jung's Dualism and Spirituality
- Jung's Depth Psychology
- Jung and Freud On The Unconscious
- The Activity Of The Collective Unconscious
- References

Article 21: Twelve Scientific Fallacies Enumerated In AC 5084: Implications for Science Education
1. The sun revolves around the earth.
2. The space between the stars and planets is a vacuum.
3. "Atoms are simple substances."
4. Nature is all there is in the universe (materialism).
5. Life ends at the death of the body.
6. The human race is on a continuum with animals.
7. It is the brain that senses our outside environment.
8. Light and heat originate in the sun (or stars).
9. Marriage evolved for adaptive purposes for the survival of the species.
10. Competitiveness is compatible with unity and love.
11 and 12. Being good to others for the sake of self merits reward, and faith alone merits salvation.

Implications For Natural And Social Science Education

Article 22: Hindu and Buddhist Nonduality: Is There A Conflict In The New Church Mind
    Introduction
    Incompatibility Between Nonduality And Duality
    Examples Of Clashing Concepts
    Danger Points

Article 23: Bryn Athyn: The City of Levites In The New Canaan
    Introduction
    Introduction by Leon Rhodes
    About Drs. Diane Nahl and Leon James
    Written questions submitted by the audience and read aloud by Dr. Ray Silverman
    End Notes

Article 24: How Regeneration Of The Individual Affects the Grand Human
    Our Thinking and Willing Affects The Entire Human Race
    The Special Role of Science in the Salvation of Humankind
    How Human Beings Are Conjoined To God
    Rational Consciousness And The Successive Levels of Regeneration
    The Greatest Of All Uses

List Of Sections For All Volumes
God, Immortality And Theistic Psychology Series
Other Books by Leon James
About the Author
End of Volume 12

Theistic Psychology - Expanding The Narrative Series—Volume 4
Correspondences, Synchronicity, And Self-Witnessing

God, Immortality And Theistic Psychology Series

REGENERATION MEDIA PUBLICATIONS KAILUA

© 2018 Leon James and Diane Nahl

Other Books by Leon James

Jung and Swedenborg on God and Life After Death (2015)

Reality Is Mental. Volume 1. Dreams and the Spiritual World. Integrating the Psychology of Jung and Swedenborg (2016)

Reality Is Mental. Volume 2. The RTS Personality. Rational Theistic Self-analysis (RTS) For Achieving Wholeness Here and in the Afterlife Based on the Theistic Psychology of Jung and Swedenborg (2016)

Reality Is Mental Volumes 3, 4, 5. The RTS Interviews: Rational Theistic Self-Analysis (RTS). Giving a New Perspective On God, Sacred Scripture, Regeneration, Collective Consciousness, Afterlife Lifestyles, and Spiritual Marriages. Based on the Theistic Psychology of Jung and Swedenborg (2017)

Experiencing Regeneration: Equipping Our Personality For Living In The Afterlife (2015)

The Conjoined Pair: Natural and Spiritual Marriage (2012)

A Man of the Field: Forming the New Church Mind in Today's World (2014)
  Volume 1: *Reformation: The Struggle Against Nonduality and Materialism*
  Volume 2: *Extracting the Spiritual Sense of the Writings*

Volume 3: *Spiritual Regeneration Disciplines For Daily Life*
Volume 4: Uses: *The New Church Mind In Old Age* (in preparation)

BOOKS POSTED ON THE WEB

The Correspondential Sense of Sacred Scriptures: Proving that there is a Unified Theistic Psychology Hidden within the World's Historical Sacred Writings (2009)
On the web at:
https://web.archive.org/web/20121129100050/http://www.soc.hawaii.edu:80/leonj/theistic/ssss.htm

Best Friends in Love and Together Forever: The Natural and Spiritual Dimension of Marriage (2009)
On the web at:
http://web.archive.org/web/20161031202655/http://theisticpsychology.org/books/best-friends-in-love.htm

Principles of Theistic Psychology: The Scientific Knowledge of God Extracted from the Correspondential Sense of Sacred Scripture (18 Volumes) (2004-2008)
On the web at:
http://web.archive.org/web/20161031202655/http://theisticpsychology.org/books/theistic/index.htm

Moses, Paul, and Swedenborg: Three Steps in Rational Spirituality (1999)
On the Web at:
http://web.archive.org/web/20161031202655/http://theisticpsychology.org/articles/moses2.htm

Swedenborg Encyclopedia of Theistic Psychology: The Ideas of Emanuel Swedenborg (1668-1772) Expressed In Modern Scientific Psychology (1995-2010) (multiple Volumes)
On the Web at: http://web.archive.org/web/20170930074343/http://www.theisticpsychology.org:80/gloss.html

OTHER LINKS

Each item in the list is a live link to the Web article.
Note that some of the articles on this list are reproduced in
Volumes 10, 11, and 12.

1. *YouTube: With Dr. Leon James Talks Freewill and our ego-centric idea of Self*
   https://www.youtube.com/watch?v=gl5N3Li1gg4

2. *YouTube: With Dr. Leon James on Spiritual discourse on understanding our non-physical nature*
   https://www.youtube.com/watch?v=rfxvoCLyYIs

   3. Avatar Psychology and Mental Anatomy
   On the Web at:
   http://web.archive.org/web/20161031202655/http://theisticpsychology.org/avatar/avatar-psychology-g29.htm

   2. Best Friends in Love: Natural and Spiritual Dimension of Marriage
   On the Web at:
   http://web.archive.org/web/20161031202655/http://theisticpsychology.org/books/best-friends-in-love.htm

   3. *Doctrine of the Wife Lecture Notes and Articles*:
   Part 1 || Part 2 || Part 3
   http://web.archive.org/web/20161031202655/http://theisticpsychology.org/articles/dow1.html (Part 1)
   http://web.archive.org/web/20161031202655/http://theisticpsychology.org/articles/dow2.html (Part 2)
   http://web.archive.org/web/20161031202655/http://theisticpsychology.org/articles/dow3.html (Part 3)

   4. *Doctrine of the Wife for Husbands: A Spiritual Practice for Achieving Unity*
   Part 1 || Part 2 || Part 3 || Part 4
   On the Web at:
   http://web.archive.org/web/20161031202655/http://www.soc.hawaii.edu/leonj/

leonj/leonpsy/instructor/gloss/wife.html (Part 1)
http://web.archive.org/web/20161031202655/http://www.soc.hawaii.edu/leonj/leonj/leonpsy/instructor/gloss/wife2.html (Part 2)
http://web.archive.org/web/20161031202655/http://www.soc.hawaii.edu/leonj/leonj/leonpsy/instructor/gloss/wife3.html (Part 3)
http://web.archive.org/web/20161031202655/http://www.soc.hawaii.edu/leonj/leonj/leonpsy/instructor/gloss/wife4.html (Part 4)

5. The Conjoined Pair
   On the Web at:
   http://web.archive.org/web/20161031202655/http://www.amazon.com/Conjoined-Pair-Leon-James-ebook/dp/B009QBSNEE/ref=la_B000APNWRS_1_5?s=books&ie=UTF8&qid=1426641444&sr=1-5

6. Further Resources on Theisticpsychology.org site
   On the Web at:
   http://web.archive.org/web/20161031202655/http://theisticpsychology.org/resources.htm

7. A Man of the Field: Forming The New Church Mind In Today's World
   http://web.archive.org/web/20161031202655/http://theisticpsychology.org/books/nonduality/index.html

8. Discoveries by Leon James

9. Site Map for Theisticpsychology.org

10. Substitution Technique for Deriving the Spiritual Sense of Sacred Scripture

11. Human Development: How We Learn and Develop Rationality

Theistic Psychology - Expanding The Narrative Series—Volume 4
Correspondences, Synchronicity, And Self-Witnessing

12. Theistic Psychology: Teaching the Scientifics Of The Interiors Of The Third Testament

13. Perizonius Thesis: What We Think Affects the Whole Race in Both Worlds

14. Religious Behaviorism

15. Swedenborg Glossary

16. Regeneration--Divine Psychotherapy

17. Spiritual Geography--Part 1--Graphic Maps of Consciousness for Regeneration

18. Genes of Consciousness: Spiritual Genetics for Regeneration

19. Substantive Dualism: Swedenborg's Integration of Biological Theology and Rational Psychology

20. De Hemelsche Leer--A Spiritual Bombshell

21. De Hemelsche Leer 3

22. De Hemelsche Leer in Swedenborg Glossary (Part 1)

23. Out Of Egypt Have I Called My Son: Teaching the Scientifics of the Internal Sense Of The Writings 1. By the Substitution Technique 2. By Diagramming

24. The Spiritual Significance of Neologisms

25. Spiritual Psychology: The Mental Technology of Self-Witnessing

26. Overcoming Objections to Swedenborg's Writings Through The Development of Scientific Dualism

27. The Organic Mind: Discovering the Mental World of Eternity

28. Spiritual Psychology in Swedenborg Glossary

29. Spiritual Psychology

30. Theistic Science in Swedenborg Glossary

31. A Guide to Spiritual Self-examination

32. Radicalist Empiricism: The Universal Modes of Enactment in Human Experience: A Self-Witnessing Account of the Discovery of Sudden Memory and My Interpretation of Its Significance for the Human Race

33. The Making Theistic Psychology

34. Spiritual Significance of Neologisms

35. The Genes of Consciousness in Spiritual Development

36. Moses, Paul, and Swedenborg: Three Steps in Rational Spirituality

37. Correspondential Sense of the World's Sacred Scriptures Proving That There Is A Unified Theistic Psychology

38. Half a Century of Science in Psychology Scientific Neologisms Coined by Leon James For the Period 1958-2008

39. Notes on De Hemelsche Leer (DHL) Part 1--Degrees of Consciousness

40. Principles of Theistic Psychology: The Scientific Knowledge of God Extracted from the Correspondential Sense of Sacred Scripture (Web document; 18 volumes)

41. Resources on Theistic Psychology
    (Web documents by Leon James and others)

42. Songs Spiritually Understood About Driving Cars on Roads and Highways

43. Swedenborg Encyclopedia of Theistic Psychology: The Ideas of Swedenborg Expressed in Modern Scientific Psychology

44. The Correspondential Sense of Sacred Scriptures: Proving that there is a Unified Theistic Psychology Hidden within the World's Historical Sacred Writings

45. The Organic Mind: Discovering the Mental World of Eternity

46. Theistic Psychology and Mental Biology
47. Various Articles on Swedenborg and Theistic Psychology

About the Author

Beauty is to behold the order of God's creation. ~Leon James

Leon James has authored a series of books on what he calls *theistic psychology*. He describes his ideas as a new modern synthesis of the works of Carl Jung (1875-1961) and Emanuel Swedenborg (1688-1772). He has been Professor of Psychology at the University of Hawaii since 1971. Today he teaches all his psychology courses online.

His current research involves the attempt to synthesize the work of Jung and Swedenborg. Jung discovered the psychic world of archetypes as having an existence of its own, and independently of the physical world. Swedenborg discovered the spiritual world of afterlife societies to be in eternity and not in time and physical space.

In the attempt to synthesize Jung and Swedenborg, Dr. James made the discovery that the "psychic world" of Jung and the "spiritual world" of Swedenborg refer to the same world. He then came to the conclusion that the psychic world and the spiritual world are the same world as the "mental world" in which we all live as human beings.

There is only one mental world and all human beings are born into it. Since there is no physical time or space in the mental world it is called the mental world of eternity. You are in it now!

A significant consequence of this identification between psychic world, spiritual world, and mental world, is to realize that we are born into the mental world of eternity with our immortal spiritual body, and therefore we are not really on earth, as it appears to be.

The *existential illusion* that we are on earth, and that our mind is in the physical body comes from the fact that our natural mind in eternity receives all its sensory input by correspondence from the physical body on earth. Our immortal spiritual body with which we are born into the mental world of eternity is connected by correspondence to our temporary physical body on earth. This is the source of our belief that we are on earth.

We are disconnected from the physical body through the two-day dying-resuscitation procedure. When this occurs we lose all contact with earth and we begin immortal life in the afterlife of mental eternity.

The purpose of being born temporarily connected to a physical body on earth is to provide the means by which human beings might acquire a natural mind that thinks with material ideas that are adapted to earth-time conditions and activities. Our natural mind becomes inactive in the afterlife of eternity but nevertheless serves as a basis for the use of our spiritual mind, which only then becomes fully active to eternity. We can then see and hear the environment of the afterlife world, and we can form normal relationships with those people who are already there.

Swedenborg's observations confirm this explanation in that the afterlife world has a similar external appearance as what can be seen and heard on earth. We are all familiar with the experience of dreaming in which the setting resembles the physical world. Without our natural mind our dreams would have no content. In the afterlife, our natural mind is needed as a basis for providing us with material content in mental eternity.

Following the two-day dying-resuscitation procedure that Swedenborg describes from empirical observation and experience, we are no longer connected by correspondence to the physical body on earth. We seem to ourselves at that point to "awaken" in the afterlife world. We then seek, find, and settle in one of the numberless afterlife societies, some of which Swedenborg explored in his dual consciousness and described in his Writings. Which of the societies we settle in is determined by our personality inclinations. We are attracted to the afterlife society whose inhabitants have a personality structure that is compatible with ours.

Dr. James' current work involves showing the details of how God instructs us in *Sacred Scripture* regarding the psychology of regeneration, which is the systematic modification of our personality from the inherited personality that is based on self-love and self-interest, to a new acquired personality that is based on altruism and mutual love.

Dr. James shows that Jung's idea of "symbolism" is the same as Swedenborg's idea of "correspondences". As well, Jung's idea of "archetype" is the same as Swedenborg's idea of "ruling love" that characterizes the personality of the people in each afterlife society.

Further, the symbolism that we use in our dreams is the same symbolism that God uses in *Sacred Scripture* to instruct us about the psychology of regeneration. Without regeneration we cannot develop a personality that is able to live in a heavenly afterlife society.

How we can be successful in regeneration is of deep interest to everyone.

Dr. Leon James
Professor of Psychology
University of Hawaii
Kailua, Hawaii
2018

End Of Volume 4

Printed in Poland
by Amazon Fulfillment
Poland Sp. z o.o., Wrocław